CARL WARBURTON'S
BUFFALOES: ADVENTURES IN ARNHEM LAND

David Andrew Roberts and Adrian Parker
Foreword, by Professor John Mulvaney

Buffaloes: Adventures in Arnhem Land

ISBN 0977511413

First Published in Australia in 1934 by Angus & Robertson Ltd, Sydney
Reprinted in 1944 by Consolidated Press Limited
This Third Edition, printed by
Gecko Books
P.O. Box 118
Marleston
South Australia 5033
Reprinted in 2009

Publication Copyright: Gecko Books
Story Copyright: Carl Warburton
Edited: David Andrew Roberts and Adrian Parker
Printed in China Through Phoenix Offset
Designed by: Robert Moller / Phoenix Offset

National Library of Australia Cataloguing-in-Publication data:

Warburton, Carl (Carl William).
Buffaloes: Life and Adventure in Arnhem Land

3 rd Edition
Includes Index
ISBN 0977511413

1. Frontier and pioneer life – Northern Territory – Arnhem Land
2. Arnhem Land (N.T.) – Description and travell. Roberts, David Andrew,
1969- . II. Parker, Adrian, 1968- . III. Title.

919.4295044

CONTENTS

CARL WARBURTON'S BUFFALOES

FOREWORD

In Carl Warburton's 1937 novel, *White Poppies*, his hero expresses the author's sentiments, that the Northern Territory was "the land of the Forgotten People". Today, Warburton is a forgotten author. He deserves republication because *Buffaloes* makes a distinctive contribution to burgeoning Territory historical studies. Carl Warburton's and Lawrence Whittaker's brief but adventurous times in early post-WWI Arnhem Land provide both a good read and a rich resource for evaluating racial relations and frontier social conditions.

Warburton was omitted from the *Australian Dictionary of Biography*, the *Northern Territory Dictionary of Biography*, and from most Territory histories extending from Ernestine Hill's *The Territory* (1952) to Alan Powell's excellent survey, *Far Country* (2000). More understandably, Warburton is absent from that 1400 page magisterial survey, H.W. Green's *A History of Australian Literature*. More recently, he was featured in the *Oxford Literary Guide to Australia* (1987).

David Roberts and Adrian Parker have provided modern readers with this lively account of how two demobilised soldiers faced life, substituting exotic freedom for army control, yet utilising their expertise as accurate marksmen.

Warburton and Whittaker departed to hunt buffaloes in what is now the Kakadu Park, an area which everyone then believed to be a region of primitive savages and crocodiles, but which they discovered was a difficult but humanised landscape. They arrived ill-equipped, but gratefully acknowledging the freely proffered advice and practical assistance from `old timers' and particularly the contribution of Aboriginal people. "You could not imagine a more cheerful crowd", was Warburton's heartfelt verdict.

Particularly valuable are Warburton's insightful and contrasting word pictures of two of the territory's first generation of buffalo shooters, Fred Smith and Paddy Cahill. Although using the current racialist idiom, Warburton showed interest in and admiration for Aboriginal people, evidently sharing the sympathetic realism of Paddy Cahill, their Oenpelli neighbour.

The post-war slump in buffalo skin prices rendered their hard-won enterprise uneconomic. Tom Cole, a third generation buffalo hunter, claimed that the industry "soon sorted the men from the boys". Certainly Warburton and Whittaker graduated as men.

Warburton's novel, *White Poppies*, drew nostalgically upon his experiences, setting the story in familiar lands between the east Alligator River and Pine Creek. In words which echo Warburton's own feelings, his hero bitterly confided to his loved one, "What is the hoodoo that hangs over the Northern territory? ... It has fine harbours, navigable rivers, mineral belts, rich agricultural and pastoral lands; and yet ... a miserable population of four thousand whites and Asiatics ... Once up here he is forgotten". Many Territorians since then echoed his individualistic exasperation: "Why should we be under the domination of southern politicians who have not the foggiest idea of the country".

While *Buffaloes* is expressive and gives a sense of place and people, White Poppies is less attractive. It is an old-fashioned romantic melodrama, in the Rider Haggard manner. It involves both heroic white frontiersmen and villains, brave women, secret caves, gold, exotic Aboriginal rites, with the added ingredient of Chinese and opium poppies present in Arnhem Land.

The central Aboriginal figure in *Buffaloes* is Koperaki, a co-operative Bunitj elder, whose brother was father to the late Bill Neidjie. The novel transforms him into T'Kala, a great warrior, ensuring that Aboriginal society plays a positive role in the story.

Warburton's novel appeared in bookshops shortly before Xavier Herbert's epic *Capricornia* achieved fame. Although set in the same environment, Herbert attained a higher aesthetic and intellectual level. His characters were more three-dimensional than Warburton's stock colonial people. While Warburton's fiction is forgettable, his realistic and vivid autobiographical recall in *Buffaloes* is both interesting and guist to the historian's mill.

It is forty years since I first researched in the Top End. I recently completed Paddy Cahill's biography and *Buffaloes* assisted me considerably; its portrayal of Cahill rings true. Roberts and Parker are in our debt for rescuing Carl Warburton from oblivion.

John Mulvaney

INTRODUCTION

Carl Warburton's *Buffaloes: Life and Adventure in Arnhem Land* recounts the author's exploits as a buffalo shooter in the Top End of Australia's Northern Territory during the early 1920s. First published in 1934 by Angus and Robertson Ltd. in Sydney (at 6 shillings a copy) and again in 1944 by Consolidated Press Ltd., *Buffaloes* struck a chord with Australia's metropolitans. Its story of adventure, mateship and freedom massaged the escapist yearnings of a society torn by economic depression and total war, and stirred a persistent curiosity and anxiety about Australia's "unknown north."

These adventures took place on the plains of the East Alligator River around Cannon Hill, now the heartland of Kakadu National Park. Today, Kakadu is one of only a few places inscribed on the World Heritage Register for a combination of natural and cultural values. This is recognition of the region's scenic beauty and ecological qualities, and acknowledgment of the antiquity and universal significance of the cultural traditions of its Aboriginal owners. Aboriginal ownership of Kakadu is formally recognised under the Aboriginal Land Rights (Northern Territory) Act of 1976. Its importance to Australians and the wider international community is reflected in its status as a National Park which attracts up to 200,000 visitors a year.

In Carl Warburton's time Kakadu was a frontier zone, still owned and occupied by "wild" Aborigines, and largely unknown to all but a small number of adventurers and mercenaries who extracted hard-won money from trades such as trepanging, pearling, mining and timber-getting. The East Alligator River region was the domain of the buffalo hunters. For around 70 years from the 1880s to the 1950s, buffalo shooting was the principal industry in the region and the main medium of contact between foreigners and local Aboriginal peoples.

Buffalo shooting was a rough and rustic pursuit, extremely hazardous and perceivably heroic. In the glamorised rendering of Banjo Paterson it was "about the last remaining relic of the old wild days ... life as it was in the beginning of things" (*Sydney Mail*, 7 January 1899). The nature of the trade and the character of its practitioners made it a popular subject in 20th Century Australian frontier-style literature. A number of notable bushmen/authors such as Allan Stewart and Frank Woerle have recounted their lives as buffalo shooters. The most acclaimed of the fraternity is the late Tom Cole, the `real-life Crocodile Dundee' of the 1920s and 30s, whose *Hell West and Crooked* (1988) and *Riding the Wildman Plains* (1992) have sold prodigiously in multiple reprints, earning him the Medal of the Order of Australia for contributions to history in 1994.

Carl Warburton's *Buffaloes* is the earliest of these first-hand, memoir-styled books, and the first to describe and document the buffalo shooting industry in such detail. Its content, themes and ideology are faithful to the popular, nationalist sentiments of old Australia, which glorified the bush as a mainspring of Australian virtue and achievement. By choosing the vocation of a buffalo shooter, Warburton placed himself in the tradition of the Australian bushman/pioneer, crusading in a land that was undomesticated and hostile. *Buffaloes* is a tale of adventure, courage, resourcefulness, mateship and close-calls, and an account of contact with an ancient Indigenous culture in the apparently inevitable process of being dispersed and dispossessed. It is both a ripping yarn and a discourse of conquest.

Carl William Warburton was born 1893 at Millthorpe near Bathurst (New South Wales), the second of three sons to the farmer, Thomas Warburton, an English emigrant from Somersetshire, and a school-teacher, Isabella Mockett, daughter of a pioneering family of the Bathurst region. Carl received a sound education, then worked as a clerk at the Milthorpe branch of the Bank of New South Wales. His life changed dramatically in March 1915, shortly after his 22nd birthday, when he enlisted in the Australian Imperial Force (AIF). Warburton joined the Australian Army Medical Corps' 5th Field Ambulance, attached to the 5th Infantry Brigade which departed Sydney on the *Ajana* on 31 May 1915 for Egypt. The 5th Field Ambulance was assigned to the newly formed AIF 2nd Division in July 1915 and posted to Gallipoli, where Warburton served in a bearer subdivision. He was admitted to hospital in Malta with rheumatism shortly before the evacuation of the Gallipoli peninsula. While serving in France he left the Medical Services and was taken on the strength of the 17th Battalion, but would spend much of the remainder of the War in England. He attended Officer's College at Oxford, where his commanding officer described him as "well educated and intelligent: should make a good officer", then rejoined his Battalion in France at the time Australian troops recaptured the town of Hamel. Weeks later he was wounded in action, floored by some shrapnel on the day the Australians advanced the line south-east of Villers-Bretonneux, and was sent back to England where he remained in convalescence until after the Armistice. Lieutenant Warburton returned to Australia in May 1919.

It was in the 5th Field Ambulance at Gallipoli, amidst the filth and misery of advanced dressing stations behind the front line at Pope's and Quinn's Post, that Warburton met his friend and co-adventurer in *Buffaloes*, Lawrence Whittaker. An

Englishman, born near Rochdale (Lancashire), a year younger than Warburton, Whittaker had been apprenticed as a mechanical engineer before emigrating to Australia. At the time he enlisted, Whittaker was said to have been taking an engineering degree at the University of Sydney. The two promised to reunite after the war and do "something with a kick in it", either in South America or northern Australia. Their destination would later be determined in a spontaneous, typical Australian fashion, "over a mixed grill and a couple of bottles" and the toss of a coin. It was an audacious decision, seemingly informed by visions and legends rather than any practical fact or plan. Warburton and Whittaker set out for Darwin with only a vague understanding of the local buffalo shooting industry, hopelessly under-supplied and with a few rifles and shotguns which they soon learnt were inadequate instruments for the task ahead. They were extremely fortunate in being the first on hand to claim land set aside for lease to returned soldiers, which proved in fact to be one of the best locations for buffalo shooting.

There were probably buffalo in the Cannon Hill area shortly after 1845, when Ludwig Leichhardt's hungry party shot one further north near Mount Borradaile. Local Aborigines told him the country was full of the beast they called "Anaborro" (Leichhardt, 1847: 524-5). The Asian water or swamp buffalo *(Bubalus bubalis)* was imported from Timor to service the early British outposts on Melville Island and the Cobourg Peninsula. They flourished in a propitious environment, fanning out across the coastal floodplains and tidal flats of northern Australia. From the 1880s their numbers were sufficient to support a profitable industry shooting for meat and hides. A nascent buffalo industry first emerged on the Adelaide and Mary Rivers, further east in the Alligator Rivers region, and on Melville Island and the Cobourg Peninsula, boosted by the demand for meat in the mining towns between the Adelaide River and Pine Creek. Hides were preserved and dried at local camps, then transported back to Darwin for shipping interstate and overseas. It spawned a generation of now legendary hunters such as Edward Oswin Robinson, Robert Joel (Joe) Cooper and the Hardy brothers, Harry and Frank, who provided a large number of the estimated 100,000 buffalo hides exported from the region in the first twenty-five years of the industry.

The most renowned of the early hunters was Paddy Cahill (1863-1923), who from around 1885 shot on both sides of the East Alligator River, probably including the Cannon Hill area. Cahill is famed for introducing the technique of horseback hunting or "scrub dashing" - training horses to gallop alongside the buffalo and placing a shot directly into the spine to immobilise the animal. For this he was widely celebrated as a frontier hero, romanticised by the likes of Banjo Paterson, who in the *Bulletin* in 1898 described Cahill "pursue[ing] the infuriated buffalo at full gallop, standing on his saddle, and dressed in a towel and a diamond ring, and yelling like a wild Indian". It was this sort of imagery that captured the imagination of many adventurers to the Territory, including Carl Warburton. Paddy Cahill is also remembered for his ten year collaboration with the anthropologist, Baldwin Spencer, whom he hosted in 1912 when Spencer was the Northern Territory's Chief Protector of Aborigines. Cahill and Spencer maintained a long correspondence that was critical to Spencer's landmark work on the Kakadu Aborigines. Cahill also helped Spencer build the brilliant collection of around 170 local bark paintings that are in the possession of the National Museum of Victoria.

When Warburton met him at Oenpelli, Cahill was an

elderly man who had long given up the hunt. Oenpelli station had been taken over by the Northern Territory administration shortly after the Commonwealth government assumed control of the Territory. Under the patronage of Administrator Gilruth, Cahill ran a state-funded experimental farm, mostly producing butter from cows imported from Queensland. The operation struggled commercially and collapsed when unions refused to handle the goods produced by Aboriginal labour, placing Cahill into effective retirement on what was now a grand and comfortable establishment in the wilderness. Oenpelli station had been gazetted as a government reserve and Cahill employed by the Commonwealth Government as a local Protector of Aborigines and Superintendent of the Alligator Rivers Reserve. Oenpelli epitomised what was achievable in the north, with its grand house, fences, domesticated stock, orchards, gardens and refrigeration unit. In Warburton's portrayal, Cahill, "the high priest of Oenpelli", is a generous but stern character whose views carry an undisputed air of authority. He was spending his final months at Oenpelli before leaving the Territory for the last time in August 1922. Cahill died in Sydney in February 1923.

Warburton also arrived just in time to meet another celebrated local character, Fred Smith, "a big-hearted, genial bushman" based at the former mission station at "Kopalgo" (Kapalga). Smith's assistance was critical to Warburton's venture. He gave them directions to Cannon Hill, provided valuable tips and equipment (including horses) and arranged for their supplies and hides to be lugged to and from Darwin. In stark contrast to Cahill's Oenpelli, Kapalga is the "unmarried bushman's idea of a home", a crude bush village of paperbark huts, albeit with a productive garden (possibly a remnant of the mission) and facilities for processing meat. Again, Warburton witnessed the end of an era. The "grand fellow"

Fred Smith died in Darwin shortly after.

Like so many before and after, Warburton came to the Territory seeking "mad adventure" with "visions of fortune swift and sure", and like many he was, at least in regard to anticipated riches, sadly disappointed. They went to the Territory in hard times. In 1920, a decade after its administration had been transferred from South Australia to the Commonwealth government, the Territory still yearned for the influx of population and capital required to realise visions of prosperity and importance. The economy remained stagnant and precarious, reeling in the wake of the much maligned administration of Dr John Anderson Gilruth, whose command was marred by mismanagement, scandal and industrial unrest. Little changed in the 1920s. Australia's boom years of "men, money and markets" did not penetrate the Territory. It remained "the Achilles heel of Australia" in the words of Prime Minister Stanley Melbourne Bruce.

Buffalo shooting offered quick returns in times when hides fetched up to £1 each, but prices and production slumped after the War, at the same time as the Northern Territory administrators began to fear the buffalo were endangered. The calculated harvest for 1922 was 800 hides, one-tenth of the number procured during the peak years of the War (Harris 1962: 37). Warburton and Whittaker, "bagging about a dozen beasts a day" during the two short seasons of 1922-23, claim to have shot 1,000 buffaloes.

The high action and extreme dangers of the vocation are described vividly and avidly in *Buffaloes*. To procure the best hides, hunters chased down the largest beasts at full gallop across uncertain and treacherous terrain, using single-shot.303 rifles and carbines, mostly Martini-Henrys and Martini Enfields, "designed to kill men, not thick-hided bovines" (Stewart 1969: 37). Warburton, from his own description, was using some type of short-barrelled, pistol-style .303, probably similar to those wielded by tiger hunters in India as a weapon of last resort, infamous for a savage recoil that unseated the rider and jarred the hand. As a thick-skinned buffalo was capable of surviving several poorly placed .303s, a shot down into the loins at close-range was essential. The ferocity of the wounded bull, and its capacity to use its horns as weapons, claimed the lives of many hunters and horses, including Warburton's Aboriginal employee, Big Head, whose sudden, horrible death in the final phases of the book reminds us "there is no more dangerous animal in the world than a wounded buffalo bull".

Warburton's Northern Territory venture was brief, cut short by plummeting prices for hides and by the misadventure described in the closing chapters of the book. But Warburton maintained a strong interest in the potential, and the vulnerability, of the north. *Buffaloes* is partly an entreaty for a greater economic development of Northern Australia, an agenda Warburton revealed more explicitly in his publicity appearances on Sydney radio in 1934. In the classic frontier paradigm it is a vacant but prospective space, one that needs to be filled with enterprise and industry in order to legitimise and secure it for White Australia. This agenda informed much thinking and writing about the Territory in the early twentieth century (McGregor 2004). As the ever-eloquent Alfred Searcy put it, "does it not behove us to bestir ourselves and prove to the world that we are worthy of the great inheritance, lest some foreign power, making our lethargy an excuse, step in and use it for us?" (Searcy 1912: 13-4). Certainly in Warburton's mind it was a source of much anxiety that the

Territory's white population remained relatively small, recently-established, and uncomfortably outnumbered by Aborigines and Asians. This sense of vulnerability was amplified in the uncertain times of the early 1930s. Following Searcy and others, Warburton advertises a land of opportunity where one could dream of domesticating buffalo, pigs, perhaps even cattle, irrespective of environmental impediments and consequences, and where one could obtain a one-year lease on 3,000 kilometres of undeveloped and largely unchartered terrain for a mere £60, in spite of Aboriginal occupation and ownership.

The land Warburton referred to as "our marvellous holding" is Bunitj country. Bunitj are one of numerous clans of the floodplain country who once spoke the Gagudju language. Cannon Hill is *Namarr-ga'naangga*, from the Gagudju lexeme *ga'naangga*, meaning high country (Harvey 1992: 8, 17). From them we derive the term Kakadu, the popularised pronunciation given by Baldwin Spencer, who recorded their traditions and customs with the assistance of Paddy Cahill of Oenpelli. The central Aboriginal character in *Buffaloes*, Koperaki, was a Bunitj man, well and favourably known to Paddy Cahill, though he apparently declined to work at Oenpelli. Baldwin Spencer met "Kopereik" at Oenpelli station in 1912, a "fully initiated" man whose "totem" was "Kunaitja, mullet" (Spencer 1914: 52, 319). One of the most precious outcomes of *Buffaloes* is its portrait of a distinguished and important Aboriginal character of whom we would otherwise know almost nothing.

Today, Bunitj country is the home of Jonathan Nadji and his sisters. They are children of the late Bill Neidjie, the

"Kakadu Man', a senior Aboriginal lawman, artist and poet who, in his later years, was one of the most celebrated and respected Aboriginal Australians of his generation. Bill was born at Alawanydjawany, the son of Nardampala, who was Koperaki's brother. Nardampala worked for Paddy Cahill but died around the time Warburton was at Cannon Hill. After travelling widely in search of employment and adventure, Bill returned to Kakadu in the 1970s and won the land back for his family as a successful claimant in the East Alligator River's Stage 2 Land Claim, and until his death in 2002 fought tirelessly for the conservation of his land and the preservation of his culture. Bill's son Jonathan is a senior Park Ranger with Parks Australia North.

Carl Warburton's *Buffaloes* has long been valued as a precious eye-witness account of the Kakadu Aborigines, taken at a pivotal moment of their history. In Warburton's time, and by the definitions of his generation, they were "myall blacks", traditionally orientated peoples who remained in possession of their land. They had barely shed a long held reputation for hostility and resistance, following numerous attacks on white explorers and entrepreneurs in the late 19th Century. Warburton amplifies the unspoiled, uncorrupted state of local Aboriginal society in a manner appealing to metropolitan audiences, who could accord some degree of nobility and respect toward such people, in stark contrast to their abhorrence of "fringe-dwelling" Aborigines and the even more reviled people of mixed descent who were perceived as degraded and impure. Though it is barely evident in Warburton's account, except in a brief reference to their perilously low birth-rate, the Kakadu Aborigines were in the midst of a demographic and cultural catastrophe. The intrusion of sojourners, mercenaries and missionaries, and the attractions of European outposts at Darwin (1869) and Pine Creek

(1872) had caused significant population shifts and the spread of disease before Warburton arrived. Some of the old languages and customs were already in serious decline. The long history of contact between the Kakadu Aborigines and outsiders was apparent in their ability to communicate via pidgin English. They were familiar with European technology and economic regimes, and evidently had great experience in the techniques and requirements of the buffalo industry. Warburton benefited inestimably from these circumstances.

Aboriginal people were crucial to the buffalo industry. Men like Warburton and Whittaker brought Aboriginal workers with them, namely Bob Cadell and Jacky Anyone, who "play an important and oft-times highly amusing part" in this adventure. But the enterprise relied on gaining the consent and assistance of locals, in this case Koperaki and his "boys", Big Head and Hobble Chain, plus several others mentioned. Procuring hides was a labour intensive business. Large parties of men and women were required to skin, wash and salt the hides, which then had to be dried, folded and loaded onto luggers for shipment to Darwin. The Kakadu Aborigines performed these tasks efficiently and productively, a "more or less humdrum business" for people who had been familiar with the industry most of their lives. It was seasonal work only, lasting around six months until the onset of the Wet Season. Workers were paid usually in tobacco, flour and tea.

The buffalo industry's reliance on Aboriginal labour was consistent with most sectors of the Northern Territory economy. As Fred Smith tells Warburton, "without the blacks the country would beat the white man". Despite their importance to the Northern Territory economy, Aboriginal welfare was ultimately subordinate to the interests of those major stakeholders who demanded that Aboriginal labour be cheap and submissive. Yet while the use of Aboriginal labour in the buffalo industry was inherently exploitative, the arrangements were also consensual and rewarding. On the Kakadu frontier provisions were more useful than wages, and European items such as firearms and axes were of enormous value. One of the key rewards was buffalo meat, an increasingly critical resource for local Aboriginal people. Warburton's account provides evidence that buffalo meat facilitated the gathering of large numbers at a time when there were fewer people to acquire food, and when some of the land's natural resources were threatened by the environmental impact of feral buffalo. In any event, Warburton was duly appreciative of the role played by his Aboriginal workers. The anthropologist A.P. Elkin, president of the Association for the Protection of Native Races, who reviewed *Buffaloes* for the journal *Oceania*, thought "one of the best features of the book is the author's willingness to give the aborigines the appreciation and thanks that is due to them".

The value of Warburton's book from an anthropological perspective is, as was noted at the time, probably limited to those who are not anthropologists - "interesting from an outsider's point of view", according to Elkin's *Oceania* review. In the course of the story there is excellent detail on Aboriginal implements, technologies, food gathering strategies, social organisation and personal relationships. There are also passages relating cultural and religious practices including burial rites, circumcision, infanticide, sorcery, rock painting and cannibalism. Naturally Warburton conveys only a vague understanding of these matters, reporting them as casual observations of the bizarre and exotic habits of "curious beggars", rather than scientific data. Some of his comments accord with or are further explicated by the work of Professor Baldwin Spencer, and we have occasionally noted this in our annotations on the text. Warburton was privileged to enjoy access to and intimacy with traditionally-orientated Aboriginal peoples, though his learning was not always consensual, as in the case of his spying on an "initiation ceremony" involving the circumcision and body scarification of young men. That Koperaki, when later asked to explain these proceedings "seemed disinclined to discuss the initiation at all" indicates that Warburton had transgressed.

Some aspects of Warburton's treatment of Aborigines will no doubt sit uncomfortably with a 21st Century readership. *Buffaloes* is underlined by an overt faith in the virtues and achievements of white civilisation in Australia - a conviction that the exploitation of the land and its people was natural and necessary. Their dealings with Kakadu Aborigines were informed by a long and often bitter history of Australian frontier relations, one that had frequently degenerated into barbarity and lawlessness. In this particular area the "shoot-up of blacks by whites" was recent history, within the living memory of those like Paddy Cahill and Koperaki. Warburton and Whittaker went to Arnhem Land with little fear of being harmed, but despite their reliance on Aboriginal labour and their apparent interest in aspects of Aboriginal society, they inevitably treated Aborigines with a degree of caution and contempt. The frontier portrayed in *Buffaloes* bristles with moments of tension, misunderstanding and potential misconduct, as in Warburton's promising to use his gun rather than suffer being "made a fool of by a black".

Buffaloes contains some examples of dated nomenclature, especially the derogatory term "nigger", considered highly offensive today. Warburton only uses that term twice, once when quoting the blunt and hardened views of Paddy Cahill. Indeed, it is mostly through the medium of other Territorians (or through his co-adventurer, Whittaker) that Warburton relates the harsher views of Aboriginal society. His own treatment and views generally express a degree of understanding and fondness that was uncommon in those times, particularly in the frontier regions. Here there may be some relevance in Warburton's status as a "blow-in" to the Territory. When *Buffaloes* was released in 1934, the gulf between the ethos of Australia's frontier/bush communities and its southern/metropolitan populations was brought into focus by a furore arising from Aboriginal attacks on Japanese trepangers at Caledon Bay and the fatal spearing of a Northern Territory policeman, Steward McColl, on Woodah Island in July 1933. These events, and the subsequent plans by the Northern Territory Administration to launch punitive expeditions against Yolngu people in eastern Arnhem Land, were widely reported in metropolitan newspapers. Public outrage and political pressure prevented the retaliatory actions, and the draconian sentence given to the Aboriginal man convicted of McColl's murder was overturned by the High Court in November 1934. This victory of humanitarian sentiment over the old Australian frontier ethos was followed by an important period of organised agitation and reform, as Australia came under increasing domestic and international pressure to address issues concerning the condition and rights of remote Aboriginal populations. These events fuelled a heightened public interest in Arnhem Land and contributed to the appeal of Warburton's *Buffaloes*, and the tone of the book is informed, in some measure, by urbane humanitarian sentiment. He, like many others, scorned and lamented the gross ingratitude of those of "our own crowd" who "treat them more like dogs than human beings." This is consistent with family accounts of Warburton's temper and personality in later years, when he was noted for his respect toward Aboriginal people.

Those terms and themes that are sensitive and potentially offensive have been retained in the current edition for historic authenticity, and in the belief that such lapses are redeemed by the otherwise insightful and empathetic qualities of the book. We present *Buffaloes* as a relic of its time, statement of the worldviews of author and audience. Where that affronts or offends, it may hopefully convey something of the experience of Aboriginal people who lived under such harsh views and values. This might remind non-Aboriginal Australians of the darker and tenser forces of their history, at a time when there are revitalised attempts to deny them.

The are no figures for the size of the original print run of *Buffaloes*, or of the volume of sales, though its' popularity is evident in the appearance of a second edition in 1944, and by the number of surviving copies held in antiquarian collections and second-hand bookshops throughout Australia. The favourable reception is apparent in the volume and tenor of personal letters received by Warburton from those who were touched by reading the book or by hearing Warburton speak on Sydney radio in April 1934. Mavis Murrell of Mosman told Warburton how "I caught my Dad looking into space this morning & asked him what he was thinking of. He replied 'Arnhem Land. Imagine a man spending a day like this in the office'". Others, like a Miss Coleman of Rockdale, were surprised to discover themselves wholly unaware of this hidden corner of Australia, "and it is surprising the number of people equally ignorant".

While *Buffaloes* is well known to researchers and residents of the Kakadu and western Arnhem Land region, it has been obscured from a broader readership by its having remained out of print for almost 60 years. It lays no claim to being a literary classic, but it is a good tale told laconically and earnestly. *Buffaloes* has considerable importance and appeal to enthusiasts of Australian history and culture. Aside from its value as an historical document, it remains a convincing and engaging story, still capable of massaging our escapist yearnings. The passage of time and the extent and speed of changes in Australian society have enhanced the nostalgic air of this romanticised frontier tale. Carl Warburton's *Buffaloes* described a world in transition. Now it is a record of a world that is largely lost. It illustrates how much has changed, while highlighting some impulses and scenarios that have remained constant.

This project has been undertaken with the kind permission and assistance of Carl Warburton's son, Robert, and daughter Carolyn. The editors are grateful to them for entrusting them with the task, and for providing personal reminiscences of their father and access to some of his papers and photos. We are also indebted to Jonathan Nadji of Cannon Hill, who has long been our good friend and assistant, and has provided us with vital access to and knowledge of his country and heritage.

This 3rd edition of *Buffaloes* has been prepared from the text of the 1st edition (1934). There were in fact at least two prints of the 1934 edition, one retitled *Adventure and Discovery in Arnhem Land*. We have made only a few minor corrections, including those made for the 2nd edition (1944). We have retained antiquated and accepted variations of spelling (as in "loth" for loathe, "conjuror" for conjurer), and have retained the predominantly Americanised spellings of words such as civilize, realize, recognize, organize. This 3rd edition features some annotations, though we have kept them to a minimum, located as endnotes at the rear of the book. For the benefit of researchers we have also indexed the text, supplemented it with illustrations, and supplied a list of further readings. To provide further context for the story, and because it ends so abruptly, we have included an epilogue, briefly relating the later histories of the author and developments in the Kakadu region.

About the authors:

David Andrew Roberts is a lecturer in Australian History at the University of New England, Armidale. He has researched and published numerous works on nineteenth-century frontier and rural history. He is the co-editor, with Martin Crotty, of *The Great Mistakes of Australian History* (2006).

Adrian Parker is an artist, musician and author who has lived and worked in Kakadu National park since 1994. His interests include studying Aboriginal rock and bark paintings, and playing didgeridoo. He is the author of *Images in Ochre* and *Didgeridoo Dreaming.*

Together, Adrian and David co-authored *Ancient Ochres: The Aboriginal Rock Paintings of Mount Borradaile,* western Arnhem Land (2003).

CHAPTER I

WE "SHAKE" ON IT

IT was a night on Gallipoli.

The 5th Brigade was in occupation at Quinn's Post, and four of us - Bert Rockliffe, who had been assistant town clerk at Orange, Bob Hayward, a butcher, Lawrence Whittaker, a Sydney engineer, and myself - had established a dugout.

Darkness had fallen. It was a reasonably quiet night, only an occasional bomb bursting, and the whine of a few bullets passing high overhead to remind us that life was likely to be a very precarious thing.

We were squatting in the unlit dugout smoking cigarettes, and passing the time in desultory chatter. Strange what men will talk about in such circumstances! But surely there could have been no more remote topic than: "What will we do after the war?"

I forget which of us started it. However, there we were after four months of war-quite long enough to know the cheapness of human life-calmly discussing plans for the future. Only youth with its regardless enthusiasm could have done so.

Bert Rockcliffe had had a row with his girl over enlisting, but he fancied all would be well on his return. He intended to get married, pick up the threads of his Local Government work, and live a peaceful, settled life in some country town in New South Wales.

Poor Bert! He was hit in the leg at Pozieres. When the stretcher-bearers arrived he waved them on, in his generous way, to others more badly wounded. When they returned, fragments of tunic were all they found of Bert; a shell had landed where he had been lying.[1]

Bob Hayward spoke of becoming a master-butcher, with a string of hunters for country shows as a sideline. Bob came through the mess all right, and is now handling carcasses somewhere in Sydney. I don't know about the hunters, but you could bet that Bob would not be far away from a horse. He was a fine and fearless rider.[2]

Whittaker and I were unanimous on one point.

We agreed that after the war we would have to do something with a "kick" in it. Although I was born and bred on my father's holding at Millthorpe, a few miles out of Orange, I was in a bank when I enlisted, and the thought of returning to that life appalled me.

Whittaker had been studying for an engineering degree at the University of Sydney, but he was definite that he had had sufficient academic learning to do him for all time. In future he would seek the practical, and the more adventure that could be mixed with it the better. A shell burst near at hand and shook the walls of the dugout.

"Still feel enthusiastic about the future?" asked Whittaker.

"Never more," I said. As though a bursting shell could dampen the ardour of twenty-one!

Whittaker, thereupon, suggested we should seek our post-war fortunes in Brazil. He was a great reader. I listened while he painted a fascinating picture of the probable adventures we should meet with on the Amazon and Rio Negro.

"But why leave Australia?" I asked, and proceeded to tell him something of what I had heard of the vast and little-known lands in the Northern Territory.

I recounted many tales of the great north which my uncle, Arthur Mockett, had told me when I was a boy.[3] Mockett was a station-owner who had spent many years in the Gulf country and on the borders of the Territory. His experiences with the blacks, and his exploits had stirred my youthful imagination; I remember well the thrill I got when he allowed me to handle one of his horse-pistols. A hankering to explore the Territory was one of my earliest desires, but that night on the shell-swept peninsula, with death always just around the corner, the hankering became almost an obsession.

I did my utmost to persuade Whittaker to go with me to the Territory - I laugh now when I think how earnest was that conversation in the midst of war! But his mind was set on Brazil.

"Well, say we decide where we'll go when we get back," I suggested.

This suited him. We shook hands, and pledged ourselves to the great adventure when the little business in hand was completed.

It was my turn to go outside and remake the fire, and that brief excursion nearly upset our plans for all time. Foolishly I struck a match to light a cigarette, and my silhouette, thrown on the waterproof sheet hanging in front of the dugout, made an admirable target.

Immediately there was a tearing sound, and a plonk behind me; a bullet had passed through my trouser-leg, and smacked against the side of the dugout. One would need to take a little more care if Brazil or the Northern Territory was to be explored.

Whittaker and I had enlisted together. We escaped without hurt at Gallipoli, and went with the 5th Brigade to France.

At Passchendaele in 1917 I got my first hit; and there Bob Hayward made us feel mighty proud of him. A shell had burst near an ambulance-wagon, killing the driver, wounding the other, and killing two of the horses. Hayward took in the situation at a glance. Under raking fire he cut the dead animals clear, put the wounded driver in the wagon, which was full of maimed men, and mounting one of the other two horses, brought them to safety. For that exceptionally gallant piece of work he received the Military Medal.

My wound was caused by a bullet in the stomach. The bullet, however, had done its deadly work by passing first through another man. Still, it was sufficient to put me out of action for a while, and it gave me the opportunity to get a commission at the Officers' College at Oxford.[4]

Returning to France I sought out Whittaker. Although I was now commissioned, our plans for the future were more important to me than army regulations, of which I had had more than enough. So, whenever the chance offered, we discussed our great future.

Some pieces of shell in the head floored me at Villers Bretonneux, and the armistice was signed while I was convalescing at Cobham Hall in Kent.[5]

I wrote to Whittaker, who was still in France, and outlined what I thought we ought to do. The one who first got back to Australia was to make a definite point of meeting the other at the wharf in Sydney; then, without undue delay, we would formulate plans.

Whittaker got the letter all right; for when I landed in Sydney at the end of April 1919, he was there to meet me. While most of the chaps seemed content with the hectic glamour of those times, we straightway got down to the now serious matter of our immediate movements.[6]

We went to a familiar restaurant and, over a mixed grill and a couple of bottles, resumed discussion of the project born on the hills of Gallipoli.

Whittaker was still keen on Brazil, while the Northern Territory still had its lure for me. We broke the deadlock by doing what the average Australian generally does.

When Whittaker spun the coin I called heads for the Northern Territory. Tails turned up. But as the coin in falling had hit the table, we, luckily for me, barred the toss. I spun next. Whittaker called tails: it was heads - and our compass was set for the unknown north.

CHAPTER II

WE HEAD FOR DARWIN

NEITHER of us had a particularly clear idea of what form our fortunes would take when we reached the Territory. What little information I could gather about the buffalo shooting possibilities impressed me. I had read of the exploits of two crack buffalo-shooters, Fred Smith and Paddy Cahill, and how they had shot up to two thousand beasts a year. As the hides were bringing £2 each I had visions of fortune swift and sure.

Before making final arrangements, we agreed that Whittaker should go to Melbourne and gather what facts he could from the Home and Territories Department concerning the Territory. He returned after a futile trip. We were both astounded at the small amount of information available.

(That was fourteen years ago; and I am just as astounded today at how little is known of that wonderful country.)

We decided to waste no more time, but to go and find out for ourselves. We got together our kit - a medicine chest, two .303, one .32 and one .22 rifles, two shot-guns, two .45 revolvers, half a dozen curved butcher's knives, tent, fly, swag-covers, rugs, army clothes, and odds and ends - and boarded the *Mataram* bound for Darwin.

Our enthusiasm, now at a high pitch, got its first setback from a prospector who joined the boat at Brisbane. He had lived at Darwin and thereabouts for years, and knew intimately the country, its needs and difficulties. He overhauled our equipment and found little right with it.

First of all he told us our rifles were useless for buffalo shooting and explained why. Buffaloes, he said, were shot from horseback, and not from foot as we had imagined. The idea was to ride on to a herd, armed with a carbine, shoot one, reload, shoot another, and perhaps get a dozen or more on the one charge.

You could bring down a buffalo shooting from the ground he said, but that would be the last you would see of the herd for the day. Martini-Henry carbines were what we needed.[7] We determined to wire the Defence Department for them when we got to Darwin.

Then our prospecting friend discovered we had no snakebite outfit. Thereupon he proceeded to give us a useful demonstration of the bushman's treatment. This was to place a ligature above the bite, make a wound, scarify it with Condy's crystals, and keep on gently loosening and fastening the ligature so that the poison would be taken into the system almost imperceptibly.[8]

He also told us our supply of quinine was inadequate; that we were without chlorodyne, so essential for dysentery;[9] that our mosquito-netting was useless (we should have had cheese-cloth instead of the usual net); and one or two other things, all of which somewhat disheartened us.

Still, he gave us much information about the Territory, but in a manner which suggested he was releasing a secret which none but the men of the north should know.

On the trip to Darwin, one point of interest particularly stirred me. It was a monument on Albany Island to the memory of Kennedy, the explorer. Kennedy had set out in 1848 to find a way to Cape York Peninsula, but he was speared by blacks when within sight of Albany Island, where he was to await the supply-ship. His two mates whom he had left, were speared later, his black boy Jacky Jacky being the only survivor.[10]

It was a solemn moment when the *Mataram's* siren sounded a salute to the memory of the hundred and thirty-four lives which were lost when the *Quetta* went down in the same locality on her way from Brisbane to London in 1890.

As we approached Darwin, Vestey's meat-works were pointed out to us, and the tragedy of this great enterprise was told.

The Federal Government had offered Vestey's large land concessions on the undertaking that they would erect the works. Vestey's did so at a cost of £1,000,000, and carried on for four years when the extreme demands made by the unions compelled them to close.[11]

(Most of the machinery has since been removed, and there seems no likelihood of the works re-opening for many years.)

Darwin, last port of call for the East! It is a quaint old place built on the cliffs, and its history goes back to 1869 when the site was selected. The population of fifteen hundred embraces forty-five nationalities, including Chinese, Japanese, Malayans, Cingalese, Greeks, Patagonians, Argentinians, Maltese, and the government officials who are, of course, whites. The Chinese predominate; the town's business is almost exclusively in their hands.

The one beauty spot in Darwin is the botanical gardens. There we saw a blaze of colour-hibiscus, frangipanni, cannas, mock-orange, jasmine, honeysuckle, wax-flowers, as well as some six hundred tropical plants, rubber, coffee, tea, cassava and the rest. The sense of peace and joy which the gardens gave us was a little upset when we saw opposite, the British cemetery with its freshly dug and open graves. The dead cannot remain long unburied in Darwin; graves have always to be ready.

Strange stories were told us of the Chinese cemetery not far away. When the bodies have lain buried for two years they may be disinterred and removed to the home of their ancestors, and it is the gruesome duty of the customs officials to examine them. Frequently they have found gold-dust and pearls cunningly secreted in the bones.

There were then three government hotels in Darwin, but now there is only one, and that is privately owned. The government enterprise had been a dismal failure. We were later to learn that the government's business activities were regarded with scorn, and justly so, by the men of the north.

We made a trip out to Myilly Point, the residential area; saw the hospital, a fine institution on the cliff edge, and later had a look at the gaol at Fanny Bay. Adjoining the bay is the aerodrome where Sir Ross and Sir Keith Smith made the first historic landing.[12]

We had seen all we wanted to see of Darwin for the moment and were anxious to set our expedition moving.

Full of hope and confidence we made a call upon the Administrator, Staniforth Smith.[13] Although he wore only a singlet and white ducks his attire lost him no dignity, and he gave us a warm welcome. We told him we were there to shoot buffaloes, and he suggested we should see Horace Trower, Director of Lands.

Trower was courtesy itself, but when we told him we hoped to make a modest living from buffalo-hides he smiled sympathetically.

"I'm sorry, boys," he said, "but all the buffalo country has been leased."

A puff of wind would have knocked us down, so great was the disappointment. All our dreams, all our plans blasted in a few words. Why the devil couldn't the Department have told Whittaker that in Melbourne!

It was a staggering blow, and after we had partially recovered we found ourselves listening to Trower again.

"Yes, it's tough luck," he was saying, "but now you're here why not look at some grazing country? There's money in that. I can let you have about six hundred square miles in the ironstone bore country, five hundred miles south, at 2s. a square mile. There is a government bore on the block, and plenty of stock pass through there. The halfpenny a head watering-fee you'll get will more than pay the cost of the lease."

Trower suggested we should inspect the country, and offered us an outfit of horses and packs to take us over the rest of the journey from the rail-head at Katherine River, one hundred and eighty miles from Darwin.

I looked at Whittaker, and I'll wager the same thought passed through our minds. Here was a chance to see some of the Northern Territory at the government's expense which might, in a small measure, mollify us.

We agreed to look the country over. After thanking Trower, who had been very decent to us, we made for the pub, there to make less real the disappointment we felt so acutely.

CHAPTER III

ALL ABOARD FOR KATHERINE

The trip from Darwin to Katherine I shall never forget. The train was due to leave at eight o'clock in the morning - it made fortnightly trips - and when that hour approached the guard would clang a huge fire-bell. There would be last-minute drinks at the pub, a scurrying to gather belongings, and a rush for the train. But as the guard knew everyone who was travelling there was little chance of being left behind.

It was a weird collection of passengers. There was a government official, immaculate in helmet and white ducks, stockmen you could easily identify by their elastic-side boots, prospectors with that look of hope deferred in their tired eyes, and blacks returning after a "walkabout," which is their expressive term for a short holiday in Darwin, or elsewhere.

At the last moment a stockman jumped aboard, and when the guard came for the tickets he said he did not know how far he was going. His horses had got away, and he expected to pick them up somewhere along the railway track. Sure enough he sighted them about eight miles south, signalled to the driver to stop the train, paid his fare, and left us. That, I learned, was the easygoing way they did things in the north.

We were passing through uninteresting country. There were miles upon miles of open forest with occasional clay-pans, and liberally dotting the landscape were huge white-ant beds, some as high as the telegraph wires. The magnetic ant-beds were especially intriguing. They were fashioned like huge tombstones, with the edges pointing due north and south.

It was December, and, with the temperature hovering around 112 degrees of sticky heat, we were already getting tired of the trip. When we reached Rum Jungle, forty miles from Darwin,[14] we saw the first sign of life since leaving. An old prospector met the train and took away his mail and a fortnight's supply of salt and fresh beef. He had been on a wellnigh hopeless quest for tin for years, and was still carrying on.

We also saw about a dozen blacks, the gins with dresses made from flour-bags by the simple process of cutting arm-and neck-holes and slitting the bottom, and the boys in long, ragged trousers, discarded by white men, and carrying hunting-spears. They were a hungry, miserable lot, vastly different from the warriors and their gins we were to encounter later.

After leaving Rum Jungle the country began to improve; the big trees and the grasses told us we were passing through more fertile lands. When we arrived at Bachelor Farm, ten miles farther along, we were told a priceless story of government ineptitude. At a cost of some £20,000 the government had established this experimental farm for the purpose of improving agriculture in the Territory.

There were first-class stables and outbuildings, and any wealthy man would have been content with the manager's quarters. Windmills were erected, and the ground cleared, at considerable expense, for the cultivation of peanuts, tropical fruits, vegetables, grasses, and other experimental growths.

After this grand flourish the farm succeeded in producing one pumpkin which was stolen by a black! This farm was abandoned in 1912; implements and machinery were left to rust away, and a caretaker is now there to keep the white ants out of the buildings.[15]

A striking contrast to this government effort is at Stapleton a few miles farther down the line. An Australian farmer had, after a courageous fight against adverse conditions, established a farm on which flourished all the things which the government had failed to grow at Bachelor. On one side of the line ran a clear-water creek lined with immense trees and pandanus palms, and on the other was this prosperous farm. The sight gave us our first really encouraging impression of the

Territory. But we were longing to see a buffalo, although we knew we were hundreds of miles away from their country.

Leaving Stapleton we continued to pass through fertile country, and at last reached Adelaide River where lunch awaited us. And it was a lunch which no one would, in his wildest dreams, have expected in a place so remote from civilization.

The menu was something like this: - soup; fish (barramundi, which abound in the fresh waters of the Territory and weigh up to forty pounds); roast pork, duck, goose, beef or mutton; vegetables (potatoes, turnips, cabbage, pumpkin); fruit (papaw, oranges, mangoes, melon); and tea. And the cost was 2s. 6d.

Except for tea, sugar, and flour everything was produced on the river. There were hundreds of wild pigs, progeny of a few Berkshires which had been imported some years before, and flocks of wild ducks and geese.

The river looked cool and inviting, but when we suggested a dip we were promptly told it was infested with crocodiles. At this same spot some time later a friend of mine, Leo Angusson, met with a frightful experience. Leo, a farmer in a small way, was standing in the long grass which lined the river-banks, looking for the tracks of his horses. His back was to the river when, without any warning, he was grabbed around the knee by a crocodile and dragged into the water. Leo did not lose his presence of mind, and jabbing his thumb into the crocodile's eye, its one vulnerable spot, he released himself.

Suffering terrible pain he was struggling up the bank when the crocodile came at him again, this time clamping its fearsome jaws around his arm. He was dragged back into the water. Although semi-conscious with agony Leo luckily found the crocodile's other eye with his thumb and, temporarily blinded, the animal let go. His cries brought his brother who helped the terribly mutilated fellow to safety.

After a nightmare journey they got Leo to Darwin hospital

where he suffered indescribable torture. As the crocodile lives only on decayed food the wounds it inflicts are immediately poisoned. Leo was in such a shocking condition that the slightest movement of his bed increased his pain nearly to breaking point. Splendid nursing patched him up sufficiently to enable him to be removed to Sydney where great surgical and medical skill saved both his leg and his arm.

Soon after leaving Adelaide River the character of the country changed perceptibly. Rocky hills, sparsely covered with stunted timber, and innumerable dry watercourses told us we were in the actual mineral belt of the north.

The country became more and more rugged until we reached Brock's Creek, the most important stopping-place in the hundred and twelve miles from Darwin. A pub was there. Brock's Creek was the remnant of a prosperous gold-mining settlement, as the abandoned shafts and dismantled machinery bore witness. About half a mile from the township were the Chinese quarters. Some of the descendants of the coolies who worked on the construction of the railway line from Darwin to Pine Creek in 1887 were living there.[16]

After the line was completed the Chinese, instead of settling on the land like the whites might have done, went prospecting and fossicking. How much gold they won from this once rich area nobody knows.

The pub was a tin shanty. Adjoining it was a general store, and the police station was across the line a couple of hundred yards away. The publican was one Mrs Haynes, widow of Tom Crush, the first parliamentary representative of the Territory. She was a fine buxom woman who would give long credit to the thirsty hard-ups in the same spontaneous manner as she would pitch a man on to the road if he annoyed her.[17]

"Keep in with Mrs Haynes," was the slogan in those parts. As she also owned the store, it seemed good policy.

Another fifty miles of mining country and we arrived at

Pine Creek at six o'clock, having taken just on ten hours to cover a hundred and sixty.

Pine Creek was more like civilization than anything we had seen since leaving Darwin. There was a fine hotel with about a dozen rooms, a court house, hospital and shops. There were over a hundred residents, about 60 per cent being white; the rest Chinese.

Here the first gold in the Territory was discovered in 1871: it was alluvial gold, reef-mining came later. This, being a low-grade proposition, has now ceased because it would be highly expensive to work profitably. A little fossicking by Chinese and whites is practically all that is now done on the field.[18]

Before we left for the rail-head at the Katherine next morning, we had an amusing experience of how justice is interpreted at the Pine Creek court.

A local justice of the peace, who had a slaughtering licence, had before him a Chinaman on a minor charge.

" I fine you 17s. 6d.," he said, "which, with the £1 10s. you owe me for beef, makes £2 7s. 6d. - or seven days." The Chinaman paid up without a murmur.

When we reached Katherine, forty miles farther southeast, we were met by a black boy with a buck-board and pair which was to take us to the government station a Mataranka, where we were to pick up the outfit promised us by Trower.

The black boy seemed a sulky little fellow, for not once in the forty miles journey did he speak. Our pidgin-English, though not expert, was not so bad that we couldn't make ourselves understood.

At Mataranka we were given a cheery greeting by Percy Love, the manager. He was a genial soul and appeared only too anxious to see that we were equipped adequately for the two-hundred-mile trip to the promised land of the ironstone bore country.

With twelve horses, saddles, guns, ammunition, enough salt

beef to see us part of the way, and a black boy, we waved good-bye to Percy Love, who, no doubt, was wondering if he would ever see us again.

CHAPTER IV

HOPES DASHED AND RAISED

ON our first night out we shot a kangaroo, and I revealed to Whittaker the secret of making kangaroo-tail soup, and of cutting and grilling a steak. I had lived my young life in the bush, but Whittaker was new to it, and since the cooking was to be his particular charge, I decided that the sooner he learnt how to do it, the better.

One thing I early impressed upon him, a thing which no bushman ever forgets. Make certain the lid of the golden syrup tin is firmly on! There is nothing in the bush more calculated to make a man murder his best friend than to find, when opening the tucker-bags, that everything is smothered in syrup.

A couple of days out we passed through Elsey Downs and saw what remained of the homestead around which Mrs Gunn wrote her famous *We of the Never Never.*[19]

For eight days we rode leisurely and without excitement or adventure. Not even a black came our way. The only animal - and bird-life we saw were kangaroos and pigeons.

At last we came to the bore (we knew it by its marking No. 3) and gazed upon the country on which Trower told us we could do well with cattle.

We examined the bore first. It was sunk about three hundred feet, and was surmounted by a huge windmill about which circled thousands of pigeons. That was the first set-back, since their presence told me more definitely than any words could have done, that there was no surface water within miles.

I scanned the thickly-timbered, well-grassed country (an excellent grazing proposition had there been surface water) and once more cursed the spin of the coin which had brought us to the Territory. The bore was in a state of disrepair, and since it was supposed to water an area of six hundred square miles, settling there was out of the question.

However, we made camp and put ourselves in a more or less contented frame of mind with some delicious pigeon-pie.

Next morning after saddling our mounts we hobbled the remaining horses, and with the black boy, turned west to see if my belief that there was no surface water would be confirmed. We scoured the country for fifteen miles, circling to the south and returning to camp without seeing a drop.

Before finally giving in, we decided to try east next day on what I was convinced would be another hopeless quest. There was no sign of water anywhere.

"This about puts the lid on things," I said that night. "What about heading straight for Darwin, and catching the first boat south?"

"I'm on," said Whittaker. "And then the first boat to Brazil."

"Do me," I said. And we shook hands upon it as we had done that night on Gallipoli.

So at daybreak we followed our tracks back to Mataranka. A day away from the station we ran out of supplies, and were feeling pretty hungry, when Whittaker pointed to what appeared to be a duck in a waterhole. It was about fifty yards away, and taking swift aim with his rifle, he made a good hit.

We sent the black boy to recover the kill, and my mind dwelt pleasantly upon thoughts of roast duck until I saw the boy grinning broadly. Pointing to the bird he was carrying, he said:

"This fella no more duck."

The wretched thing was a shag.[20] I told Whittaker he could cook it if he liked, and I made up my bunk and turned in, telling him to call me when the meal was ready. After four hours cooking Whittaker sampled the shag, and wasted no time in getting rid of the first mouthful.

"Filthy stuff," he said between spits. He gave it to the black boy. The little fellow fell upon it with a hungry gleam in his roving eye, for shag is appreciated by the blacks.

Back again at Mataranka we had a much needed bath, and a good meal. After dinner that night we were smoking on the spacious veranda of the homestead and talking to Percy Love when it occurred to one of us to mention that we had come to the Territory to shoot buffaloes.

"Why didn't you say so before," said Love. "I might have wondered what you were doing in these parts, but it's not the custom here to ask questions. It is always good policy to wait until you're told."

I began to take notice immediately.

"Don't say you know where we can get some buffalo country," I said in some excitement. "We were told at Darwin that all the leases had gone."

"That's funny," said Love, "because I know that there's a block of twelve hundred square miles between the East and South Alligator rivers, about three hundred miles north of here, and north-east of Darwin. It's on the way to Port Essington. The country's been put aside for returned soldiers, and you should be able to get it for the asking. Buffaloes are there by the thousands."

We almost fell upon Love's neck. What great news - if it turned out to be true. But the memory of our recent disappointments sobered me at once.

Love, however, assured us there could be no hitch to prevent us getting the lease. Further, he said that he was a sleeping partner with a buffalo-shooter who had "shot out" his own territory and was not able to get this particular lease because he was not a returned soldier. [21] Moreover, Love's partner was going south and wanted to sell his outfit of packs, saddles, knives, steels, guns, and the rest.

This sounded like luck at last and we promptly made

arrangements with Love for the outfit to be left for us at Kopalgo on the South Alligator River.

We were both a bit too excited to sleep much that night. Our dream had become reality at last. I set to figuring out the best selection of words with which to bring shame to the face of one Trower - and the sooner we could get to Darwin and see him, the better.

We took our leave of Love and Mataranka with kindly feelings for both, and boarded the train at Katherine with hopes higher than they had yet been.

On the tedious trip to Darwin I frequently found myself bestirred by misgivings, and asked myself, and Whittaker too, innumerable, questions. Why had not Trower told us about that buffalo country? Why had Trower sent us on that wild-goose chase to look at country where there was no water? Why had not a dozen or more people mentioned something about that buffalo lease? Could it have been because they were all like Love, happy to answer questions, and content not to ask them?

Then I pursued a further line of thought. If we got the lease how would we fare? I knew enough about the bush to know we would not starve or (as long as I retained my army compass) get lost. But would we get the "kick" out of potting buffaloes I dreamed about on Gallipoli? Would we be able to turn the hides to profit? Would, in fact, the Territory give us the adventure which we sought?

I fancy the inactivity on that train trip caused these questions to arise; but at the moment they were very real, and when we alighted at Darwin I was far from being in the exalted frame of mind I was in when Percy Love indicated to us the seeming waywardness of Trower.

We wasted no time in getting another interview with Trower, and told him in no uncertain terms that the iron-stone bore block we had seen was no use to us.

Trower offered no apologies or explanations, but proceeded airily to suggest that we should take up an agricultural block on the Daly River, about a hundred miles away.

We listened impatiently while he extolled the virtues of this land, and at last I said:

"What about that buffalo country on the East Alligator River?"

Trower seemed surprised that we knew about it.

"That's reserved for returned soldiers."

"Well, we're returned soldiers."

He opened his eyes.

"Now, why didn't you tell me that before. Yes, there are twelve hundred square miles, and you can have the lot at 2s. a square mile."

I looked at him squarely, but thought it best to refrain from comment.

Being forewarned by a tip from Percy Love, we decided to take half the block on the East Alligator River, which was by a long way the best country, and since there were no boundaries we should not need to worry if our operations extended into the other half.

With a grand flourish we gave Trower a cheque for £60, a year's rental for the lease in advance, and left him still wondering why he had not mentioned of his own accord the buffalo country which, barring accidents, was now ours.

In due course our application was returned from Melbourne, granted, and with the lease in our pockets, we thought we owned the world.[22]

We made immediate arrangements to take ten week's supplies with us; a further six months' supplies to go around by lugger from Darwin to Oenpelli on the East Alligator River.

We supplemented our equipment on the lines suggested by the prospector we had met on the *Mataram*, and wired the Defence Department at Sydney for half a dozen

Martini-Henry carbines and two thousand rounds of ammunition.

We made a rush trip to Pine Creek where Trower told us we could pick up twenty young horses. I looked them over and found them good sorts.

We promptly bought pack- and riding-saddles, and engaged two black boys. These were called Bob Cadell (no doubt after a former employer, as the blacks often name themselves) and Jacky Anyone. They were to play an important and oft-times highly amusing part in our future adventures.

I left Whittaker and the boys to bring the horses to Burrundie, a railway-siding fifteen miles from Pine Creek, and about a hundred and sixty miles from our property.

Trower had also told us we could have ten of his horses and equipment from Bachelor Farm - to be returned after we reached the East Alligator River.

I went back to Darwin for the ten weeks' supplies which I entrained to Burrundie, and left on the same train for Bachelor Farm for the other horses.

It was a hard job droving these animals as they always wanted to make for home. After the first night out it took me three hours to get them together the next morning.

However, I got to Burrundie, and found Whittaker had made camp five miles out on three freshwater billabongs.

After tea that night we rode to Mount Wells, a couple of miles from camp. It was a tin-mine cut in the side of a hill, and from all accounts should have been a payable proposition. But the whites who first owned it could not agree on who should boss the show, and it ultimately passed into the hands of Chinese who today are making a good thing of it.

To make a few purchases we drifted into Wing On's store. The crowd hanging around outside made us think he had a prosperous business; but once inside we saw the reason. It was Wing On's daughter. Standing there with her long pigtails, and in Chinese dress, this full-blooded Oriental lady made a beautiful picture.

Whittaker and I were pretty well dressed at the time, and our appearance, no doubt, caused the Chinaman to imagine that affluence went with it.

We had hardly put foot in the store when Wing On approached us, rubbing his hands and smiling and bowing.

With a wave of his long yellow hand towards the little beauty, he said:

"You likee missus longa yourself?"

I didn't quite see the point, but agreed with him that the lady was very desirable.

"Me selle you missus you want im."

Wanting to gaze a little longer upon the striking child I carried on.

"Might be. How much?"

The Chinaman with a bland smile:

"You plenty good fella. Plenty money. £100 for you."

I told him that was a lot of money, and asked him what she could do.

He said she was a wonderful rice-cook, could make bread, and, above all, he was sure she could produce a large family.

Feeling a little sorry for the exquisite piece of Oriental ware, who, apparently, fully understood what the talk was about, I told Wing On that maybe I would think about it some other time. And so we left.

The old chap sold his lovely daughter to a countryman at Pine Creek, and Whittaker and I took part in the festivities in celebration of the birth of their first child.

CHAPTER V

ON THE TRAIL

WE returned to camp and had a good night's rest in preparation for an early start on the long trail in the morning.

At daybreak the horses were brought in and the loads apportioned and balanced. The end of the first stage of our journey was to be Mary River, twenty-five miles away. Percy Love had given us a rough map on which were noted the landmarks which, with luck, should guide us to our ultimate destination.

Before making a move I asked Whittaker had he selected a mount for himself. He said he had his eye on a chestnut mare and invited me to try it out for him. I found the mare of lamb-like quality, and just the thing for Whittaker who was not much of a horseman, and knew it.

I was a little amazed to see Whittaker produce a stockwhip from his baggage.

"You'd better give that to one of the boys," I suggested.

"Not on your life. A bushman's not a bushman without a stockwhip," said Whittaker from the city.

"Have you ever tried to use one?"

He said he had once and succeeded in tying it around his neck.

I let him have his way. We had been going only a couple of minutes when I heard a yell, and looking round saw Whittaker lying on the broad of his back with the whip firmly clenched in his hands. Unfortunately for him his horse was one of the many to take umbrage at the sight of a whip. After that discomforting incident the whip was handed to the care of Bob Cadell.

About half an hour later a white man galloped up and introduced himself as Charlie Fez, a cattle-owner on whose property we were travelling.

"On the track?" was his cheery greeting.

"Yes," we said. "We are hitting towards Oenpelli. Any buffaloes about?"

"Very few," he said, "but I saw tracks ahead a couple of days ago. I'll go on and see if I can come across them for you." He rode away.

We discovered later that Fez had made up his mind that we couldn't tell the difference between a bullock and a buffalo, and would, likely as not, shoot down some of his stock.

That was a fine impression for two great hunters to create! We also learnt later that Fez had told them at Mount Wells of having seen two new-chums on the trail, and that he was sure that no one else was ever likely to see them again. When I look back I am forced to realize that the assumption of Fez was a perfectly natural one.

We were moving along at an even pace, I in the lead, when a packmare made her way up from the rear and took her place beside Whittaker. The animal then pushed her way in front of him. I realized something must be wrong and dismounted. Sure enough the surcingle was chafing her. That's horse-sense for you!

There was one thing about the incident which pleased me tremendously. The mare was, obviously, a trained leader, and I immediately placed her in the lead of the horses following Whittaker.

We were passing through undulating country, heavily timbered. It was hot and close, and I fell to dreaming about what lay ahead when I heard a shout from Whittaker:

"Spur!"

Automatically I gripped the saddle with my knees, dug the spurs in, and Dandy (a beautiful bay standing sixteen hands) bounded forward. Whittaker's cry was followed immediately by a shot and looking around I saw the mangled head of a black snake hanging from a hole in a tree some feet from the ground.

Whittaker told me he had seen the snake strike at Dandy's foreleg, then withdraw its head to strike at my leg, and as it did he fired. It was a sweet shot.

I have often thought why I acted so promptly at Whittaker's cry; I suppose the war had a lot to do with it. We were on so many patrols and raiding-parties together that there was almost perfect co-ordination of thought and action between us.

The incident, though slight, was a reminder that our adventures were only just beginning.

About eleven o'clock we dismounted and set about preparing for the midday meal on the bank of a sandy-bottomed creek with clear running water and fringed with pandanus palms, and paper-bark or tea-trees.

Whittaker wanted to know why we crossed the creek before camping. I impressed upon him the point that a bushman, if he has to cross a creek as well as camp, will cross first. I didn't realize how soon we were to get a very practical illustration of the wisdom of this custom. We were removing the heavy packs from the horses - always the first job on making camp, owing to their weight - when Bob Cadell came up to me:

"Big fella storm close up, boss," he said, pointing with his charred and stumpy pipe to the horizon where a cluster of heavy black clouds had gathered.

Suddenly the whole atmosphere seemed to become close and tense with an occasional puff of wind, which rustled the leaves ominously.

We pitched the Birkmyre fly between two small saplings and placed all the food-stuffs and perishables underneath.[23] The storm was gathering quickly. In a few moments the wind had risen to gale force, and great black clouds swept across the sky. Lightning such as I had never seen before slashed the blackness above, and the thunder reminded me of Flanders.

The black boys, who had crept under the tent, were huddled together and trying to bury their faces in the ground. Then came the rain. It began with a few large drops, but increased until it fell upon us like a wall of water. The tent stood up to the deluge splendidly.

The storm passed as quickly as it came and the air was once more heavy with moisture. A mighty roar drew us from cover. The placid creek we had crossed was transformed into a raging torrent. I reminded Whittaker that had we camped on the other side we probably would have been held up for a couple of days.

For the next ten miles we passed over desert country covered with stunted growths of lancewood and wild quinine bush. The lancewood is particularly dangerous. In dry spells it sheds its foliage, leaving the branches brittle, hard, and pointed: small stock have frequently been found impaled on them.

Just before coming to Mary River we passed through about half a mile of dense bamboo thickets. They grew from twenty to thirty feet high, with a diameter up to four inches; and so closely packed were they that we had to use our tomahawks to clear a path for the packhorses. I thought, at the time, what wonderful tropical huts could be built with the bamboo.

At Mary River we found a wide course of deep waterholes beautifully clear. We crossed at the shallows and made camp on a bank in the shade of a great fig-tree.

I opened some of the figs and found them full of worms.

This, unfortunately, is also the trouble with most of the wild apples and pears in the Territory. Unfortunately, too, goats find the figs a delicacy with the result that their milk has a strong flavour.

Leaving the blacks to unsaddle and hobble the horses, make the fire, and get bundles of grass for bedding, we took our towels and selected a clear pool. After a delightful dip Whittaker got out his fishing-line and flies he had bought in

Sydney, and I took my shot-gun.

Our individual excursions were highly profitable. I bagged eight pigeons, and Whittaker brought back several fish weighing about a pound and a half each. I don't know what they were, but they closely resembled our speckled trout.

The black boys cleaned the catch, and we had a great meal of fish and pigeon.

After tea we went for a stroll, when the mosquitoes acquainted us of their presence. They were mostly the famous Scots Greys; they literally stood on their heads and bored in. The small black ones, with their remindful bites were also present.

Before it was dark they drove us underneath the cheesecloth netting. I realized then what flimsy defence ordinary netting would have been against the grey battalions.

Bob Cadell and Jacky Anyone had made their camp about a quarter of a mile away. I was thankful that that distance separated us, for Bob had his *didgeridoo* (a hollow piece of bamboo about four feet long) from which he blew a mournful dirge, while Jacky beat an incessant tat-a-tat with two sticks upon a flat piece of stone. We were settling down when Whittaker asked:

"Sure we haven't forgotten something?"

"Not that I know of, Whit."

With a look of smug self-satisfaction he produced a bottle of whisky and poured out two good nips. He had brought four bottles with him, from which we were to have only one spot each before retiring, and a few bottles of brandy to be used only when needed medicinally.

I lay awake for some time that night enjoying the wonderful loneliness that surrounded us. We might never get through this mad adventure, but it looked as if we were going to get some "kick" out of it. I was just about asleep when Whittaker called out:

"What on earth's that?"

I listened, and although all was quiet about us, there seemed to be a high wind blowing some distance up. I dragged on my trousers (when we had the chance we always changed into pyjamas throughout the war, and intended to do so now), and went out to investigate. Above, I saw thousands of flying foxes making their way down the river.[24] Next morning Whittaker said he had scarcely slept a wink.

"Those cursed horse-bells nearly drove me mad," he said.

We had fastened bells of different tones to eight of the horses. I knew that as the horses would mate up, we would have little trouble in locating them. I told Whittaker that he would soon get used to it.

"A bushman," I said, "goes to sleep with the tinkle of the bells in his ears. It is when they stop ringing that he wakes up."

He looked at me dubiously, and said he would risk trying to sleep without the aid of the bell music.

After a refreshing swim I took the shot-gun while Whittaker prepared the breakfast. On my way back to the camp with a few pigeons, the smell of sizzling bacon quickened my footsteps. To anyone who has lived in the bush there is no more marvellous sensation than that early morning smell of bacon cooking.

CHAPTER VI

A FIGHT WITH THE BLACKS

BEFORE hitting the trail again I asked Bob Cadell to ride with me in the lead as I wanted to get some information from him about what we were likely to encounter.

Bob looked rather sullen until I remembered that I had forgotten his and Jacky's daily allowance of half a stick of tobacco. This forthcoming, he was soon his grinning self again.

We were heading for a place called Flynn's Grave which was marked on Love's map. Flynn was an old prospector who had met a tragic death some years before. He had apparently been making his way back to Mount Wells when he was bitten by a snake. He knew he was beyond help and dying, and had scribbled his last farewell to the world on a scrap of paper which was found in a tin by the grave, which it was thought the blacks had dug for him.[25]

I asked Bob about the possibilities of meeting any blacks and he said that he belonged to a tribe on the side of the Mary River we had left, and he did not know the country we were now in.

I was chatting to Bob and endeavouring to improve my pidgin-English vocabulary, when his quick and ever-restless eye alighted upon something off the track. He rode over, dismounted and beckoned to me. To my astonishment I saw, stuck in the fork of a tree, the skeleton of a crocodile. I whistled Whittaker over, and remembering our swim that morning we exchanged meaning glances.

I was struck by the extremely long snout, which differed considerably from the snouts of crocodiles I had seen in the Zoological Gardens.

I said to Bob Cadell.

"What name this one?"

He grinned.

"Im halligator. No more cheeky fella."

Always believing that all crocodiles were dangerous I hardly got the point of this remark. But I found later that what Cadell had meant was perfectly true. The skeleton was that of what is known throughout the north as a freshwater crocodile. It is only found in northern Queensland and the Northern Territory; it grows to a length of seven feet, and its long slender snout with sword-like teeth distinguishes it from the man-eater with its blunt snout and totally different tooth-formation. These freshwater crocodiles live on wild pigs, dogs, fowl, and the rest, but have never been known to touch human flesh.[26]

Incorrectly, the crocodiles of the north are frequently referred to as alligators. The alligator is found in China and in the southern states of North America. It has a more rounded head, but the chief difference is in the formation of the teeth. The fourth tooth on each side of the lower jaw of the crocodile is much larger; it fits into a notch in the upper jaw and is visible when the mouth is closed. The same tooth in an alligator fits into a socket, and is invisible.[27]

As we gained the summit of a hill, Cadell hastily pulled his pipe from his mouth and, pointing to two or three columns of smoke in the distance ahead, he said:

"Im blackfella, close up."

"Cheeky fella, Bob?" I asked.

"Might be longa nother fella black - but no more longa white man."

My interpretation of this was that there were blacks ahead who would not harm Whittaker or me, but Bob and Jacky would not be safe with them. I gave the question no further thought, and we moved steadily on.

I observed Cadell reaching now and again and plucking berries, which he ate with relish. I tried one and found it a luscious fruit; it was the size of a cherry, but green. I was later told that they were a specie of wild plum and excellent eating.

We passed by dozens of big grey kangaroos which gazed at us inquisitively. We did not interfere with them as we had resolved only to shoot for food. These animals hardly bothered to hop from our tracks: apparently they had never been gun-hunted and knew nothing of the danger the white man carried.

We made a midday halt on a billabong near which were the ruins of an old homestead. We were told afterwards that a man had established a small cattle-station there, but so many head were speared by blacks and led wild by buffaloes, that he had abandoned it.

Shortly after hitting the trail again, Cadell, who was still riding with me, appeared anxious. His eyes were darting first to the ground and then to right and left. Not asking questions I tried to follow his gaze, but could see nothing to cause concern.

Topping another small rise we again saw the smoke columns.

"Blackfella close up, boss," said Cadell.

He appeared to be uneasy and gave me to understand that a black was all right in his own country, but in pretty real danger anywhere else. I was becoming more and more interested, and for the next mile or so I was very much on the alert. Suddenly Bob Cadell, whose eyes had been glued to the ground, jumped from his horse and pointing excitedly, said:

"Im white man come up."

I jumped down and saw what Bob had discovered. It was the fresh imprint of an iron-shod heel which could only have been made by a white man.

I called Whittaker up, showed him the marks, and told him

to keep a sharp look out. I left Whittaker in the lead and cantered about half a mile ahead with Cadell. Those smoke columns and the evident presence of a white man were disturbing.

We were riding through dense palms and heavy timber, when Cadell grabbed Dandy's bridle, bringing him to a sudden stop.

"Listen, boss!"

I could hear faint shouting, then suddenly there pierced the air a terrible cry of "Help!" - a cry I had heard before when death was close at hand. I plunged the spurs into Dandy and galloped in the direction of the shout. Never before have I been so thankful for such a horse. He threaded his way through the trees at amazing speed, and at last we came to the edge of a clearing.

In a glance I took in the sight before me. There were some fifty black warriors with spears and nulla-nullas, yelling and dancing, and in the midst of them I caught a glimpse of the arm of a white man gripping a black by the ankle.

I drew my army .45, and, firing two shots into the air, galloped at them. The clearing was about a hundred yards across, and the blacks were in the centre of it. By the time I got there most of them had scampered to the shelter of the trees, but I could see there were two in the process of throttling the white man, while others were jumping around and howling horribly.

The impact of Dandy's shoulder sent several of them spinning, and I managed to fell one with a hit behind the ear from the pistol. I dismounted and fired two more quick shots into the air, which sent the rest of them scattering.

I made a swift examination of the white man, and saw that he was still alive, but the position then was desperate for both of us. He was a man of about fourteen stone, and the thought of dragging him to safety was out of the question. Dandy had cleared away. There was no sign of Whittaker, and I had two shots left in my gun.

I was looking wildly around when, with a chill of horror, I saw the blacks emerging from the trees and advancing as they fitted their spears into their wommeras. They were obviously only waiting until they got well within range before throwing.

It looked like the end and I was about to pull the trigger when I heard the thunder of hoofs on the left and saw the blacks vanishing as if touched by magic.

Six men galloped into the clearing almost coincidental with the arrival of Whittaker. The new-comers rode up to me and their leader said:

"What the hell's up here? What's happened to Bill?"

"We can talk about that later," I said. "Let's fix your mate up first!"

I gave a cursory glance at the black I had stunned with the revolver and guessed that he would recover in time.

We dragged the unconscious white man to the shelter of the trees, and found that, apart from the ugly bruises around his neck and a jagged cut on his temple from which the blood welled, he was not seriously hurt. A drop of brandy which Whittaker produced revived him, and we heard the story.

It appeared that the party had been prospecting towards Arnhem Land and their mate had left them to do a little on his own. While having a drink his horse had broken away, and he was making his way back to camp when the blacks came across him.

They asked him for tobacco and he said he had none. This did not seem to satisfy them and one of them caught him by the shirt. He lashed out with his fist and knocked the black down. That was almost the beginning of his end.

When he had not returned to camp the next morning his mates had set out for him, and had been attracted by the cries the same as I.

Before leaving, I asked the leader what the chances were of a further attack by the blacks. Curiously enough, he said there was no likelihood, and I often pondered upon this confident statement.

It was not until some time later that I discovered that the man called Bill was what is known in the Territory as a "marked" man by the blacks. It seems that he had been guilty of interfering with their women, and of violating all their tribal customs - unforgivable sins which are only washed out by death.

And I was not surprised when I heard that his body had been found pinned to the ground with spears. The black man's honour had been vindicated.

After we got our party on the move again I asked Bob Cadell what had happened to him when I rode in among the blacks. He said he had gone back to hurry Whittaker up. I said:

"I think you bin frightened alonga the cheeky fella."

He poked out his chest.

"Me no flite alonga those poor myall blacks." But I had my own opinion about it.

It was mid-afternoon when the affair ended and we pushed on, eventually striking camp not very long before sunset. We chose a site of considerable strategic value in case the blacks decided upon a visit. We pitched tent at the mouth of a gorge with flat country behind us, and ran the horses ahead. It was an ideal spot.

Acting upon Bob's advice we took our bunks to a place about twelve yards away from where the tents were pitched, leaving them to act as dummies. Bob said there would be no chance of an attack during the night as the blacks were frightened of the debil-debils which prowled after dark, but their favourite time was at daybreak.

All the same we noticed that the black boys camped as close to us as we would allow them. I slept very little and the low murmurings of Bob and Jacky and Whittaker tossing restlessly, assured me that the rest of the party was as much on edge as I was.

We were all heartily glad to see daybreak which brought its own balm. After breakfast Whittaker and I consulted Love's map, and from it had little difficulty in finding the last resting-place of Flynn. The small wooden cross had been partly burnt away, and scrub was growing on the cairn. We straightened it out as best we could, and gave a thought to the old prospector who had met such a tragic and lonely death.

After a breakfast of cold pigeon and damper, washed down with tea, we were on the move again. It was a glorious morning. As we passed through the gorge the air was alive with the shrill cries of parrots, parrakeets, white cockatoos, jackasses, and birds of every hue and cry.[28]

With what I thought was considerable relief Bob Cadell pointed to the blacks' smoke signals at the rear of us. Their formation, he told me, indicated that they had no further interest in us.

After travelling a couple of hours through fertile country we came across a battalion of native companions or brolgas. They were forming quadrille parties and when we whistled they seemed to be dancing for us.

By midday we alighted upon another ideal camping ground.

Fifty acres of young, green grass were surrounded by half a dozen waterholes like great white sapphires around an emerald. The waterholes were up to two hundred yards wide and five hundred in length, and splashing gently in and out of the reeds were hundreds of ducks.

Tea-trees and bloodwoods fringed the banks, casting inviting shades, and Whittaker and I sat still upon our horses drinking in the beauty of the scene.

There was a sudden and violent movement in the reeds, and

Dandy gave a startled rear. I was thrown around his neck and when I regained my seat two fearsome horns came into view, followed by a huge bulk smothered in white clay. Instantly I knew we had seen our first buffalo.

The great beast had been lying in its mud-bath, as is their wont. The moment it sighted us, it scrambled out of the waterhole and tore through the undergrowth, crashing saplings in its charge.

At the sight of the buffalo our packhorses bolted, with Jacky Anyone in pursuit, but whether of Jacky's own volition I didn't know.

However, he soon returned with the horses, and taking our .303s Whittaker and I left the boys in charge and set after the buffalo. We followed the trail for about a mile, but as the buffalo still seemed to be going at top speed, we gave up the chase and returned to camp.

There had apparently been an argument between Jacky and Bob Cadell. Jacky was asserting that the beast was a bullock, and Bob, with contemptuous snorts, was trying to convince him it was a buffalo. When we rode up to them Jacky ran over to me, and, pointing excitedly to where the animal had disappeared, said:

"What name that fella, boss?"

"Him buffalo, Jacky."

Poor Jacky! His face went a greyish colour, and his big eyes rolled in abject fear. He would shoot fearful glances to the scrub where the buffalo had disappeared, and then look appealingly at us as though for protection. Jacky had never seen a buffalo before, but he had heard at corroborees terrifying legends of the wickedness of the buffalo, and had lived in mortal dread of the beast.

In the afternoon Whittaker and I took our shot-guns, and went hunting for game. We were lucky enough to bring down a number of teal (small wild duck), and some pygmy geese - the exact replica in miniature of the goose we know in civilization. And delicious eating they are; the best, I think, of all wild birds.

During the preparation of the evening meal we were puzzled as to how the black boys had cooked theirs, and thoroughly cooked too, long before us. We discovered that they had filleted their birds which, as Bob Cadell explained, was invariably the custom.

Whittaker and I were lazing and smoking in that contented frame of mind which only a full stomach can produce when my thoughts were disturbed by a deep-throated "Coo, coo." I tried to place the weird cry, when I suddenly remembered my uncle Arthur Mockett telling me of the Torres Strait pigeon and how easily one could distinguish it.

Grabbing my gun I left Whittaker to his meditations, and returned in a while with a brace. They are very large black and white birds, and migrate from the Malayan islands to the Australian coast at regular intervals. They are berry-eaters, differing in this respect from the ordinary pigeon, which lives on grain.

It was too early to turn in, so Whittaker and I strolled down to the waterhole, where I watched him set a line baited with a chunk of corned beef. The mosquitoes soon drove us back, however. On reaching camp we were surprised to find there were none there. I was struck by the sweet smell of smoke from our fire. Whittaker hit upon the explanation.

"That's sandalwood burning on the fire," he said. "Don't you know sandalwood oil keeps mosquitoes away?"

I did; but what might have been a pleasant night was disturbed by the howling and yapping of mobs of dingoes. We had nothing to fear from them, but their unceasing noise was extremely annoying.

I felt sorry for that poor little devil Jacky Anyone. He was still trembling from the shock the buffalo had given him and all night long he sat hunched before the fire throwing one stick after another upon it, and peering into the bush.

A restless night at last ended. With break of day Whittaker and I went to see if his line had snared anything. Sure enough on the end of it was a huge catfish. We skinned it and had it for breakfast. It tasted right enough, but later I was to remember that catfish.

We got ready for the pad again and left with some regrets the most beautiful spot we had so far seen in the Territory. Kadauke (meaning plenty of everything) is the name now given it. We were carrying our .303s across our saddles, since having seen one buffalo one could never tell when another would come across our path.

There was not a breath of wind, and the sun beat down with a burning ray, but as time was not pressing it was a leisurely procession.

A mile or so farther on, we came upon a small clearing, and there saw a pack of dingoes slinking away from a carcass. It was that of a buffalo. At last it seemed we were getting amongst them.

We then passed through some of the most wonderful plain country I have ever seen in any part of Australia. It was covered with rich water couch and kangaroo grasses which came up to our shoulders. Sparkling waterholes were dotted everywhere.

We were making for Kunkamoula lagoon, marked on our map, and we had little trouble in locating it. The first realization we had that we were near the camping-ground was the flight from the trees of hundreds of white cockatoos, which told us there was an expanse of water near by.

No time was wasted in getting the heavy packs from the horses. Then I left Whittaker at the camp while I took my .32

and went exploring. The lagoon was about half a mile wide and two miles long, stringing out into a number of fair-sized waterholes.

I spotted a big grey kangaroo, and taking a running shot, brought him down. I dragged the big fellow into the shade of a tree, and covered him with leaves to save him from ants, heat, and dingoes.

Where the bank was accessible I had a look for tracks, and saw those of kangaroos, wallabies, dingoes, and native companions, and, yes, the unmistakable print of the cloven hoof of the buffalo! I examined it closely, but found it was not recent enough to be worth following.

Going along warily, not knowing what I might meet, I saw a big reddish-brown dingo almost as large as a full-grown Alsatian dog, playing with her five cubs. She would grab them by the throat in turn, toss them aside, and wait for them to come at her, which they did with inherent viciousness.

I watched them fascinated, and it was some minutes before I could bring myself to shoot. I killed the mother first and then three of the cubs: two of them got away. This may seem heartless, but the dingo is the sworn enemy of every bushman, be he black or white, and it is the unwritten law to kill them with the same dispatch as you would a snake.

Returning to camp I told Jacky to collect the kangaroo, which he did, and as we only wanted the tail the boys had a great meal of choice cuts from rump and shoulder. After the salt beef and tinned stuff we had been having that soup was great!

CHAPTER VII

A BUFFALO-SHOOTER - AND TWO DESPERATE SOULS

WE were sitting around the fire that night when Bob Cadell startled me by exclaiming:

"White man come up, boss."

I listened intently, and could hear the faint creaking of leather on packhorses. We jumped up, and, throwing a couple of sticks on the fire, put the billy on. It is an old custom in the bush to offer a man a pot of tea before asking any questions.

An outfit of about twelve horses, headed by a white man and followed by two blacks, appeared out of the darkness. The stranger was a thick-set, bearded man wearing a sombrero and khaki shirt open at the neck. He halted about ten paces from us. His quick movements and the decisive commands to his boys marked him at once as a man of competence and self-possession.

In no time the horses were relieved of their heavy loads, and turned out hobbled and belled. Meanwhile Whittaker and I were standing there, certainly admiring the completeness of the stranger's outfit, but feeling a little peeved that we had been so completely ignored. At last he came over to us and said:

"I'm Fred Smith from Kopalgo." Just that. Not, who are you, or how are you, or where are you making for?

Such casual treatment rather hurt our dignity, for we regarded ourselves as people of no little importance. Of course, I had heard of this man. It was the accounts of the exploits of Fred Smith and Paddy Cahill which had fired my early enthusiasm for the Territory. But big man though he was, we would have appreciated more sociable treatment.

We mumbled something about being pleased to meet him, and invited him to have some salt beef and tea with us. He accepted the tea, but declining the beef, whistled to one of his boys who produced half a roast goat.

It was a silent, rather uncomfortable meal; I know Whittaker and I were glad when it was over.

When Smith had finished, he slowly filled and lit his pipe; then rummaging in his swag, he drew forth a bottle of "square" gin and asked us to join him. We had a spot of the potent fluid, but even a liberal dash of water did not prevent us from gasping. Smith threw his down neat in one gulp.

"Great stuff for the kidneys. You should never travel without it," he said.

I was beginning to think it must be great stuff if it could extract conversation from Fred Smith. It must have been the gin, because he went on:

"I've heard of you two chaps. You had a bit of a brush with blacks back on Mary River."

"How on earth did you hear that?" we asked in surprise.

"News travels fast up here; nothing goes on without my boys knowing. What was it all about?"

In spite of the stranger's abrupt manner, I found myself thawing a little, and condescended to tell him the story from the beginning. When I had concluded Fred Smith shook his head:

"That fellow's doomed. The blacks have been after him for some time, and they'll get him yet."

Knowing Smith's wonderful reputation, we began asking him questions, and it was not long before he revealed himself for what he was - a big-hearted, genial bushman. He said he had seen our tracks, and could tell by them that we were strangers. He had overtaken us to see if he could be of any assistance.

That is the way of the north. The life of many a man has been saved by the timely arrival of a bushman, such as Fred Smith, to put him on the right track when he was heading for certain death from thirst.

After another round of stiff gins, Smith invited us to visit him at Kopalgo, about a hundred miles from our holding, and very generously offered us the use of a couple of trained buffalo horses.

He warned us of the danger of shooting from an untrained horse, pointing out that the trained animal will swerve outwards immediately a shot is fired, and so avoid crashing into the fallen buffalo. So interesting and useful was the talk, that it was well after midnight when we turned in.

Next morning our boys brought our horses to the camp, and Fred Smith gave them the once-over. Dandy, he said, was a splendid horse, but he thought he would be too highly strung for buffalo-shooting. He selected my second mount, a golden chestnut named Sovereign, saying he could be trained to be a perfect horse. It was an excellent tip to get. Now I knew what type of horse would be required for what promised to be a dangerous game.

Smith's arrival was fortunate in other ways. In the hundred miles we had covered from Burrundie, we had followed a more or less defined pad, but now we would have to depend upon our sense of direction and compass. He drew for us a rough plan on which he marked sandstone ridges, small hills, creeks, and one particular creek, named Jim Jim, which we could only cross at one spot.

"Are we likely to run across the blacks again?" asked Whittaker.

"You can bet you're being well watched by them, but I don't think they'll interfere with you. It's that other chap they're after. There's only one way to get on with blacks," he went on.

"Treat them fairly, but firmly, and don't on any account mix with them. If you do, in no time you'll be 'brother belonga them' and then the trouble will start."

After a final drink Smith departed as swiftly and efficiently as he had come, saying as he was going that he had left us a "bit of mutton" in a flour-bag. We opened the bag and found the other half of the delicious roast goat, as well as sweet potatoes and pea-nuts. That was typical of him.

When Fred Smith had gone, we felt our spirits slump a little. The bushman had demonstrated how poorly equipped in knowledge we were, and we felt how far short of him we measured. Still, we were learning rapidly, and we were as keen as ever on the big adventure.

Not intending to move until the following morning, we spent the remainder of the day overhauling our gear, and putting new rivets in the broken harness. We were determined to leave little to chance on the final and risky stages of the trip.

This completed, we were lolling in the shade, when Jacky Anyone pointed to two horsemen coming slowly along a couple of hundred yards away.

Immediately they sighted us, they rode into the scrub, reappearing in a few minutes, and one of them had magically been transformed into a woman. They came straight up to us, and the man introduced himself as Bert Evans, and his companion as his wife.

They looked hungry and ragged; and the woman, though only young, bore the tell-tale marks on her face and hands of privation and suffering. She seemed on the verge of collapse.

Seeing that their urgent need was food, Whittaker produced a freshly cooked damper, some broiled goose and sweet potatoes, and not wishing to be witnesses to the ravenous attack, we left them to it.

After a lapse of time which we considered decent, we returned and found the pair somewhat cheered. Evans seemed disposed to talk of their misfortunes, and we listened with considerable interest while he unfolded his tale.

"We were mighty lucky to come across you people," he said by ways of thanks for the meal. "I don't think we could have hung out much longer. We've had a stiff trot, and this looked like being the end."

He seemed anxious to spill the story, and the words literally poured from his lips. Jerking his thumb towards his wife he said:

"I met Rose in Brisbane a while back, and we got engaged. I returned here and promised to send for her when I'd got enough together. Vestey's were going then, and I was in a fair way doing stock work. I sent for Rose about eighteen months ago, but before she arrived Vestey's closed, and I was out of a job. I put it to her straight, and told her she ought to go back home." Turning to his wife he said: "Didn't I, Rose? But you were all for getting married, and sticking."

"I'd do the same again," she said, with a brave smile.

"Well, we got married at Pine Creek, when I heard from a prospector that there was gold on the border of Arnhem Land. I wanted to leave Rose at the creek, but she insisted on coming with me. I told her it was no journey for a woman, and she said she hadn't expected to find feather-beds in the north. She had her way, and so we set out on the hundred-and-eighty-mile trip with two saddle-horses and two packhorses. We got there all right and prospected around, meeting with a little luck, but nothing large. Then came our first blow. One of our packhorses broke its hobbles, and we never saw it again. A few days later the other packhorse was speared by the blacks.

"If that wasn't bad enough, we returned to camp after being away a few hours, and found the blacks had collared our food and everything we had. I was left with my rifle and three rounds of ammunition; and with the nearest known white man a hundred and twenty miles away, it looked as if our numbers were up. Anyhow, we hit the trail. God knows what would have been the end if we hadn't heard your horse-bells. I used my last shot two days ago."

We were deeply moved by this recital of hardship and fortitude, and I could not help casting admiring glances at the brave woman who had stuck by her mate.

"You must be wondering why the change-over in my clothes," said Mrs Evans with a little laugh. "We thought it safer that the blacks should take me for a man; but I like to look like a woman sometimes."

As a matter of fact, I had been wondering, and I thought this explanation pathetically splendid.

They stayed with us that night, and in the morning I gave Evans my shot-gun. He was not long in returning with a goodly supply of geese and ducks, which we supplemented with damper, potatoes, and oil - some call it butter. After handing Evans enough ammunition for his .32 to see him through, we bade them good journey.

The area on which Evans and his wife were prospecting is now being worked at considerable profit by a syndicate of which Evans is not a member. Which only goes to show that the original prospector can expect little of the world's gifts.

CHAPTER VIII

A BUFFALO VISITS US

AFTER a spell of a day and a half we moved on again, setting our compass north-east. We hoped to strike a spring at the foot of the centre of three hills: it was marked so on Fred Smith's map, and the distance was about eight miles away. The horses were reluctant to leave the wonderful grass, but we eventually got them going, Whittaker and I riding in the lead of the column.

We crossed a marshy plain for about two miles, finally coming to a stream of fresh water which we at once recognized as the upper end of the South Alligator River, knowing that the lower end was salt.

As we approached the water, the horses snorted and pulled back. We dismounted, and examining the banks, saw the cause of the danger which the horses had sensed before us. There were the claw-marks and tracks made by crocodiles as they had dragged themselves along the sand after sun-baking.

A good place to keep away from; so we rode down the river for about half a mile, where the horses, although they pricked their ears, and their eyes were wide, consented to cross.

Safely on the other side we took our bearings, and I must admit that the outlook appeared pretty hopeless. We beheld miles upon miles of bush, with long grass and heavy forest trees, and no sign of a track of any description. We were in the wilds of the Territory for the first time; whether we'd ever get out of them remained to be seen.

Taking the compass from me and facing north-east, Whittaker said with a grin:

"Somewhere about a hundred miles away is our country. We're in for it now, so here goes."

I agreed, and we began to force our way through the bush.

I now had the compass, but decided to discard it, and be guided by the sun. The influence of the steel barrel of my gun upon the needle of the compass was sufficient to throw us many miles out.

After about four miles of heavy going, the country became hilly and gravelly, with indications of diorite and quartzite. Although not geologists, we were always on the look out for minerals, and knew enough to be sure of the type of country we were passing over. We saw many wallabies and kangaroos, and there were flocks of squatter pigeons which almost allowed us to trample on them. At any rate there seemed little likelihood of being without food.

From an eminence we sighted the three hills, and finally arrived at the spring, a wonderful supply of bubbling fresh water. The eight miles had taken us four hours to traverse, which gives an idea of the roughness of the country.

We stayed there a couple of hours and pushed on again. We had not been on the move long when we found ourselves in the midst of fan-palms up to fifty feet high, and so dense that the packhorses had difficulty in getting through them.

A bush-fire had been through recently, and some of the huge palms were so loose in their sandy beds that they could be pushed over. One of the packhorses became wedged between two palms, but being an old stager, he simply waited until we released him by cutting one of the palms down.

We emerged from this bewilderment on to a flat clay country with tea-trees and pandanus palms, which told us we were getting near water. We were soon in the scrub again, and the tea-trees added to the damage already done to our packs by the fan-palms.

At last we came to a clear, dry, swampy plain of about five hundred acres. Our horses had only stepped upon the edge of it when I noticed a well-defined pad about two feet wide. I thought it possibly a track made by Paddy Cahill of Oenpelli, whom I understood occasionally came across that way to the railway line at Burrundie.

I examined the track more carefully, and saw it was too well worn to have been made by a pack-team. We followed it a little way, and where the ground was softer noticed with a thrill the unmistakable splay imprint of the buffalo-hoof.

We were making for the large creek with only one crossing, marked on our map as Jim Jim and as we knew the pad might lead to water, we decided to follow it in the belief that it would take us to some point on the creek.

As we proceeded along this pleasant change to easy going, we observed signs that buffaloes had passed along the track quite recently. There were freshly twisted saplings, and bark torn from trees showed where the buffaloes had been giving their great horns gentle exercise.

Still farther on we saw where buffalo bulls had been pawing the soft soil, and on a small clearing clods of earth and broken ground gave indications of a recent conflict between, probably, two young bulls, but whether in earnest or in play we had no means of judging.

We were getting into even more swampy country. Whittaker whistled to me as he pointed to a hole in the soft ground half-full of liquid mud, with the edges splashed with lumps of mud not quite dry. We had read a good deal of the habits of the buffalo and knew we were looking at a mud-bath, or wallow, which is one of the animal's pet recreations.

We were naturally excited, believing that had we been there a little earlier we would have found the buffalo in his bath. We stopped our horses and listened intently, expecting any minute to hear an animal crashing through the bush.

Jacky Anyone seemed to sense that his dreaded enemy was near about, for the wild expression on his face as he crouched on his horse at the rear of the outfit would have been laughable had it not been so pathetic. Although Bob Cadell was puffing at his pipe and grinning horribly at Jacky, I knew where he would be if a buffalo appeared.

Not wishing to be caught on the narrow track by a surprise buffalo charge, which would have gone hardly with the heavily laden horses, and perhaps ourselves for that matter, we pushed on hoping soon to come upon open country.

After going another mile or so, the track led us to an open clearing, through the trees on the other side of which we caught a welcome glimpse of glittering water. The buffalo-track swung sharply to the left, but we proceeded straight on until we reached the banks of the creek.

At this point it was impassable, so we turned to the right, looking for the crossing mentioned by Fred Smith. Rounding a bend, about a mile farther on, we saw what appeared to be large, old English beehives. On drawing near, however, we recognized a deserted blacks' camp. Whittaker truthfully remarked:

"This looks good to me. You can bet it's safe where these jokers make their camp."

We moved on about a hundred yards, and after ascertaining that the horses could reach the water, we unloaded. For once we gave the boys a hand to unpack, mainly to see what damage had been done to our packs after the rough trip through the palms and tea-scrub.

Bad enough, but not so bad as it might have been. The pack containing Whittaker's syrup-tin was in a filthy state, potatoes, onions, flour, tea, sugar, all mixed up with the treacle.

We told the boys to clean it up, and they had a great time digging their fingers into the sticky mess, and licking them with relish.

When we had straightened things out, I asked Bob Cadell about the blacks' camp; he told me it had been built only for the wet season.

"Come alonga me, Bob. We go look," I said. He looked startled.

"No more go alonga that one camp, boss. Might be plenty debil-debil there."

I laughed at him, and Whittaker and I went to have a look ourselves.

It consisted of about a dozen oval huts about three feet high and five feet in the longer diameter, and made with native simplicity.

Hickory sticks had been stuck in the ground and bent until the other ends formed an arch, and over them had been placed large sheets of paper-bark; finally the lot were thatched. The entrance was merely a loose piece of bark. Bob Cadell told us the blacks with their gins and dogs would creep inside and light a small fire to ward off the mosquitoes, only emerging when hunger drove them out in search of food.

Bob also informed us that the huts were never used for more than one season. When the wet weather came again, the blacks would return and burn the huts, thereby destroying the debil-debils which they knew would have inhabited them during their absence. On hearing this Whittaker raised an interesting point:

"Maybe these debil-debils are the name for vermin. Perhaps some wise old bird invented this superstition to teach the abos clean habits."

I have often thought about the origin of many similar superstitions among the Australian blacks and believe there is a heap of truth in what Whittaker suggested.

Seeing that the huts bore signs of recent occupation, I asked Bob where he thought the blacks would be now. He said:

"Mine tinkit, boss, he might be close up."

He then took me to several tea-trees and showed me freshly-cut holes in branches, explaining that the blacks had made them within the last few days hunting for "sugar-bags" - the honey of the native bee.

We decided to forget about the blacks for the time being, and in the hour which remained before dark, to have a scout round for any further buffalo-tracks, and also to make sure that there was adequate feed for the horses.

It had been a long and tiring day, so after a satisfying meal of roast goat, we turned in early. There was a bright moon shining through the trees, and Whittaker and I were lying awake chatting, when we heard a gurgling bellow, followed by a heavy splash.

"What in the hell's that?" called Whittaker.

We listened, and the eerie sound was repeated.

"It must be a crocodile," I said, and fell to wondering if the couple of hundred yards which separated us from the water's edge was far enough.

A few minutes later there was another bellow, but of a different tone, and full-throated. This was immediately followed by the violent jingling of the horse-bells, which told us our horses, though hobbled, were galloping.

We started to pull on our gum-boots when the bells began to tinkle normally again, and we knew the horses had quietened, and were feeding.

We let it go at that, and after a while dropped off to sleep.

About four o'clock in the morning I woke suddenly with an uneasy feeling that something unusual was happening. I peered around, and felt a chill run down my back when I saw the huge head and terrifying horns of a buffalo within hand's reach of me.

He was sniffing, sniffing. I had my revolver by my side, but I dared not move or scarcely even breathe. I was frankly scared stiff, and prayed that the others were still sleeping.

Then the big beast began to snort and paw the ground, and I thought any minute he would trample me to death, or toss me into kingdom-come with his horns.

I was on the point of taking the risk and pumping a couple of quick shots into his head, when a piercing yell came from the boys who were camped a little to the rear of us. They had seen him.

The buffalo threw up his head, gave one startled look around, wheeled swiftly, caught the tip of his horn in Whittaker's mosquito-net, and carrying it with him, dashed into the bush.

Whittaker and I jumped up together and took several flying shots at him, and although we heard the thud of the bullets on his hide, he continued unchecked.

We knew we would have no chance of getting him then, and decided to postpone any further attack until later in the morning. We collected Jacky and Bob Cadell from the branches of a Moreton Bay ash about a hundred yards away, and after considerable persuasion, put their fears partially at rest.

Neither of us felt like further sleep, so we kindled the fire and made some coffee to fill in time until the dawn broke.

Chatting over the buffalo's visit, Whittaker told me he had been awake all the time. For some reason, he took it for granted I was awake, and said he was waiting [for] a move from me before deciding what part he would play.

Daylight was not long in coming. We were still sitting by the camp-fire when Jacky Anyone came up to us, shuffling his feet and with downcast eyes.

"Boss," he said, "I want talk alonga you."

Whittaker looked at me with a grin. We both guessed what was coming.

"What is it, Jacky?"

"This fella country no good alonga me. Him full up buffalo, crocodile, and cheeky fella blackfella. Might be they killem me all about."

"All right, Jacky," I said, tossing him a stick of tobacco.

"You bin catchem tucker alonga bag. You go alonga your own country now."

Jacky walked away; but after an earnest talk with Bob Cadell he came back to me, looking a little less dejected, and said:

"Might be boss, my country little bit too far. More better I stoppem alonga gun."

"Right-oh! Jacky," I said. "Bimeby I send im you back alonga home all right."

I had a shrewd suspicion that Bob, whom I knew was just as scared as Jacky, had put him up to tell me he wanted to go home. But they knew their only safety lay with us.

CHAPTER IX

WHITTAKER'S DEADLY SHOT

WE dispensed with an early breakfast that morning, optimistically thinking it would not be long before we were sitting down to a sizzling piece of buffalo-steak.

We told the boys to bring the horses into camp, and gave instructions to Cadell to get the rivets out and repair the damages of the previous day.

We cleaned and oiled our guns, strapped on our ammunition-belts and hunting-knives, and, after leaving a shot-gun with the boys, we set off on foot to trail our visitor of the night before.

We had no trouble in following the beast. The soft earth had been churned up by the pounding hoofs, and small trees and shrubs had been torn down. Pieces of Whittaker's mosquito-net were scattered here and there, and occasional splashes of blood assured us that some of our bullets had taken effect.

The buffalo's track led us to the creek, which at this spot was about half a mile across and split into numerous channels. We crossed and picked up the track again, which took us into dense scrub.

Having heard quite enough of the ferocity of a wounded buffalo, we proceeded with the utmost caution. Our track at last turned on to a defined pad, and we thought our quarry had made back to the main herd.

I was in the lead, and both of us were tense with excitement. With the safety-catches of our rifles forward, we came out of the scrub into a small clearing of hard ground, where the pad forked. Whittaker suggested he should go to the left, and I to the right to see if the branches of the track joined up again with the main pad. This we did.

We were about sixty yards apart when the buffalo came out of the scrub on my side, and with head lowered charged Whittaker.

"Whit! Whit!" I yelled, at the same time bringing up my rifle and pressing the trigger. I was horrified to hear a click; the cartridge was a dud. Feverishly I jammed another cartridge into the breach. This time my heart jumped with joy as I heard the explosion.

The shot did not drop the infuriated beast, but it had the effect of making him swerve from Whittaker's path. He hesitated, trembling for a split second, and sighted me. Down went his enormous head again, and with a bellow of rage he came for me.

I had no time to consider what had happened to Whittaker, but reloading as quickly as my excitement would allow, I fired again. Through hurry or rotten aim I heard the whine of the bullet ricocheting, and knew it must have glanced off the solid bone at the base of the horns.

With no time to reload, I looked around desperately and saw a small tree a few paces away. With one leap I was behind it.

The buffalo was then almost on top of me, and my heart gave a jump as I heard the report of Whittaker's rifle. Simultaneously, the tree shook to its roots. Blinking my eyes I saw the buffalo lying on its side, tossing its head and breathing its last gasps.

Whittaker ran up waving his arms in wild excitement.

"By God, that was a wonderful shot, Whit! The best you've ever done."

That was as much as I could say at the moment, for I was quivering from the reaction. When the mist cleared from my eyes, I added:

"Where in hell did you get to?"

Whittaker was gazing fascinated at his kill.

"Eh?"

"What happened to you?"

He came to life with a jerk.

"I heard you yell, saw what was coming at me, and dived for the timber. Then I heard your shot and saw the big fellow after you. I couldn't shoot when I wanted to, because you and the buffalo were in a direct line. But when you ducked behind the tree, I let go, aiming for just behind the shoulder; and that's where I must have got him."

We had a look at the buffalo, and saw the hole made by Whittaker's bullet exactly where he had aimed for. The bullet had gone straight to the heart. It was the only vital spot open to Whittaker, and I again patted him on the back for one of the best bits of marksmanship I had ever seen.

As we gazed upon the beast, I was at once struck by the great sweeping horns which must have been at least six feet from tip to tip. Unlike the horns of the bullock, they were triangular at the base and about six inches through, flattening out until they came to almost needle-point. Their colour was dark grey, and their general appearance as sinister as you could wish. I could well imagine the fate of any man who was tossed by them.

I was next surprised by the animal's hide and the massive head and shoulders. The hair, in parts long, was on the back and flanks short and bristly, for all the world resembling a pig's skin. He was about seven feet in length and about four feet high from the shoulder. The hoofs were like those of a bullock, but much larger; no doubt because the buffalo spends most of his time in swampy and marshy ground.

Later, I learned a good deal about the buffalo, which even now is to be found in tens of thousands on the coastal areas of the Territory from about ten miles north of Port Darwin to the Gulf of Carpentaria. Stray bulls have been found as far south as Victoria River Downs, five hundred milesaway,[29] and also over the Queensland border.

The Northern Territory buffalo is a native of India, and is commonly known as the water buffalo. When Major Campbell was appointed commandant of the British Military Depot on Melville Island (about fifteen miles north of Darwin) in 1824, he took charge of a population of a hundred and fifteen white men and six white women (including fifty-four prisoners), sixteen cattle, twenty-three sheep, fifty-four pigs, and sixteen buffaloes, which had been landed from Timor, three hundred and fifty miles north-west of Melville Island. That settlement was abandoned in 1828 and removed to Raffles Bay on the mainland, which in turn was also abandoned in 1830.[30] But the buffaloes became quickly established, and have been thriving in the Territory ever since. The millions of acres of swampy ground, and the tropical climate, provide a natural habitat which exists nowhere else in Australia.

For food the buffalo prefers coarse herbage, and for recreation he delights in immersing himself in water until only his head appears above the surface. He will remain thus for hours. Frequently he will envelop himself in white clay as protection against stinging insects. It further adds to his fearsome appearance. He is a much more powerful animal than the ox, and in his wild state is savage and dangerous. Alone of all wild animals he will attack unprovoked, and in single combat is more than a match for a tiger. It is the pleasant pastime of some Indian princes to stage such combats for the entertainment of their guests.

In spite of his ferocity, the buffalo when caught as a calf is easily domesticated, and the Chinese in and around Darwin are utilising some of them as beasts of burden.[31]

Buffalo milk is very nourishing though of peculiar flavour. Other features of the buffalo are that it cannot be crossed with our cattle, being an entirely different species of animal. Its freedom from disease and its immunity from attack by other animals account for its remarkable increase.[32]

It was still early in the morning, so we set about taking back the steak we had promised ourselves for breakfast. Not having time at the moment to skin the whole beast, I proceeded to skin the hide from the hind-quarters as I have done with a bullock.

But I found it an entirely different proposition. In places the hide was two inches thick, and not having brought a steel, the knives soon lost their edge. Finally I cut about five pounds from the rump, and we made back to the camp.

I told the boys that Whittaker had shot a buffalo, and they were mildly excited but seemed dubious as to whether the meat was really buffalo-steak. After a careful inspection, Bob Cadell said:

"All same bullock, that one."

"No more bullock, Bob, that one buffalo," I said.

I knew he would want to see the buffalo before believing, so I let it go at that.

We threw the juicy steak in to the frying-pan, and in a short while we were attacking it in the fashion of hungry hunters. Unhappily, it was rather a disappointing meal. The flavour was good, but the meat was coarser in grain than everyday steak, and it was tough going. We discovered later that we should have hung the cut for some hours and that the best meat by far came from a young cow. Our kill happened to be an old bull who had been driven away from the herd by younger bulls. His isolation had made him resentful and unusually vicious.

Still, it was the first definite niche in our adventurous programme, and there was no stopping Whittaker from talking
about it. Not that I wasn't thrilled about it, but Whittaker was
a more effervescent type of chap.

Breakfast over, we got the boys to bring in a packhorse, and
armed with half a dozen knives, steels, and an axe, the four of
us made off for the scene of the kill. We were just in time to
chase away a scavenging eagle who had alighted on the carcass,
and a few dingoes who were sniffing around.

When Jacky Anyone saw the beast from about fifteen yards
away, he stopped in his tracks, fear written large upon his
troubled face. I said to him:

"Him all about dead now, Jacky. You look alonga me." I
walked over and, grabbing the horns, shook them.

That satisfied him. Turning to Bob Cadell with an air of
"there's nothing to worry about. I'm here," he said:

"Plenty beef alonga this one." Swaggering across, he placed
a foot on the animal's neck and gripped one of the horns, the
while expanding his chest and grinning broadly at us.

At that moment there was a crash in the bushes behind, and
an old-man kangaroo thumped into the clearing, gave us one
startled look, and was off again. It was enough, however, to
cause Jacky to leap back from the buffalo and cast anxious eyes
about for a safe retreat, much to the amusement of Bob
Cadell.

"Jacky, you plurry fool," he said, and added, with heavy
sarcasm: "You no more plenty frightened all right. More
better you bin sit alonga camp alonga lubra."

Jacky, who looked rather shamefaced, ignored the insult. As
both Bob and Jacky were expert butchers, we tossed them the
knives and steels and told them to go to it.

Whittaker and I concentrated upon the head. We wanted
the brains and the tongue, and I was anxious to learn more
about the animal. We got the axe and hacked away at the

skull, which we found abnormally thick, so thick that no ordinary bullet would penetrate. Eventually we got through and found the brain, which was a good deal smaller than that of a bullock, and it was located well at the back of the head. We next removed the tongue.

Whittaker turned his attention to the horns and wanted to take them, but I pointed out that they would have to remain part of the head for some months before they could be knocked off with an axe.

For once he took my word for it without wanting to experiment, and we agreed to collect them on the first trip from our holding to Pine Creek. More optimism!

The horns, although a fine pair, were badly scarred, indicating that the old bull had had many a battle.

Jacky and Bob worked well, and the skinning was completed in about three-quarters of an hour. We next opened up the beast.

I found the heart was larger than that of a bullock. The kidneys were the shape of a pig's, and entirely different from those of a bullock, which are quartered. The fat surrounding them was white, also resembling the pig.

My father, who knew a lot about animals, had led me to believe that a pig's kidneys were not good, and rightly or wrongly, I could never be induced to eat them.

We removed the heart, liver, and kidney fat, and as we wanted both salt and fresh meat, we took a couple of good-sized loin roasts, a little more steak, and the tail, a miserable thing of a couple of feet, almost bare and with a tuft at the end of it.

Packing the hide and meat on our horse, we made back for camp, leaving the boys with blood up to their armpits to collect what, according to their own ideas, were titbits.

Straightway I began making preparations to salt the beef when I noticed Whittaker lolling in the shade of a tree reading.

"Here, you, what's the big idea?" I called.

"Don't be in a hurry. I'm looking for something," he said.

I waited, wondering what brain-wave was surging over him. At last he jumped up and came over to me with a gleam in his eye.

"See here," he said, brandishing a cookery book, "I've found the real thing - a recipe for making biltong". (A South African dried-meat product). He read to me:

"Take any quantity of water, using sufficient salt to float an egg. Bring it almost to the boil. Cut your meat into thin strips; allow it to remain in the water for a minute or so; and then hang out in the sun to dry."

We decided to give it a go, but there being no egg about, we had to guess the salt. By placing green branches on the fire we smoked the meat as well, which was an idea of our own. It was really beautiful; from then on we were rarely without biltong.

Whittaker was very proud of his discovery, and not to be outdone, I sent the boys back to what remained of the buffalo, telling them to get the legs.

These I skinned to the hoofs, and after smashing them, put the lot into an old petrol-tin, tossed in a couple of onions and some salt, and kept a fire under it all day. The result was a delicious dish. So rich was it that we had to eat sparingly.

Next day we did a little exploring. We came upon a plain of several thousand acres, and there saw a herd of fifty or so buffaloes. The sight did not surprise us as much, perhaps, as it should. We knew we were getting right into the buffalo country, and having killed our first beast, our appetites were satisfied for the time being.

The buffaloes went on quietly grazing, taking not the slightest notice of us, and we didn't interfere with them. On this plain was a wonderful waterhole a mile long and hundreds of yards wide, and rippling its surface and on its banks was every conceivable type of game. There were kangaroos, wallabies, pademelons (small wallabies), quail, wild ducks, pheasants, geese, pigeons, white ibis, cranes, and white cockatoos in thousands.

I had never seen such a sight.

We next went up and down the creek, looking to see if there was any crossing other than the one over which we followed the buffalo. We found none; so knew we had made no mistake about the Jim Jim marked on the map by Fred Smith.

On returning to camp Bob Cadell called me aside, and in an apprehensive voice said he thought there were blacks in the locality. He had seen fires, and had come across fresh footprints.

We soon had the feeling that we were being watched, although we could see nothing. We didn't like it. We wanted them either to show themselves or clear out.

That afternoon, having a further look around, we came upon the tracks of crocodiles, and later saw several of them swimming down the river. They were very wary however. We took a couple of long shots, but I don't think did much damage.

All turned in early that night, but with the mosquitoes which were particularly vicious, and the ever-present uneasiness about the blacks, I for one had a restless night.

The next morning we got ready to move off to Magela Creek, twenty-five miles away, and only about fourteen miles from the boundary of our longed-for holding. The boys had seemed uneasy since breakfast. Suddenly Jacky, with his eyes rolling, shuffled up to me, crossing and uncrossing his toes in his agitation.

"Blackfella come up, boss," he whispered. Looking where he indicated, I saw a company of about fifteen blacks appear through the trees.

They stood watching us; I beckoned them on. They came slowly forward. The party consisted of half a dozen old men, lubras with children, and a few likely looking young bloods.

Several were carrying spears, but the rest were without them.

Instantly, I remembered a warning given me by my uncle Arthur Mockett, and I watched their feet closely, looking to see if they were trailing spears with their toes. I did not see any, so called them still closer.

One of the young ones came up to me and I offered him a piece of damper and treacle. He looked at it suspiciously, at length stuck his finger on the treacle, and tasting, appeared to find it good, for he took the offering to the others, and mutual goodwill was established.

They were an unimpressive lot, vastly different from the Mary River warriors. They wore no clothing, and the bucks had been rolling in the mud as protection against the mosquitoes.

Bob Cadell was eyeing them with that contempt which he reserved for all the blacks, although I noticed he was favouring the lubras with speculative glances.

The lubras! They were the first wild ones we had seen, and their sagging breasts, flat noses, huge mouths, and filthy hair made me feel ill.

Bob endeavoured to get some information from the old buck who seemed to be leader of the party, and after trying every dialect he knew, gave up in disgust. By sign language, which included frequent pointing to the sun, we managed to tell the old fellow where we were making for.

We commenced to pack for the trip to Magela, when Whittaker said:

"Where are we going to load this?" pointing to the buffalo-hide which he had carefully folded.

"Surely you don't think we're going to take that with us ?"

"Well, what did we bring it back to camp for?"

"I'm going to cut a strip off the belly for hobbles. We don't want the rest of it."

Whittaker gave a cry of pain.

"Cut it? You can't do that. There's two quids' worth there. We must take it with us."

Whittaker full of that cheerful unthinking enthusiasm again! What use to argue.

"Right-oh!" I said. "Shove it on a horse."

He told Bob Cadell to bring a spare packhorse, and give him a hand.

Bob obeyed, grinning broadly. He knew that the hide, being unsalted, would be a stench about us within a day.

He brought along old Ted, a sturdy roan entire, that was usually very placid and obedient. But, unfortunately for Whittaker, one of the many things about horses which he did not know was that an entire has a pronounced aversion to the smell of blood, and the hide simply reeked of it.

"Hold his head, Bob," said Whittaker, and lifting the eighty pounds of folded hide, he approached from the side, and was about to hoist it on when the smell of blood reached the nostrils of old Ted.

He turned his head, gave one swift look at the apparition and, pivoting neatly, lashed out with both hind-feet. They landed squarely on the hide, and the force of the kick sent Whittaker tumbling fifteen feet away, the breath knocked clean out of him.

When he picked himself up his temper was not improved by the sight of Jacky Anyone squatting under a bush doubled up with laughter. For many days after Jacky and Bob chuckled together, and it didn't take much guessing to know what it was about.

Whittaker was never long in recovering his good humour. He said:

"P'raps we'd better leave the blasted thing here. Shame to give two quid to the dingoes all the same."

At last we got going, leaving the blacks to finish off a fair quantity and variety of food.

CHAPTER X

PYTHON AND WALLABY

WE did not make Magela that day, but reached a place called Paralpa, fifteen miles away. To our astonishment, there were the old black and his tribe!

They had a fire going, and I was curious to know if they had lit it by their own primitive methods. But Bob Cadell told me they had carried a fire-stick over the fifteen miles, every now and then waving it around their heads to keep it alive.

The blacks soon made it clear why they had anticipated our arrival. Food was the attraction - particularly the damper and treacle, which had made a big hit with them. We gave them a fair supply, and there were delighted jabberings from the lubras when Whittaker produced several lengths of red Turkey twill, and some boiled lollies.

They twisted the twill around their necks, breasts, and loins to see which position created the best impression. Eventually modesty won, and the twill came to rest about their loins.

The country was teeming with game, and quite the equal of Jim Jim. We shot a few squatter pigeons and grilled them on the coals. They were large breasted and plump, and cooked as we cooked them, were delicious.

The boys had returned after gathering a supply of good hardwood for damper making, which was a nightly job. Practically all timber lying upon the ground is dry-rotted and plastered with mud by white ants, and when burned quickly leaves an ash. That makes it totally unsuitable for damper cooking.

We left Paralpa a little later, throwing a further supply of food to the myall blacks and not expecting to see them again. We knew they would not venture beyond their own territory.

We passed many fine billabongs; the country was still beautifully fertile and full of game. Magela Creek was reached shortly after midday. This creek is similar to most of the others we had seen: broken into several deep channels with sandy bottoms. The debris piled high in the trees told us it would be a good place to avoid in the rainy season.

After resting a while, we got a couple of fresh mounts, and taking our guns rode ahead to see what the country was made of. We passed half a dozen emus, the first we had seen in the north; I had wondered why we had not seen them before. We learned later that they are nothing like as plentiful as in the western plains of New South Wales.

We left the track and climbed to the summit of a hill; the picture seen through our powerful field-glasses was wonderful. Towards the east as far as the eye could see there were sandstone ridges several hundred feet high rising sheer and extending for many miles south. Such rivers as the Mary, West Alligator and South Alligator and numbers of smaller streams are fed by innumerable springs at the foot of these great ridges.

About ten miles away, as near as we could estimate, the northern portion of the ridges seemed to break and form a valley. That valley, through which we had to pass, would, we thought, be the eastern boundary of our territory.

To the west, as far as we could see, were vast plains and open forest country. Numerous columns of smoke indicated that there were plenty of blacks about.

On the way back to camp we saw any number of squatter pigeons, but we were after something different. Suddenly we almost rode on to a couple of birds, which as soon as they lifted, I recognized as curlews. I dismounted and stalked them through the timber getting one with each barrel.

We had listened night after night to their weird cry, but these were the first we had seen. They are sometimes called the stone-plover, but are very much larger than any variety of plover and have longer legs and sharper beak. Their plumage is brown flecked with white, and their eyes are large and yellowish-brown. We stewed those birds for tea, and they were as good as anything I had tasted.

Later we went fishing in the creek, using for bait the innards of the curlews. We caught a couple of fair sized fish very much like bream. While waiting for something more substantial to attack the bait, I noticed a round, white object, about the size of a plate, bobbing up and down. The longer I looked at it the more curious I became. At last I stripped off and swam out, having beforehand made quite certain that there were no crocodiles about.

The mysterious object was a fish of sorts, and alive. Not caring to grab hold of it, I propelled it ashore by splashing. With bushes we got it on to the bank and found it to be a large catfish. The belly had been abnormally distended, causing it to float wrong side up. Still curious, I put my knife into it and, with a rush of foul gas, it collapsed like a pricked balloon. Then we discovered what had caused the trouble; the catfish had swallowed a jew lizard almost as large as itself.[33]

We looked at each other, and both thought of the catfish we had for breakfast back at Kadauke. That finished me with catfish for all time.

When we got back to camp Bob and Jacky had made a fire of their own, and with broad grins were cooking small freshwater turtles. They had dug a small hole in the ground, covered the bottom with hot coals, and, having placed the decapitated turtles on them, had covered them with ashes. They left the turtles there about an hour, and when hauled out the shell dropped away, leaving white flesh. I sampled some, but although tender, it tasted too strong and fishy for my palate, quite different from the delicious salt-water turtle.

Bob Cadell, who always took an intelligent interest in what

was going on, came up to me.

"What name this place, boss?" he asked.

"Magela, Bob."

This seemed to satisfy him. He grunted and said:

"Plenty blackfella sit down here bimeby."

I asked him how he knew that, and he told me that while fishing for turtles, he had happened across hundreds of mussels buried in the moist sand alongside a waterhole. He explained that the blacks collected the mussels and placed them fairly deep in the sand to fatten, and to keep them from the reach of water birds. They would return in a couple of weeks and collect their store.

That night a fearful yell from Jacky woke us and shattered the stillness. We jumped up and, grabbing our pistols, rushed over to the boys' camp. There was Jacky shivering and stuttering. We couldn't understand a word he was saying, but thought all the dangers of the north must have descended upon us at once. I shook him by the shoulder and he managed to squeak out:

"Full up plurry snake alonga my bunk, boss."

Was that all!

I got my shot-gun, and Whittaker, with a big stick in his hand, began to drag Jacky's swag cover back. It was almost off when Bob Cadell exploded with laughter.

"I bin tellem you before, Jacky, you all same lubra. That one no more snake, him rat."

Bob was about right, for a sand-gopher about the size of an ordinary rat scuttled from beneath the cover. Jacky had thrown his swag cover over its burrow, and in trying to get out the little animal had found Jacky's back barring his path.

Jacky looked as silly as he always did when Bob had the laugh on him, but no doubt squared things with his own conscience by killing the gopher and eating it next morning.

Before moving off next morning, I missed my pipe. After hunting for it everywhere I noticed Bob smoking a stemless briar: he always did, but this looked familiar. I asked him where he got it.

"I bin find him long way, boss."

Jacky who was standing behind him began scratching his woolly pate just above the ear, and grinning. Instinctively I looked at the same spot on Bob's head and behind his ear I saw a pipe-stem. Bob looked guilty, but still maintained:

"I bin pick him alonga nother place, boss."

It is one temptation which the blacks find hard to resist, and they will thieve a pipe whenever they get the chance.

I gave him a lecture; told him I would send him back if I caught him at anything like that again; presented the pipe to Jacky; and cut out Bob's tobacco ration for the day. But as all blacks are true socialists, I knew Jacky would give him half his.

To show his appreciation, Jacky blew a cloud of smoke in Bob's face.

"This good fella pipe, Bob. All same pipe belonga boss." And he chuckled to himself. Jacky was one up on his mate for the first time since they had been with us.

Discussing our plans for the next stage, we decided to skirt the sandstone ridges, and so cut off many miles. That was not according to the directions given us by Fred Smith, but we thought we knew enough by now about the bush to do something on our own initiative.

We soon left the timber behind us and reached the plains we had seen the day before. The going looked easy enough, but it was not long before we found ourselves in swampy country, and finding long detours necessary.

We were making very slow progress, when we emerged from a belt of tea-trees on to a grassy plain, and came suddenly upon a mob of buffaloes grazing. When they sighted us they started to come forward.

Our horses were very restless, and I was afraid they would bolt and become bogged in the swampy ground, or that the buffaloes would charge.

The boys were told to move the outfit to the right. Then Whittaker and I set spurs to our horses, at the same time firing over the heads of the buffaloes. They had evidently been shot at before, because they turned tail and cleared out.

We were beginning to feel sorry we had taken the present track, and seeing the sandstone ridges, for which we should have made direct, set off on a bee-line for them.

Night was falling, and as we found ourselves getting more and more entangled in the swamp mazes, we pulled up on the banks of a large waterhole and made camp. So bad had been the going that I don't suppose we had covered more than five or six miles.

The air was alive with mosquitoes, vicious brutes which swarmed all over us. There was no sandalwood about, so we collected heaps of dry buffalo manure, made a ring of it around the camp and set it alight. The smell was pretty dreadful, but it was better than the mosquitoes.

We were about to start the meal when an old gin wandered into the camp. She must have been eighty. Her hair was white, and her bones were showing through the shrivelled flesh. A loin-cloth was her only covering, and she carried a dilly-bag and a tomahawk.

Speaking to her in my best pidgin-English, I asked where she had come from, and she replied that she was on a walkabout from Oenpelli. I then asked her how far we were from the East Alligator River.

"Bimeby my boy come up. More better you talk alonga him."

She gave a long, low cooee, which only the Australian aboriginal can give effectively, and in a few moments there was a faint answer. In ten minutes or so the "boy" arrived. He was an old grey-headed man of the same skeleton appearance as his gin. He stood before us scratching his shin with his big toe, as a white man might rub his hands together, and looked at us curiously. I put the same questions to him that I had to his gin. Proudly he said:

"I bin alonga Paddy Cahill long time and speakem English all same alonga boss. You no more speakem English all some alonga boss."

This was hard criticism because I fancied my pidgin English was becoming really first-class. I gave him some tobacco, and a good helping of beef, damper, treacle, and tea which he and his gin ate ravenously.

Afterwards I told him we were making for a place called Gaernin on the East Alligator River. It was the only aboriginal name I knew on the river, and I thought he might recognize it. He did. I asked him if we cut across the swamp would we strike the river. Being a little bushed at the moment, we were not sanguine about the immediate future.

"Might be," was his answer.

That was one of the many occasions when I felt inclined to curse the blackfellow's "might be." They have about half a dozen shades of meaning to the phrase. I asked the old black and his gin to stay the night with us.

In the morning I pumped him again and at last gathered that we would have no earthly chance of crossing the swamps. He told us to follow him, which we did for the rest of the day.

We finally came to rest two miles from where we had started at Magela! Two days had been wasted in trying a track of our own. We decided to act upon instructions in future. It was our first setback on the journey, and we accepted, with some humility, the demonstration that we were not yet the last word in bushmen. Heaven alone knows where we would have finished - probably bogged hopelessly in the swamps - if we had not met the old black.

We rewarded the black and his gin with tobacco and Turkey twill, and they left us to continue their walkabout. After a good night's rest we set off early next morning, intending to make for the gap between the sandstone ridges, which we had seen through our binoculars, keeping all the time to the higher ground and avoiding those swamps as we would the devil.

We reached our destination without mishap about midday. The break between the ridges was only a few hundred yards wide, but once through it there lay before us about fifty square miles of exceptionally heavy-timbered country. Selecting a suitable spot we made camp. When the horses were unloaded we left Bob to straighten things out and, taking Jacky, went on a short tour of exploration.

We were at the foot of the great red and white sandstone ridges which rose perpendicularly from the ground and towered two hundred feet above. Around us were huge boulders, weighing up to hundreds of tons, which must at some time have been dislodged from the cliffs by earth tremors or continual washing away by water. The tall iron and stringybark trees added further to the loneliness and majesty of the surroundings.

Presently the silence was broken by a thrashing behind a large boulder. We crept around it, and were just in time to see a python and a big rock wallaby in mortal combat. The python had one coil around the wallaby's body above the hind-legs, and the animal was clawing and kicking with the light of horrible fear in its brown eyes. The python's head was swaying from side to side, and its beady eyes were watching every move of the wallaby.[34]

With a slithering movement of its body, quick as lightning, the reptile had another coil around the unfortunate wallaby, and as the terrible pressure was applied, we could hear the

ETERAN BUFFALO-SHOOTER AT ADELAIDE RIVER, WITH A PAIR OF HORNS MEASURING SEVEN FEET ACROS

erstood that this so-called "jungle" is similar to the forest   more bulls have been sho   in the timber   the shooter are

An elderly Fred Smith. Courtesy of N.T. Library.

Oenpelli Homestead. Courtesy of N.T. Library.

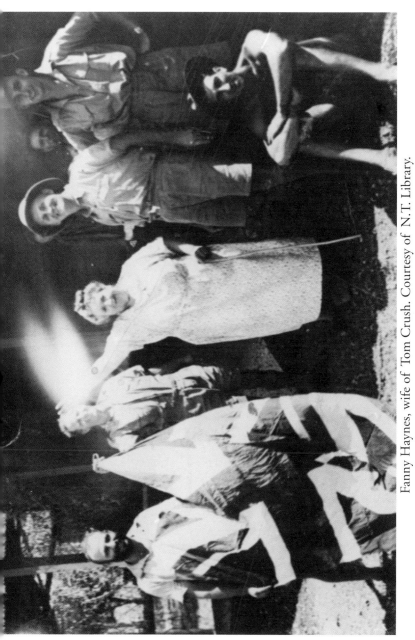

Fanny Haynes, wife of Tom Crush. Courtesy of N.T. Library.

Paddy Cahill and family with stockmen. Courtesy of N.T. Library.

Fred Smith and shooting party. Fred Smith is third on horseback from right. Courtesy of N.T. Library.

Previous Page: L. Carl Warburton.
R. Lawrence Whittaker.

bones cracking. Too late to save the wallaby, and unable to watch the sickening sight any longer, Whittaker sent a bullet through the python's head.

Even dead, the reptile's hold relaxed but slightly. After putting the wallaby out of its misery, we unwound the python, not without difficulty. Stretched out, it measured sixteen feet.

Pythons are found up to twenty-two feet in the Territory. They are mostly black on the back and yellow beneath, and in the middle as thick through as a man's leg. They wait in the crevices of the rocks until they see animals grazing, and are upon them in a flash. The python is non-venomous. It crushes the life out of its victim, slimes it over, swallows it whole, then writhes to its lair, where it stays until the food digests. Then it goes on the hunt again. A large-sized python is quite capable of killing and swallowing a full-grown kangaroo.

We asked Jacky which of the two he wanted. He had not seen a python before, and saying he might be "cheeky fella," claimed the wallaby. We sent him back to camp with it and continued our mooch around.

Returning a little later we came across a large wallaroo (one of the kangaroo family), and I could not help being struck with the manner in which nature had done her job. The python, the wallaby, the wallaroo, and most of the birds we saw were almost the exact colour of the rocks around.

We were anxious to get out of this particular country as soon as possible. The immenseness of the ridges and the trees had an overpowering effect. I wanted to make the open country once again.

By mid-afternoon we were ready to move on, our intention being to go as far as we could before nightfall. For an hour and a half we passed through the centre of the valley, the tall trees still all about us. At last we saw an opening, and beyond it, open country. The air was alive with the singing of birds, and calm contentment fell upon us. Suddenly everything became hushed; the birds were silent and the horses pulled up quivering. There was an uncanny stillness, and the atmosphere seemed charged with something ominous. With a start of fear I realized in a flash that an earth tremor was imminent. I had been in an earthquake before.

Yelling to the others to make like hell for the opening, we simply thundered out. On the way, loose rocks falling from the cliffs and a stir among the trees made us gallop the harder.

Once in the open we halted, and looking back saw the rocks shaking like a child's wooden blocks in a wind. The tremors soon passed, but they had been severe enough to put fear into our hearts.

The boys had been as scared as we, and it was some minutes before even the phlegmatic Bob could find his voice.

When he did, he asked:

"What name that one, boss?"

"God knows, Bob," I said. "I think it earth shake."

He rolled his eyes in greater fear.

"Cripes, boss, that one bin flite me. Him white missus alonga Pine Creek tellem me when ole man up above gettim wild him bin sendim big fella debil-debil alonga hearth, shakem hearth, killem white fella, black fella all about."

"Him finish now, Bob. That ole man up above he good fella, if you good fella. You bad fella, he killem."

This rough piece of theology seemed to appeal to Bob, for he said:

"Me be good fella alonga you, boss. I catchem horse, plenty tucker, and lubra you want him, and all about work alonga you. Might be you tell him ole man I bin good fella."

"I tell him all time you good fella, Bob," I said assuringly [sic].

I was to find from then on what a tremendous effect the tremor had upon Bob. He took more of a personal interest in the trip, and instead of making Jacky do most of the work, did more than a fair share himself.

It was a timely lesson for old Bob.

Jacky, not having felt the influence of a missionary, had heard nothing about the "ole man," and knew naught of even the rudiments of religion. He was, of course, scared out of his wits, but when it was all over, he was soon himself again.

Grinning, Jacky said to Bob, who was still a nasty greyish colour:

"Who bin all same lubra now?"

Bob made a step towards Jacky and said sourly:

"You bin shut up. Might be I bin showem you nother way which one lubra."

Jacky retreated hastily.

CHAPTER XI

OUR MARVELLOUS HOLDING

OUR horses had ceased to tremble, when a sudden, thrilling thought struck me.

"I say, Whit," I said, "do you realize we are now standing in our own country. Our very own. Every bit of this belongs to us."

"By the Lord Harry, we are," he exclaimed.

We should have both known that when we had passed through the valley. We were on the Whittaker-Warburton holding - six hundred square miles in extent - and paid for! It was a great feeling, and would have been more so had the earth tremor not catapulted us into it with such suddenness.

We had now been in the Territory about three months, and at last we were on a fair share of it which was legally ours. Looking swiftly back over those months, I thought we were damned fortunate to be there when we were. Luck certainly had been on our side so far.

A mile farther on we reached a swampy waterhole about fifty yards wide. It was getting dark, and we decided not to attempt to cross that night, and, so, made camp.

After tea we settled down to a serious talk. We were on our own block; but to strike a suitable camping-ground, to locate the buffaloes, and to determine upon a landing-ground on the river were vital matters to be thrashed out.

A recent track we had seen would lead to Oenpelli, and it must meet the East Alligator River at some point. Knowing that that redoubtable bushman and buffalo-shooter, Paddy Cahill, owned Oenpelli (about forty miles away), Whittaker suggested we should make for there.

I argued that any sudden rain-storm might wash away the tracks and we might find ourselves stranded for an indefinite period. My idea was to strike the river and establish a suitable landing-place in case the lugger arrived with our supplies from Darwin before we expected it.

Further, I was keen to show some independence on our own dunghill and explore it before worrying about Paddy Cahill's.

We talked well into the night, each making suggestions and approving and discarding them in turn. The upshot was that in the morning we headed in a north-westerly direction for the river which we judged to be about fifteen miles away.

We were now taking an even keener interest in our surroundings. It was that proud sense of possession, in which Bob and Jacky shared. Their chests were thrown out, as if the country was actually theirs. So it was, when you come to think of it.

I regret to say the first sight of our holding did not impress me. The soil was light and sandy, with a prolific growth of dry spear and kangaroo grasses. The timber was mostly bloodwoods, Moreton Bay ash and gum-trees, while fan palms and pandanus palms were present in profusion. Bob Cadell rode up to me with an informative look in his eye.

"More better you puttem match alonga grass, boss."

"Why, Bob?"

"Might be you come back this way soon. Full up dry grass. No good alonga horse. You puttem match, burnem grass, bimeby plenty green grass come up."

This sounded sense. Anyhow, it was our country, and we were going to do as we liked with it.

We found out later that, on the coastal areas north of Katherine, it is the custom to burn the grass after the wet season - about March or April. Then the whole countryside is ablaze without any danger of bush-fires as we know them in New South Wales or Victoria. There is not the same amount of herbage, and dense undergrowth, and they burn away until the blaze is stopped by some river or creek.

We acted upon Bob's suggestion, and set the grass alight. No sooner had the first column of smoke soared upward, when a swarm of large hawks, better known as kites, appeared. They circled round and round, and one by one swooped down through the smoke and swiftly rose again with snakes, lizards, and rats, which had been driven out of their hiding by the heat.

We rode on leaving a great blaze and dense clouds of smoke in our wake.

I was surprised at the amount of dead timber lying about, and examining some of it I found that worms had made a clear ringbark on the trees, and that white ants had come up the centre, causing the trunk to snap as though cut with an axe. The Moreton Bay ash was the tree mostly affected. Strangely, the bloodwoods and the ironbarks had been left severely alone.

We passed a number of kangaroos and well-fed dingoes, which were so cheeky that they would hardly get out of our tracks. We had a few shots at them with our revolvers, but the horses were more scared than they. Those mounts of ours would have to get used to shooting from their backs when we started on the buffaloes in earnest.

We halted for lunch under a shady tree. For the first time since leaving Pine Creek, a hundred and fifty miles away, there was no water handy, and we had to have recourse to our water-bags, which we always kept filled.

We soon moved on again, and had been travelling about an hour when we saw flocks of wild ducks, and thousands of wild geese, flying in V formation and converging at a point on the right - a sure sign that water was there. So, instead of keeping straight up the watershed we were on, we followed the birds.

Presently we found ourselves in dense palm-tree thickets similar to those which had given us trouble before. It was about four o'clock when we finally succeeded in forcing a way through. Like coming from darkness into bright sunshine, we suddenly burst upon a scene I am never likely to forget. The horses were brought to an abrupt halt, and we feasted our eyes upon the marvellous sight before us.

Away to the north, as far as vision would carry, stretched plains of grass, emerald green, and as high as a horse's shoulder. In front of us, about four miles distant, we could see lanes of mangroves fringing what we took to be the East Alligator River. Beyond them were more miles of green plains, with here and there large hills rising abruptly with great rugged rocks protruding from their faces.

"By heavens, this is wonderful, Warby," exclaimed Whittaker.

I agreed. It was worth coming that far for the sight alone.

The plains must have been studded with waterholes, for as we moved on there arose from the midst of the green splendour, tens of thousands of birds-ducks, geese, white cranes, plovers, pelicans, and goodness knows what else: in one great black mass they soared skywards, almost obliterating the sun.

To make the scene complete a herd of buffaloes was quietly grazing in the distance.

Whittaker and I sat on our horses enraptured. It was by far the most wonderful grazing-country we had ever laid eyes on; at a glance one could tell that thousands of head of cattle could be accommodated.

After the long dry trip across the sandy country, the horses were attacking the luscious, sweet grass; and it was with some difficulty that we got them on the move again. As the river seemed to swing towards us in a northerly direction, we decided to skirt the plain and meet it. After travelling about a mile and a half, we reached a fine billabong easy of approach, and camped.

Wanting something tasty for tea, I sent Bob off with a shot-gun. He soon returned with a dozen black ducks, the best eating of all wild ducks. It seemed like slaughter, but so thick were they that Bob's haul was the result of the discharge of only one barrel.

After settling things, Whittaker and I took a couple of the lighter guns and set off through the plain to see what was about. We had tramped for a mile or so when from the swampy ground before us there arose a graceful bird, which I instantly recognized by its plumes as the greatly prized egret.

The thought of sending some beautiful egret-feathers to one of his many ladies down south appealed immediately to the romantic Whittaker, and he promptly fired. It was a bad shot, for the bird flew about half a mile before dropping. We followed it.

Finding ourselves getting into water, we moved on to a large patch of green water couch; no sooner had we walked a few yards on it than it began to dip and rise beneath our feet. It had become matted together and formed a floating carpet. We kept on and recovered the egret.

Later, we found that the matted grass covered waterholes which were infested with crocodiles, and a shiver went through me as I thought how easy it would have been for us to have fallen through.

The egret was plumed and also had the ornamental feathers on the neck. Back at the camp we removed the feathers, but did not eat the bird, as Bob had prepared ducks. We cooked them in the fashion of the blacks, slitting them open, removing the bones, and spreading them on the coals. They were plump and juicy, and we made a delicious meal.

The mosquitoes were bad that night, and I crawled under my net early. Whittaker, however, was restless; he passed the time by taking pot-shots at flying geese in the moonlight, the while keeping the mosquitoes at bay with a towel. Hundreds of geese were passing overhead, and each shot was followed by a dull thud as a bird hit the ground.

Jacky had been lying under his net smoking contentedly, when he suddenly emitted a frightful howl. One of

Whittaker's geese had crashed on to him. This pleased Bob immensely. Giving a loud guffaw, he said:

"That one snake alonga sky, Jacky."

Whittaker decided he had shot enough geese, and was about to call it a night, when something caught his eye.

"What in the blazes is that?" he asked, pointing.

In the distance I saw what appeared to be lights dancing amongst the trees. We could not make out what they were, so I called to Bob Cadell. He was beside us in a moment - you would think those boys had had army training! - and Jacky was, of course, with him. Bob looked for only a second, then said:

"Him blackfella, boss, close up. Plenty sit down alonga this place."

He said that during the day he had noticed bones, turtle-shells, and where trees had been cut recently for sugar-bag, and knew there were blacks about.

Bob had not bothered to tell us about it. I had found that the boys very seldom proffered information; no doubt he had taken it for granted that we had seen the same signs as he had. We watched the lights bobbing about in eerie fashion, until they finally disappeared. We crawled under the nets again and slept.

After an early breakfast, Whittaker and I got a couple of horses, put some damper and pieces of biltong in our pockets, strapped pannikins to our saddles, and taking a .32 and a .303 rifle, set out on a day's exploration, leaving the boys in charge of the camp.

Our first intention was to see if we could find a suitable landing-place on the river, since we were anxious to establish a semi-permanent camp as early as possible.

We had skirted the plain for about a mile and a half when we noticed a group of sandstone hills. As the ground between us and the hills was too boggy for the horses, we tethered them and reached one of the hills on foot. Climbing to the top we gazed upon the river about half a mile ahead.

About four miles away, in almost the same direction, three large hills formed a triangle. On the top of one was a large, flat rock which was surmounted by another rock, for all the world resembling a cannon.

Fred Smith had told us to look for this place - known as Cannon Hill. He also said that at the foot of it we would find a splendid lagoon, and an excellent camping ground, which would do as our temporary headquarters. Oenpelli landing was almost opposite, Smith told us, and on the river, about a mile away, we would find a suitable place for a temporary landing for our provisions.

As far as we could see in every direction, were those wonderful grassy plains dotted with waterholes; the quantity of game about convinced me that we were looking upon some of the finest country in the world. We decided to make for Cannon Hill next morning.

We reached level ground again and strolled over to a waterhole for a drink, chatting gaily about the wonders of the country. I was sitting on a log watching Whittaker have his fill, when there was a scurry, followed by a splash, and into the water disappeared a huge crocodile. Whittaker had almost put his foot on it. Unfortunately, the reptile slithered out of sight before we could get in a shot.

Pushing back to camp, Whittaker rode in front, and so high was the beautiful, green, water couch that at times I almost lost sight of him. About a quarter of a mile from camp we came to the banks of a small lagoon fringed with dense thickets of reeds. Out of them jumped fifteen or twenty pigs, grunting and squealing. There were old boars and sows and a number of young ones - the first pigs we had seen in the Territory.

Whittaker, all excitement, called to me for my revolver,

which I threw him, and he set sail after the pigs. I left him to it. I had only gone a few yards when six shots rang out in quick succession. I smiled; a revolver in old Whittaker's hands was about as useless as nothing, and I imagined the pigs were leading him a merry dance.

He arrived back at camp not long after, and to my astonishment, he was proudly carrying a young porker across his saddle. And he told me the amazing story.

"I emptied the gun at this little brute," he said, "but couldn't hit him. Then I lost my block and threw it at him and managed to clout him behind the ear. You can see how I finished the job."

I certainly could; the porker's throat had been neatly slit. There was great jubilation in the camp at the prospect of some roast pork.

One of the geese Whittaker had shot the night before had been plucked and cleaned. I stuffed it with onions, damper crumbs, and herbs, which we always carried with us, and shoved it in our smaller camp-oven to stew in its own juice, as it were.

Then we turned our attention to the pig. After giving it a bath in boiling water, the boys scraped the bristles off, cleaned it, and placed half in our larger oven with the last of our potatoes and onions. If we never had another meal, this was going to be one!

Bob and Jacky, after cleaning the pig, had wandered down to the lagoon with the innards, and we saw Bob scrubbing the tripe like fury, while Jacky seemed to be entangled in yards of intestine.

When they returned with their washing, I asked Bob what he was going to do with it. He looked surprised that I should ask, telling me that he had worked for a Chinese butcher at Pine Creek who had told him that all the innards of the pig were excellent to eat. We left them to their own choice morsels.

It was hard waiting for that porker to cook, for, of all things, I know of nothing more tantalizing than the smell of crackling pork.

At last the feast was ready. It makes me hungry every time I think of that meal, as it makes me wince when I remember its after-effects.

The pork was so tender it actually melted in the mouth, and the crisp and brown crackle added a flavour that the epicure dreams of. Allowing for a liberal helping to the boys, Whittaker and I wolfed the entire half of that pig; and without bothering to tidy up afterwards we tottered to our bunks like drunken men.

But alas! Early in the morning I awoke with violent pains in the stomach, and judging by Whittaker's moans he was in like travail. We suffered until daylight, when we dosed ourselves with chlorodyne. But there was no hope of making Cannon Hill that day. The pig had played the very devil with our tummies.

We realized, of course, too late, that after all the game we had been eating, our stomachs were in no state to withstand such an inrush of young, rich pork. Our food for that day consisted of a few bits of salt biltong, which we washed down at night with a little duck broth.

When I was in a fit condition to think dispassionately about pigs, I wondered how they got there. I learned later that Paddy Cahill, the high priest of Oenpelli, had had some Berkshires sent to him from the south years before. A few of them had got away, swum the river and bred on our side in thousands. There was everything there to gladden the heart of any pig - yams by the cartload, all varieties of green food, and swampy water to wallow in.

In that day of internal distress we overhauled our outfit, and I gave some attention to the horses' hoofs. As they were never shod, it was necessary on occasion to pare them. They grow quickly in the soft country, and frequently split.

Further, the horses had developed a sort of mange, running from the middle of the back to the tail and on the rump. I gave this close scrutiny. Not being able to determine what it was, I asked Bob's opinion. Again the old fool had noticed it, no doubt before I did, but had said nothing because he hadn't been asked. I often think those black villains must have had many a quiet laugh at us. I said to him:

"What makem this one mange, Bob? Him hair come off alonga rump."

Of course, he *would* grin.

"That one no more mange, boss. That one burn."

"Burn?" I said. "You tellem."

"First horse go alonga drink, catchem water alonga tail, fliten fly alonga back with tail. Bimeby hot sun come up burn him alonga back."

So that was the explanation!

CHAPTER XII

HELD UP BY THE BLACKS

WE got away early next morning, both feeling a little weak after our gruelling over-indulgence in pig. We were making for the three hills, of which Cannon Hill was the landmark, about five miles away.

On our way over this magnificent country we had to skirt some pretty dense jungle into which pademelons and wallabies hopped in hundreds. And the air was charged with the screeching and the song of thousands of birds.

At length we reached the first of the hills. There was a splendid lagoon on our right, beyond us was the second hill, and on the other side and at the end of the lagoon was Cannon Hill.

We were moving in single file (as we always rode) along the base of the first hill, when a frightful smell hit us full in the face. We had smelt decayed flesh too often at the war to be mistaken as to what it was. As soon as he whiffed it, Bob rode up to us, followed by Jacky.

"Blackfella close up, boss, I tinkit," Bob said.

We halted, but could see no sign of blacks. With a sharp yelp Jacky suddenly pointed to the side of the hill, and in a hushed voice said:

"Might be there."

Looking through our glasses we saw what appeared to be a large cave.

Whittaker and I left the horses in charge of the boys, and picking our way through the rocks and scrub, we began to ascend the hill. We came across a well-used track, and, following it, were led to the mouth of the cave. The stench was fearful. In front of the cave were strewn the bones of kangaroos and other animals and the head of a crocodile with rotten meat hanging to them. Inside it was too dark to see beyond a few yards; so we gathered some dry bracken and made a torch. We entered warily, not knowing what might be lurking within.

It was a revelation. The walls rose to about forty feet, and along one side was a ledge of stone. Whether it was nature's work, or had been cut by the blacks, we had no means of telling, but it was as smooth as glass, and so was the stone floor. Apparently the cave had been used for hundreds of years. There was now no sign of life.

In the flickering light of the torch our eyes suddenly alighted upon a group of aboriginal paintings along one side. They held us in amazement. Exceptionally lifelike reproductions of kangaroos, turtles, crocodiles, emus, nude lubras with well-developed breasts, and hands, had been painted with red, yellow, and white ochre. We tested the paint, but it gave no sign of smearing.

There were also drawings and carvings. I had no idea that aboriginal art could reach such a high level.[35] In spite of the filthy atmosphere, we spent some time in the cave; but we were both glad to get out in the open again, although there was nothing of a spring morning about it there.

The boys greeted us with happy smiles when we returned. They had been worried over our long absence, and thought we had fallen among "cheeky fellas." I told Bob about the cave, and asked him to have a look at it. He shook his head knowingly.

"Full up debil-debil, that one, boss."

I had a hurried lunch and was off again, telling Whittaker to follow later. I wanted to see if it would be wise to try and make Cannon Hill before dark; if not, to select a suitable camping-ground.

Turning the foot of the second hill, I came to a huge flat stone some fifty feet high, a hundred feet wide, lying between the hill and the lagoon, and completely blocking, except for a narrow passage, the entrance to the little valley.

I was about to pass through the passage, when Dandy stopped short, throwing up his head and pricking his ears. Immediately through the small opening appeared about thirty blacks, fearsomely painted, and armed with spears.

A chill of fear swept over me, for I at once took them to be warriors on the war-path.

Before I could think what next to do, they rushed towards me, fitting their spears into their wommeras. I had no time to turn and gallop away, for those spears were soon ready to throw. Whatever was to happen next, I knew it was certain death to attempt to clear out.

So, with a ghastly feeling, I sat as still in the saddle as the prancing Dandy would allow me, and waited. I made no move to get my pistol from its holster, knowing full well that I was a gone coon if they had decided to get me.

Howling and grimacing, the blacks rushed to within a few feet of me, and came to a dead halt, with an ominous grunt, which as much as said:

"Got you!"

I endeavoured to appear unconcerned, but I was as scared as a rabbit.

They were the finest specimens of natives I had seen or have seen since. Their colouring was more coffee than the dead black of Bob and Jacky, and they were all about six feet and over, and marvellously muscled. Their hair had a reddish tinge in it, through the cartilage of their noses were stuck teeth of animals, pieces of sharpened shell or carved wood, and they were painted in red and white stripes across the belly and chest, and down the thighs and face.

It was a sight to put the fear of God in any man, and as I stared at them, they stared back at me for some moments. Then happened one of those extraordinary things which one dreams of.

They all burst out laughing.

I was so dumbfounded that a sudden movement by dandy nearly unseated me. My fear swiftly changed to anger. I was being made a fool of and didn't like it.

One of them stepped from the rest and came closer. He was the pick of a splendid bunch; perhaps not quite as tall as the others, but more powerfully built, and I could see the muscles rippling under the skin of his thighs and arms. He carried a grim-looking jagged spear, and I noticed that it was tipped with iron. He also wore a few beads, and had an air of authority about him which told me plainly that he was the leader. I said nothing, preferring to be told first what was to happen to me. Then came shock number two. In a musical bass voice, he said with a grin:

"Good day!"

I recovered quickly, and was still very angry. I did not return his greeting, but said:

"What the hell's the meaning of this?"

"They no more harm. They, bin makem fun," he answered, laughing.

Feeling I was at any rate safe, I snapped at him:

"I no more wantem fun like that. Next time I shoot quick."

He grinned again, and told me that it was just as well I hadn't tried to run, because his boys would have speared me in the back. I asked him where he came from:

"This my country. I sit down here."

"You bin work alonga white man?"

"Plenty time I go alonga mission station, but no more work alonga white man."

He seemed friendly enough, but I was still damned annoyed.

No white man will suffer himself to be made a fool of by a black if he can help it.

Seeing my anger, he seemed anxious to establish good relations.

"Me friend alonga you. Might be you gottem bacca?"

I gave him some.

Just then Whittaker and the outfit came into view, and he galloped up to me.

"Started another war, Warby?" he called.

"These __ __ have been having a bit of a circus, and scaring the life out of me," I said with disgust. Whittaker took a hand.

"What name you?" he demanded.

"My name Koperaki. Me king alonga this country." - and it was not long before I discovered that he was indeed king, and wielded great power.

Out of the corner of my eye, I saw Bob and Jacky looking open-mouthed at what was going on, and so engrossed were they that they had forgotten all about the horses which were wandering towards the reedy banks of the lagoon.

All of a sudden there was a startling yell from Koperaki, and for a moment I thought some more "fun" was beginning. But he was yelling at Bob Cadell.

"Catchem, turnem plurry horse, plurry fool. That one water full up halligator."

Bob jumped as if he had been shot, and darting after the horses, brought them back just as they were about to enter the water.

Koperaki was becoming very affable - no doubt the stick of tobacco I had given him was in a good measure responsible. He had told his tribe to retire, and they were squatting on their haunches with their chins in their hands, in the shade, watching us intently.

We asked Koperaki about a camping-ground, and he told us

to pitch our tents where we were. We could send our horses through the narrow passage. On the other side was a small billabong of fresh water in which there were no crocodiles, and there was plenty of good tucker for them.

Incidentally, that was the beginning of a friendship with Koperaki which lasted for many years. He was the finest type of black man I ever met. Always strictly honourable and honest, he was yet as wild as the day he was born. He had never bound himself to a white man, although he had taken full and profitable advantage of their company. He used to go to Oenpelli, and the old Kopalgo mission, trading bees-wax and other stuff. Everybody had an excellent word for him.

Koperaki gave his fellows a hoy, and in no time our camp was prepared. While this was going on poor Jacky had a thoroughly miserable time. The strange blacks made faces at him and uttered horrible threats of what they would do to him when the opportunity offered.

Bob appeared to ignore their gibes, but he remembered them all right. He got more than his own back a little later.

I went down to the lagoon and shot a dozen ducks, knowing that there would be a large party to feed. I gave most of them to Koperaki, who handed them to his crowd, and they departed, leaving Koperaki with us.

While our tea was being prepared, a long cooee came from the bush. It was promptly answered by Koperaki, and through the passage beside the rock wall appeared an old black buck, three lubras, and a little boy, probably four years old. Koperaki called them over, and when they were near he ran over to the boy, and picking him up in his arms, gave him a hug and a resounding kiss.

It was the first and only time I was ever to see a black man kiss a child, or anyone else, for that matter. He was a fine, plump little chap, and I assumed rightly that he was

Koperaki's son.

One of the lubras was a most striking girl of about seventeen. She alone wore a loin-cloth of human hair, and was built on graceful and splendid lines. Her features were sharpened, and her large brown eyes were magnificent. Like Koperaki, her hair was of reddish colour. Seeing me gazing so intently at her, Koperaki said:

"That one missus belonga me, and that one my boy."

And waving his hand towards the other two gins:

"No more proper missus. They belonga me all same."

He gave the gins some instructions, and they set to work, cleaned and swept the camp, collected bundles of grass for our beds, and made the fire. They also grabbed a couple of the ducks and soon had their feathers flying in all directions, which, of course, meant more sweeping.

After showing us where we could get some delightfully fresh water from the sandstone rocks, Koperaki said he would be back "bimeby." And he departed with his wife, child, and the old buck, leaving the other two gins with us. They were almost as good to look upon as Koperaki's lady.

I said to Whittaker:

"Well, what do you know about that!"

"We don't want the dirty devils here," he replied crossly.

"Oh, we'll have to treat them kindly, Whit," I said. "They're the king's property, you know."

Whittaker growled, and I noticed him take some red Turkey twill to where they were sitting under the trees.

I said to him after:

"If you intend to carry out your excellent intention of dressing all the gins in the Territory, where the devil do you think the twill's coming from?"

"I'm going to make them look decent as long as I can," echoed his noble sentiments.

We were dog-tired, but had sufficient energy to attack a

substantial meal of roast goose. When that was over, the two gins cleaned up and left us - and I couldn't even be bothered asking Whittaker if they had gone with his sanction, blessing, or curse.

I was settling into my grass bunk, at peace with the world, and was almost on the verge of sleep when I heard Jacky Anyone's voice calling me in plaintive tones.

"I tinkit more better you keep him gun to-night alonga you, boss."

There have been times when I liked Jacky; other times when I could have wrung his neck. I remembered having left my .303 rifle leaning against a tree almost five yards from me. He must have seen it.

"What for, Jacky?" I asked him, sleepily.

"Those blackfella little bit cheeky fella, boss," he said.

Bob Cadell had his ears cocked as usual, and an audible snort came from his bunk. It was too good a chance for Bob to miss.

"Might be lubra belonga myall black, stop alonga you to-night, Jacky. You plenty brave man."

Jacky jumped to his feet, and, if he could have flushed with anger, he would have done so.

"You plenty brave man all right, Bob," he said, savagely. "You bin sleepem close alonga boss to-night."

This snappy duologue could have gone on for some time, but I thought a fair thing was a fair thing.

"Shut up. Go alonga sleep. All about all right."

Jacky folded up immediately, Bob grunted, and sleep descended.

CHAPTER XIII

BLOOD-LUST - AND CORROBOREE

Just after daybreak next morning, Koperaki was back at our camp with his batman, old Jimmy, and carrying a barramundi, weighing up to twenty-five pounds, which he said he had speared in the lagoon. We slit it up, baked it in the camp-oven, and had a delicious slab for breakfast.

Koperaki joined us, sitting about five paces away.

During the meal, Whittaker and I discussed our plans. We had been three months in the Territory, and although we had accumulated a vast amount of interesting knowledge, we had come there for the definite purpose of shooting buffaloes for a living, and the sooner we got down to that serious business the better.

The life so far had been comparatively easy, and decidedly pleasant, and I could understand how content men could be to jog along in the north without any other purpose than to shoot sufficient game to live. In which case they would soon be on a par with the blacks. I could see beyond question that one could live in the Territory indefinitely - or as long as ammunition lasted.

"We must get down to tin-tacks," said Whittaker, "and start shooting those buffaloes. We've got to make some money. I haven't forgotten that two-quid hide we left for the dingoes at Jim Jim."

"We'll be shooting any minute from now, Whit," I answered.

I called Koperaki over and asked him did he know where there were buffaloes - mobs of them - and he said there were hundreds on the Magela Plains, which I figured out should be about twelve miles away.

We had the horses brought up and selected three. But Koperaki declined a mount. Shaking his head vigorously, he said:

"One time alonga Paddy Cahill ridem horse, and all time sore alonga behind."

So we started out with Koperaki leading the way on foot, and leaving Bob and Jacky to look after the camp. They were busy getting acquainted with Jimmy, the hairiest man I have ever seen, and introducing tobacco-chewing, which art curiously he had not learned.

Koperaki soon settled into a long swift stride, and we jog-trotted our horses, keeping pace with him. We passed through the entrance to our valley, and turning sharply to the right, came on the grassy plains upon which our horses were feeding. Koperaki led the way up to the banks of the lagoon which flowed past the rock between us and Cannon Hill.

Koperaki had struck a pad, and along this we proceeded at an even brisker trot until we reached the base of Cannon Hill. Keeping on the high ground, we crossed some more beautifully green plains with huge sandstone rocks which looked as though they had been ejected from the gun-like rock on the hill, and finally reached the banks of the East Alligator River.

We left our horses and went closer to the river. At this point it was about three hundred yards wide, but looking northwards, we could see it widen to over a mile. A tidal, muddy stream, and the tide was coming in and flowing swiftly.

Our black guide told us to be on the watch for crocodiles, as the river teemed with them. As he spoke we saw four sunning themselves on a mud-bank not far away.

Almost directly opposite we observed a roughly constructed platform, running about thirty yards into the water, which Koperaki told us was the Oenpelli landing.

We learned that at very low tide this was the only place on the tidal portion of the river where you could wade across, but even then it was risky unless you knew the tides. Anyhow, we were satisfied that here was the place for our landing. It was a good dry-season track back to the camp, and providing the buffaloes were on the Magela Plain as Koperaki had averred, our permanent residence looked as good as established.

We returned to camp, and after a pot of tea we stuffed some dry damper and beef into our pockets and set off for the Magela Plain, Koperaki still stretching his long muscular legs in the lead.

These blacks are tireless walkers, and can average five miles an hour for hours on end. On one occasion I rode forty miles in a day, following a black and his gin on foot. At the end of the trip I felt like dropping from the saddle, while the blacks were fresh enough to chase a bandicoot and catch it!

The track turned almost south and led us over the watershed again, and through forest country with occasional tea-tree swamps. Around about these were many signs of buffaloes. We crossed the swamps and at last were on the Magela Plain.

Although we had gone into raptures over our own plain, this was so large that in several directions it met the horizon. It was covered with the same wonderful grass we had seen on the other plains, but, if anything, was better feeding, being drier and shorter. Everyone who has been in the north has heard of Magela Plain. It is recognized as the finest of the many splendid plains in Arnhem Land.

Moving along the edge of the plain for a couple of miles, we saw to the left of us a herd of about two hundred buffaloes, and to the north-west there were hundreds more. Some were resting in the shade of the tea-trees, others wallowing in the swamps, and the rest quietly grazing.

With a thrill we realized we were looking upon the country we had come so many miles to find. We did not disturb them - "They'll keep," said Whittaker with a grin - and turned back for camp.

During our absence Bob Cadell had taken the shot-gun and had collected a few ducks. Before I could reprimand him - the boys were never allowed to touch the guns without permission - he said:

"I bin takem gun, boss, shootem duck. Might be you long time come home, plenty hungry."

As he had also cooked an excellent damper, the first he had made for us, because we didn't like the idea of the blacks handling food, I let him off lightly. Our naturally keen appetites had been pepped up by the satisfactory way things were going, and the meal was dispatched in quick time.

Koperaki's crowd had moved through the passage way in from their own camp, and had lit a fire about fifty yards from us.

Whittaker and I were chatting contentedly after tea when we heard the first ominous growl of a tropical thunderstorm on its way. Having had one experience of the suddenness of these storms, we quickly rigged our big tent-fly, a rough shelter for ourselves and our supplies.

The storm was upon us in a few minutes. The thunder rolled, shaking the earth beneath us, and forked and chain lightning slashed the blackness. Koperaki's blacks, jabbering in terror, had moved nearer to our fire, and Bob and Jacky were cringing with their heads buried in their blankets. At every clap of thunder the blacks emitted pitiful yells, and their faces, lit up by each flash of lightning, were studies of abject fear. The whites of their eyes were rolling, their teeth chattering, and their limbs trembling.

A deafening crash of thunder shook us, and with a terrifying yell Koperaki's blacks grabbed fire-sticks and disappeared into the darkness. They raced for the hills, and we could see the lights from their torches bobbing about as they crept into the small caves. There they spent the remainder of the night.

The storm hung around for two or three hours, and as there was little rain, it passed leaving the atmosphere heavy and oppressive. The very foundations of the country seemed to have been disturbed, and as each rock appeared to be balanced precariously on another, we had had the unpleasant thought of them tumbling down on us.

In the morning we agreed that Whittaker should set off for Kopalgo, which we knew was on the South Alligator about four days' ride away. There he was to buy ten horses from Fred Smith, as it was our intention to return early the horses which Trower had made available at Bachelor Farm. He was also to have a look at the buffalo-shooting outfit which was to have been left there by Percy Love's partner.

When Whittaker had left with Bob Cadell and Big Head, one of Koperaki's boys, and six horses, I got Koperaki, Jacky, and a few horses and made for the river, armed with shovels and axes, to prepare our landing.

We cleared a track through the mangroves on the bank, and having got sufficient timber, we made a corduroy path for some yards into the river. Koperaki's boys, having been kept going with tobacco, lent a willing hand, and in no time our landing was built.

A couple of nights after Whittaker had left, I was awakened about one o'clock by the furious jangling of the horse-bells, which was immediately followed by the blacks yelling:

"Anoburro! Anoburro!" (The aboriginal name for buffalo.)

It was bright moonlight. Before I had time to jump up I saw a naked black man a few paces away with a gun.

Koperaki had seen where I had left my .303 leaning against a tree, and he was at hand with it before I was properly awake.

He said a buffalo had come through the narrow opening, and was making towards the lower end of our enclosure. He had sent his boys to frighten it back from that exit.

I slipped some clothes on, and quickly took up a position beside a big rock at the narrow passage. At the shouts of the black the buffalo turned in his tracks and made straight for the opening. His head was thrown up and he seemed uncertain of what was happening.

I let him get to within about fifteen yards of me, when I fired, aiming for the centre of his forehead. He staggered and fell, but soon scrambled to his knees. As he was about to rise I pumped a couple more shots in, and he tumbled over.

It was a very tame killing, but the fact that it was my first buffalo gave me a passing thrill.

When the big beast fell the second time, one of the blacks rushed to it, and jabbed a knife into its throat, from which the blood gushed. The others ran up, waving paper-bark torches, and those who could, thrust their hands into the wound and rubbed the blood all over themselves, the while dancing and laughing.

I was horribly impressed with this exhibition of blood lust, and understood how they would kill for the joy of killing, and for the sight and the smell of blood.

Jacky Anyone, for all his vaunted civilization, was as scared as usual, and had shinned up the tallest tree, where he remained until all the ghoulish celebrations were over.

Koperaki had ordered a fire to be made, and I told him to get the beast skinned and quartered and have it hung on the limb of a tree. The blacks soon finished the job, and they were not long in getting at the innards, which they roasted and ate like ravenous dingoes.

I had no sleep after that. When daylight came, I cut some meat from the buffalo and salted it, giving the rest to Koperaki, which he handed out to his tribe.

I could get no work out of the blacks that day. They gorged themselves on roast buffalo until not a piece was left. The Australian black always lives for the day, and as long as there is food to eat, he will gorge the lot. He believes always in letting the morrow look after itself.

I decided on another look round the country, and although I didn't particularly want to take Jacky with me, I knew there was no chance of him staying at the camp alone. He was still scared of those myall blacks. But Koperaki had them well in hand, so when he said he would keep an eye on our outfit, I left knowing everything would be safe.

Jacky and I had been riding along easily for some miles, skirting patches of jungle country where everything was growing rankly, when Jacky suddenly plunged into the bush, calling me to follow. He had jumped from his horse, and was digging excitedly into a mound of dry leaves, about twenty feet in diameter and five feet high. His hands came out almost as quickly as they had gone in, and in them were white eggs, larger than ordinary hen eggs. He had found the nest of a scrub turkey.

The turkey, slightly smaller than the domesticated bird, is to be found in brush and scrub all over the north. It buries its eggs eighteen inches, or two feet in the mound, and covers them with leaves, making an ideal incubator. When hatched, the young are fully feathered, and able to fend for themselves.

Jacky broke one of the eggs, and finding nothing with feathers on inside, swallowed it. I told him to take the rest back to camp.

We were making for the horses when Jacky gave a piercing shriek and bolted for the clearing. Feeling a nip in the middle of my back, I followed him at the same speed. I was in time to see Jacky tearing off shirt and trousers, and, by heavens, I was quick to do likewise.

We were both smothered in green ants, vicious brutes as big as soldier ants, which bite and won't let go. Curiously enough, the bites have no after effects, but while the ants are busy you know all about it. They build their nests in leaves, and should you brush against one, the ants pour all over you. If you happen to get one of them in your food, you will taste the sourest thing imaginable.

Fortunately, the turkey eggs were not broken in the

scramble, and we moved along.

Getting on to higher ground, I saw something which gave me a temporary shock. I believed that Whittaker and I were the only whites within a radius of fifty miles, yet in the near distance before me was a line of what appeared to be fencing-posts placed horizontally at intervals. They stretched in a straight line towards the river, and it looked as though someone intended erecting a fence. And on our property!

I rode over and saw the posts were about six feet in length, but irregularly arranged. Following them, they led me into a thick scrub with tall timbers, where the mystery was solved. A large tree had been felled, and about twenty-two feet from the butt end had been burned and tomahawked off. It was some three feet in diameter, and the centre had been burned out with coals and chipped away. I realized, of course, that here was a native log canoe in the making. The posts which I thought were for fencing were to roll the canoe into the river. Evidently there must be a good deal of organized labour among the blacks.

A white man would have utilized about a tenth of the number of rollers by continually transferring them from the back to the front as the canoe was pushed along.

We got the eggs safely back to camp and cooked them for midday. They were a little stronger than the domestic hen-egg, but quite good, and provided a decided change in diet. They were the first eggs I had tasted in three months. We had arrived a little late for the laying season, but during it, eggs - goose, duck, plover, turkey, and others - were there in millions.

A bright moon was shining again that night, and the blacks treated me to one of their corroborees of joy. There were about a hundred of them and they were not a hundred and fifty yards from our camp. Koperaki had come over to me, and I asked him was that the extent of his tribe. He said no, there were other parties scattered about the country.

I noticed that the gins were matured mothers with their pot-bellied youngsters, and remarked to Koperaki on the absence of young girls.

Thereupon he told me an interesting thing. When they reach the age of six, he said, they are sent, for moral reasons, to what is known as the Stone Country - that is in the sandstone ridges - where they are placed in charge of a couple of old men and lubras. And they are only brought back when it is time for them to be given to certain men to whom they had been promised shortly after they were born. They are kept out of sight of the tribe, and smoke signals tell when they are to be released.

He further told me that a buck of forty will marry a girl of about thirteen, the reason being that when he gets too old to work and hunt, she will still be young enough to go after the yams and bandicoots.

Happy thought!

While I was chatting to Koperaki, the corroboree had been swinging along merrily. The blacks were seated around the fire with the gins on one side, and they were giving themselves up to a form of enjoyment which civilized folk would call a sing-song. There was one soloist in the tribe; his voice could be heard clear and musical above the din provided by the chorus. The lubras sat on their haunches, slapping their thighs in time.

Suddenly the corroboree took another turn, and the night rang with howls and wails of great grief. The gins, with heads bowed, were shaking with sobs and throwing dirt and leaves over themselves.

This dismal performance lasted until daylight.

At the first sign of light, I took my rifle and went for a stroll. I knocked a couple of fair-sized wallabies, and left them for the boys to pick up later.

On my way back I saw several black, furry animals with curly tails, looking something like monkeys, and about the size of cats. I have never been able to find out what they were, although I have asked many bushmen and zoologists. I had a number of shots at them then and afterwards, but could never manage to hit one.[36]

I was enjoying a delicious breakfast of bacon and turkey eggs, when Koperaki appeared with another barramundi. I was curious to know what all the howling had been about, and asked:

"What name big fella noise last night? All about cry?"

"Him blackfella bin die."

"Him die now?"

"Long time die."

I let it go at that. Paddy Cahill told me later that the black whose death they had been bemoaning had died three years before. He said it was not an uncommon thing for the blacks to remember the death of a brother during a corroboree, and to break into unpremeditated and distressful mourning.

Curious beggars, I thought.

CHAPTER XIV

I MEET THE FAMOUS PADDY CAHILL

ONE morning early, there was a hubbub in camp, and Koperaki came running over to tell me that he had seen smoke a long way up the river. I rushed out with him, and climbing to the top of a big rock, saw the three masts of a boat winding its way slowly along the river.

Getting hold of Jacky and a couple of horses, we made for our landing, and there saw the *John Alce*, a river steam-boat of three hundred tons. Sighting me, the skipper sent a dinghy over. I went on board and was soon sitting down to the first meal laid on a tablecloth I had had for some months.

The skipper was a very decent chap, and we found much to talk about. He said he had six months' supplies on board for Paddy Cahill (he only made two trips a year), and he thought he had everything I required.

"When do you expect Paddy down?" I asked him.

"To-night, or early in the morning."

"How will he know you are here?"

The skipper pointed towards Cannon Hill, and I saw broken columns of smoke arising.

"That's bush telegraph. Those blacks are signalling to Paddy's place!"

And looking in the direction of Oenpelli, I saw further broken smoke columns.

"There's the answer," said the skipper.

The bush telegraph is the blacks' counterpart to our Morse code. They build a fire and place on it large quantities of green leaves or grass, and when a column of smoke has arisen, they break it at various intervals by putting on and removing a blanket or green bough.

I invited the skipper to come ashore and have a shot, which

he and the engineer readily did. They spent most of the day pottering about, and got a nice bag of over a hundred geese and ducks and a few barramundi which the blacks had speared for them.

We returned to the boat and after tea settled down to a smoke, a few drinks, and a yarn.

He asked me where I came from, and when I said New South Wales I seemed to strike some chord in him of splendid enthusiasm for the Territory.

"I have been travelling along these rivers for fifteen years," said the skipper, "and it makes me wild to see this magnificent country neglected as it is. Do you know that such rivers as the Macarthur, Roper, East, South and West Alligator, Adelaide, Daly, and Victoria are navigable for from fifty to a hundred miles by a boat like the *John Forrest* with its five hundred tons? You can't get anywhere near that distance up any of the rivers on the north coast of New South Wales. And what is the difference in the country here to that around the Richmond and Clarence rivers? It's better: that's all. Then look at the rainfall - an average of ninety inches! Yet it is not settled. The trouble is that the people in the south don't know what the country here's like, and it seems to me that the young fellers prefer to hang around the cities out of jobs."

The skipper had apparently embarked on his pet topic, and I didn't interrupt. I was extremely interested.

"A few trips ago, the Gilruth administration decided to run a butter factory with Paddy Cahill at Oenpelli, which I claim is the finest dairy-country in the world. So wonderful was it, that the cows were grazing up to the bails. Butter was produced equal to the best, and I took it into Darwin. There the unions refused to take delivery on the wharves because they said it had been made with black labour. When they did decide to handle it, it was so much grease, since there was no refrigerator on the boat.

"I suppose you and your mate," he went on, "have come here at a fair amount of expense. I've got several tons of salt on board for you, and I know without you telling me what it cost."

"It cost £5 a ton in Sydney," I said, "and £35 a ton to land here. The difference was eaten up by freight and handling charges."

"If you go to the South Alligator River, have a look at the salt-pans. We were hung up by the tides one day, and I came across them. There are tons and tons of the stuff. Two Greeks in Darwin are out to catch the salt trade of the north; before you order any more south, get in touch with them.[37]"

"It's a pity some of our fellows didn't have enough imagination to get hold of the trade," I commented.

"It is," replied the skipper. "But there you are. There are sufficient salt-pans and natural deposits from five to ten miles on the South Alligator side of your boundary to supply the needs of all the Territory to the end of time."

Later I found that to be fact.

After a few more drinks we turned in.

We had an early breakfast, and shortly afterwards Paddy Cahill and about a dozen boys approached his landing. We went over to meet them and I had my first introduction to the famous bushman.

He was a man of about sixty, short, robust, and with a florid complexion which reddened the deep tan of his features. I was much impressed by his massive shoulders, which told of great strength.

Cahill was one of the earliest and greatest pioneers of the north. He went there about the time of Giles, the explorer,[38] and after working his way through Central Australia, finally took up his wonderful holding at Oenpelli. He sold his property in 1924 and took his wife and son, Tommy, south for a well-earned rest. But old Paddy's leisure hours were few, for once away from his beloved country he soon passed out.[39]

Paddy Cahill shook me warmly by the hand, and in an abrupt, jerky voice, said:

"You've arrived, have you. You've been on the track quite a time."

"How did you know that?" I asked, surprised.

"I've been acquainted with every move you and your mate have made. I know at once everything that happens in this country."

We went back on board and helped Paddy to land his supplies. When that was finished, he gave me a hand to land ours.

Just before leaving, he asked me what boys I had, and I told him of Bob and Jacky.

"They're no good," he said.

"Oh, they're all right," I replied. With all their faults, I wasn't going to have anyone running down Bob and Jacky.

"I mean what East Alligator boys have you?"

I said Koperaki had been giving us a useful hand.

"You couldn't have anyone better. You can trust that feller completely. I've many times tried to get him to work for me, but he won't. A wonderful chap. Pity he wasn't born a white man."

And with an injunction which was almost a command to visit him at Oenpelli within a fortnight, he left us.

Koperaki's boys gave me a great hand to move the supplies to the camp. It was one of the few times I have seen niggers really enjoy work. They laughed and sang, and when one of them tumbled over with two hundredweight of salt on top of him, there were howls of delight. You could not imagine a more cheerful crowd, and their strength was amazing.

The skipper and the engineer paid me another visit, did a bit more shooting, then said good-bye. They left by the first tide next morning, and I did not see them or the *John Alce* for many months.

I sorted out the stores, and was particularly keen to look over the six Martini-Henry carbines which had been sent by the Defence Department at Sydney. They were about the size of sawn-off shot-guns, single shots with pistol grips; with these we hoped to make our big buffalo kills. After cleaning the guns thoroughly, I tried them out and found them in excellent order, although, naturally, not as accurate as a long barrel.

Among the supplies were a five-pound tin of boiled lollies, a couple of dozen cheap pipes, and shirts. I gave half the lollies to the blacks, to their wild delight, pipes to Koperaki and Jimmy, and a bright blue shirt and a pipe to Jacky. His old shirt was torn and dirty. I told him he could give it to Jimmy, but the next time I saw that aged black he was wearing Jacky's new shirt, which Jacky, true to his inborn socialism, had given him.

The caricature he cut, dancing about on his hairy legs in that dazzling shirt, was one to be remembered. I made him give it back to Jacky, and the old shirt went the rounds of the tribe before being discarded.

I idled about for a couple of days, enjoying the lazy life, but anxious to begin the attack on the buffaloes. One afternoon Koperaki came to me and said Whittaker would be there on the following day. He had seen Big Head's smoke signals.

I was again astounded by this remarkable means of communication, for sure enough Whittaker arrived next afternoon. He had been away just eight days.

I was pleased to see the old grin still on his face. We shook hands, and slapped each other on the back, both jolly glad to be in one another's company again. Old Bob Cadell was there too, with a broad grin spread all over his cheerful face.

Whittaker unloaded his pack, and while the boys were looking after things I passed an eye over the horses from Fred Smith. Those we got at Pine Creek were good, but these were better. There was this big difference. The Kopalgo animals had been born and bred on the plains and swamps, and I knew they would never hesitate to go into them. Ours had been foaled on the hills and granite country, and were always extremely nervous in boggy ground, and had to be forced into it.

I gave special attention to the two buffalo horses Fred Smith had lent us. One was a very fine black called Wark-Wark (aboriginal for crow) and the other a creamy mare which answered to Dinah. She proved to be one of the most intelligent animals I had ever ridden; she certainly displayed more sense than I on more than one occasion.

Next, I had a look at the shooting-outfit we had bought from Percy Love's partner. There were half a dozen pack-saddles, bags, steels, a dozen or more knives, and several long-barrelled Martini-Henrys with ammunition. I was well satisfied that for £6 we had a bargain.

Whittaker also brought a bag of sweet potatoes, some spinach and fresh goat, or mutton as it is called in the north. Both of us ate hungrily of the good food. When we had finished the meal and lit our pipes, I said:

"Well, tell us about the trip, Whit. Strike any fun?"

"Not a darned thing happened," he said. "But a lot could've. I'd have been finished a dozen times if it hadn't been for Bob and Big Head. I only saw Fred Smith for a couple of hours. He was setting out for Wild Man River [Wildman River] shooting-ground, but he wants us to come across as soon as we can. By the way, he said he would make arrangements for his lugger to pick up our hides as well as his. Decent of him, wasn't it?"

I agreed that it certainly was.

We chatted awhile about this and that, and turned in early even for us. Old Whittaker was dead beat.

CHAPTER XV

THE GREAT STAMPEDE

WE spent next morning making our plans for the first onslaught upon the buffaloes. We gave our horses a thorough overhaul to see if any were lame, girth galled, or footsore, and tried out Fred Smith's two buffalo horses. Whittaker chose the black and I had the creamy mare. Both were exceptionally quick on their feet, and answered to the slightest pressure of the knees. They would be ideally suited for the hunt.

We decided to establish a depot on the Magela Plain, and to take our entire outfit, leaving Bob and Jacky with two or three horses to look after the general supplies.

Koperaki and his tribe were to come with us. When we told Bob and Jacky they were very downcast. Not that they were anxious to be within cooee of buffaloes, but no doubt they figured that they would be safer in such a large party than remaining by themselves at camp. However, it had to be done. We couldn't leave our valuable stuff at the mercy of wandering blacks, wild pigs, or dingoes (I have known dingoes to tear packs to pieces in their fury to find food).

It was a weird procession that moved off towards the plain. Koperaki led the way on foot, carrying a hunting-spear, and I followed, with Whittaker close up. Then came Koperaki's warriors, about a hundred of them. We had thirty-five horses in the outfit, and that many of the blacks were mounted, most of them bare-back. Behind them followed the gins carrying infants, billy-cans, yam-sticks, and short spears; and trailing the party were the old men with bundles of spears belonging to the blacks on horseback, and boys.

Koperaki had left his wife and his two fancy ladies behind, and to keep them company a couple of other gins and old men. I wondered how Bob and Jacky would fare with them, but I was far from anticipating what did happen.

Riding leisurely we followed the track we had made on our first trip to Magela Plain, and finally called a halt near a fair-sized waterhole, a couple of hundred yards from the edge of the plain and some ten miles from our camp.

While the blacks were fixing up the horses and making camp, Whittaker and I cantered on to the plain to see if the buffaloes were still there. They were grazing in hundreds.

As a big and adventurous day lay ahead, we made for our bunks early after tea; the blacks, no doubt sensing the excitement in the air, gave us a more or less peaceful night for a change.

But for me sleep was a long time coming. As I lay awake gazing at the stars in the clear and cloudless sky, I felt as I had felt on many a night on Gallipoli and France before a morn attack. If anything, I think I was more honest-to-God windy.

Everything had been comparatively plain sailing up till now. We had laughed about riding into a herd of buffaloes and shooting down; and we had talked about it as a cold and logical commercial proposition.

But now, here were Whittaker and I - two new-chums - in a wilderness with a mob of supposedly savage blacks around us, and decidedly savage buffaloes in the offing.

There was nobody to guide us; nobody to tell us what to do. All we knew about buffalo-shooting was what we had read, and been told by Fred Smith. Now it came to the pinch, what the devil was going to happen? I realized, vividly, how vast can be the breach between theory and practice. I didn't dwell upon what might, and possibly would, happen to one or both of us.

Anyhow, we were in this mad stunt up to our necks, and come what may, we would have to see it through; with which unnerving reflection I went to sleep.

We were up at daybreak, and after a substantial breakfast, began to lay our plans. We would come through the tea-trees at the rear of the grazing buffaloes, and Whittaker would take one wing and I the other. We would get the beasts on the run, gallop alongside them, and shoot them through the spine at the small of the back, as we went. It sounded simple enough. God alone knew how it was going to turn out.

I arranged for the blacks, who would be able to see what was happening from the depot, to be divided into two parties - skinners and salters. When the buffaloes fell, the skinners were to follow up, take the hides off and leave them for the salters to collect. The salters were then to take them back to the camp, scrape them clean and throw on from ten to twenty pounds of salt, according to the size of the hide.

We mounted our horses. Each had a carbine, a pocketful of ammunition, and a revolver strapped to the saddle.

As we moved off, the blacks began yelling and dancing, outlets for their wild excitement at the prospect either of blood flowing freely, or of slaughter (us or the buffaloes; I don't suppose it would have mattered) or the prospect of an orgy of beef-eating. I gave Whittaker a sickly grin, and he returned it.

"Well, we're for it now, cocker," he said. "If we get out of this show alive, what about trying a quiet spell in Brazil?"

"It's not the first rough thing we've taken on, Whit," I answered. "Pity some of the old mob aren't here to give us a cheer."

We made up the plain for about three-quarters of a mile until we reached a peak in the tea-trees which extended into the plain. From this cover we could see the buffalo herd grazing a couple of hundred yards away. There were, also, half a dozen of them among the trees.

I said to Whittaker:

"Remember we don't want cows or young bulls. Go for the big old fellows. We'll get these coves in the trees started first, and when the mob clears, you take the left flank and I'll take the right."

"Good for me," he said, with the perennial Whittaker grin. I'm darned if I could see anything to smile about.

As we moved the horses forward, the buffaloes in the tea-trees sighted us, and started off after the herd. We put our horses to the gallop and set sail. And then something happened which we had not reckoned on.

Instead of catching up with the herd, as we had logically anticipated, they suddenly stopped, turned, and began to come slowly towards us. Hell! They were only about fifty yards away, and we were going full tilt at them.

I hadn't the faintest idea what was going to happen. The thought flashed through my mind that all we could do would be to swerve when we got to them, take a chance shot - and suffer the humiliation before the blacks of being chased by them.

But luckily for us, the main herd had by now been aroused and were moving off. The stray bulls gave one more look at us, and to our intense relief they spun round and began to charge after their mates. We galloped at top speed in pursuit.

As we raced over the plain, I became aware of the potholes in the ground, and I had the uneasy feeling that any moment our horses would get their hoofs into one. That would have been the end.

The strays had now reached the mob which, given the impetus we wanted, tore off with a thunder of hoofs like a cavalry charge, and leaving a cloud of thick white dust.

I waved to Whittaker as I swung away to the right, leaving him to the left attack.

Dinah was going like a dream, and I thanked my stars for such a horse. As I came through the first great cloud of dust, I found myself nearly on top of a huge buffalo bull, almost smothered in white clay. My eyes were stinging from flying dirt, but I could see well enough to shoot.

The terrified beast was on my right, and as Dinah drew

alongside I fired, aiming for the small of the buffalo's back. I had not tried the pistol-grip with the carbine before, and the gun almost kicked out of my hand.

Simultaneously with the explosion of the cartridge, my horse swerved almost at right-angles to the left, and I was as near as a touch thrown. When I had Dinah under control, I saw the buffalo had not fallen, and again I went after him hell-for-leather, the while reloading, which was no easy job.

Dinah's great speed soon brought me beside the animal once more, and I could see from where the blood welled out of a large-sized hole, that my shot had been too far in front of the back, and too much to the left to be immediately fatal.

This time I leaned over the buffalo, and almost placing the muzzle of the gun on its back fired, and the animal dropped in his tracks.

I was now more prepared for Dinah's swerve, and before I realized it, we were tearing full belt after the herd. In the excitement of the charge I remembered vaguely hearing two shots from Whittaker. Looking towards him, I saw a buffalo lying in his track, and knew that for the second time he had made the first kill.

I got two more bulls in quick succession, and was still careering on, tingling with the excitement of the hunt, when with a sudden shock, I felt the mare's legs sink in a swamp. Hell again!

The buffalo herd was in it too, and they looked at me as much as to say, "Come on now. Have a go on our home ground."

I immediately realized the danger of getting at close quarters with them in the swamp, which was up to my horse's belly, so I scrambled out as fast as I could. The swamp was about half a mile wide and extended for some miles right and left.

With mortification I saw the whole herd make the other

side of the marsh, and gallop away across the plain.

Whittaker was riding over to me, and as he came I saw that he had dropped a second buffalo. Five beasts out of a herd of a couple of hundred! It was enough to make a man curse, which I did luridly.

"What a ——," said Whittaker as he came up.

I agreed with him warmly that it was.

Holding out his right hand, he said:

"Have a look at this."

I did the same.

"Well, have a look at this," I replied.

Both our hands were bruised, swollen, and raw between the thumb and forefinger from the recoil of the guns. We must have been very soft.

We were riding over to have a look at our kills, when Whittaker said:

"I don't know how you got on, but my first shot nearly blew the gun out of my hand, and Wark-Wark almost tossed me. When I got the second buffalo, the gun flew to the ground, and the horse took me a hundred yards before I could pull him up and go back for it."

I told him I had had a similar experience, although I did not actually lose my gun. Well, there was this about it. We had both learned a couple of lessons which should be useful for the future.

The skinning party was already on the job. We got to the buffalo I had put two shots into in time to see the result of the first ineffective hit. The bullet had almost penetrated the abdomen, but it had been too far along the back, and too much to the left. That sort of shooting, I thought, would soon get me into trouble. I could see that the muzzle would have to be almost touching the buffalo's back before firing.

We noticed Koperaki go over to one of the fallen beasts and shake it by the horns in a gesture of man's triumph. But the buffalo was apparently not quite dead, for he gave a twist of his powerful neck and spun Koperaki over his back some yards away. The black got the surprise of his life, but he was soon grinning about it. One of his boys immediately plunged a knife into its neck, no doubt in defence of his chief's dignity.

Whittaker and I removed the tongues of the five beasts, leaving the blacks to finish the skinning and help themselves to whatever meat they wanted.

It was a gory sight. The plain, where the blood had poured from the great beasts, was stained a deep red and the behaviour of the blacks made more bloody the spectacle. They seemed to get great enjoyment by throwing pieces of entrails at each other, and generally smothering themselves in blood.

When the hides were brought over to the depot, we found that Koperaki had arranged for the gins to do the salting, and we supervised, telling them to be sure to rub the salt well into all the corners. As each hide was salted it was placed so that salted side would face salted side.

After the skinning party had helped themselves to the best cuts and titbits, the rest of the tribe, even the gins and boys, rushed over and hacked at the carcasses until little more than skeletons remained.

A meal and a rest, then Whittaker and I got a couple of fresh horses and rode over to investigate the swamp which had blasted what had promised to be a highly profitable morning's shooting. Several miles along from where I had entered it earlier, we found a place to cross, and on the other side we could see the buffaloes grazing in the distance. We thereupon decided to approach them from the different angle on the following day.

There was not much sleep that night. Hordes of dingoes had scented out the dead buffaloes, and they snarled and fought while the blacks ate and sang songs of thanksgiving.

We fell to talking, which, by the way, we didn't do a great

deal of at any time. We had knocked around so many years together that both knew the tremendous value of silence, and could appreciate the other's moods. Without this understanding such a companionship as ours would have been impossible.

We discussed the thrills of the day, and as is mostly the case with men accustomed to danger, we looked back upon our excitement calmly and unwonderingly. We had not done as well as we should, but perhaps better than we had a right to expect.

Still, there was the morrow to come. If only those blasted dingoes and blacks would stop howling, we might get some sleep in preparation for it. But they wouldn't. With nightmares of charging buffaloes, I had a rotten night, and Whittaker's frequent cursing told me he had the same.

We welcomed daylight with open arms. After we had each made short work of a pound of grilled buffalo steak, we looked upon the day's possibilities with a more friendly eye than I had thought possible during the restless night.

Koperaki came over and suggested we should take a couple of his boys to shoot on foot the buffaloes in the tea-trees. I gave this proposition some thought. I didn't at all like the idea of the blacks handling the guns, but when Koperaki assured me that the two boys he had in mind had often shot for Fred Smith and Paddy Cahill, I agreed. But I took good care to give them a minimum of ammunition, and when it was all over, I made them account for every shot, which I checked, and hand back what cartridges were left.

We set off again, this time with three blacks, two carrying rifles, and with a deal more confidence than we had on the previous morning. But one thing was worrying us: how with swollen and painful hands were we going to grip those guns? Still, we supposed buffalo-shooters were not reared on pap.

After crossing the fateful swamp, we came on to dense tea-tree scrub, where we left the boys. I was still rather regretful that we had brought them. I knew that to kill a buffalo on foot you would need to get in a dead shot, either behind the shoulder or between the eyes. And I didn't relish the thought of a wounded buffalo at large; for one reason it would be needless cruelty, and for another - there is no more dangerous animal in the world than a wounded buffalo bull. We could only hope for the best.

When we got through the tea-trees, we saw the herd grazing on the plain about three hundred yards away. This time I was to take the left wing, and endeavour to head them away from the scrub, while Whittaker was to head for the right.

As I set Dinah at the gallop a thrill went through me, but it was nothing compared to the surging emotions of the previous day. If accustomed to the bush and used to roughing it, it is surprising how you learn to take each new experience in your stride.

I brought down five big bulls in quick succession without difficulty, and without anything sensational happening. Looking to the right I saw Whittaker had done the same. My hand hurt like fury at the first shot, but once it got warm I forgot about it.

I was riding hard to the left to try and keep the buffaloes from getting into the infernal tea-trees, but one might as well have tried to stem the rush of an avalanche. Seeing the futility of further pursuit, I dropped back a little. The beasts would reach the shelter of the thick trees any minute.

Glancing towards Whittaker again, I saw he was about to place the muzzle of his gun at the back of his sixth victim. Good old Whit! He was doing remarkably well for an indifferent horseman.

He was about seventy yards from me. I heard the explosion of his gun, and saw the buffalo fall sideways, Wark-Wark swerving at the same moment. Whether the horse got his hoof in a pothole or the tip of the horns touched him as he swerved, I did not know, but down he came, turning a complete somersault and throwing Whittaker heavily several yards away.

Apparently only a nasty everyday buster. But to my horror the buffalo slowly rose to his knees. The horse was also struggling to his feet. Whittaker was lying motionless. The situation was desperate. As I galloped on I saw the wounded beast look from Whittaker to the horse, evidently trying to determine which to charge. With inexpressible relief I saw the buffalo lower his head, and charge the trembling horse.

The animal seemed too terror stricken to move. With a fearful lunge the buffalo had his horns underneath Wark-Wark's belly, and with a wrench of his massive neck, tossed the horse. Wark-Wark's screams sent a chill down my spine.

Before the buffalo could disengage his horns, I was upon it. A shot in the vital spot on his back toppled him over, with his horns still buried in the horse's belly - a ghastly, bloody heap.

The horse was still screaming, and any man who has heard a mortally wounded horse knows there is no more terrible cry.

Whipping out my revolver I put an end to poor Wark-Wark's agony. Whittaker, now on his feet, stumbled over sobbing with rage and sorrow. Reloading his gun and shrieking curses, he poured two vicious shots into the buffalo's head. That was the true Whittaker when he saw an animal in pain.

As for me, I felt as I had done in France when I saw a good cobber go down; I wanted to shoot every damn buffalo in the north.

When Whittaker calmed a little, I asked if he was hurt.

"I don't think so," he said. "I feel pretty dicky, but I don't believe anything's broken."

The skinning parties had now arrived, with Koperaki in the lead, greatly concerned when he had seen Whittaker fall.

I hauled Whittaker on to Dinah with me, and left for camp, leaving the boys to finish their jobs, and telling them to bring back Wark-Wark's bridle and saddle.

The black shooters returned a couple of hours later, and said they had got two buffaloes. I sent a party to skin them, and it was practically dark when they finally returned. They must have had a great little party among the tea-trees.

Whittaker and I broke our hard and fast rule, and before lunch had a couple of stiff whiskies. It had been an unnerving morning.

That afternoon I left Whittaker to have a spell, and to supervise the salting of the hides. I got hold of Sovereign, selected by Fred Smith as a likely looking buffalo horse, and set out to put him through his paces, taking one of the blacks with me.

I followed without difficulty the trail of the buffaloes. After riding for about a mile and a half, I came upon them grazing at the far end of another plain, similar to the Magela, but not so large.

I was cantering along the grassy edges, dense with reeds, when a buffalo which had evidently been drowsing there jumped to his feet. One sight of him was enough for Sovereign. He turned and bolted. We must have travelled three-quarters of a mile at breakneck speed before I could pull him up.

I forced him back, and got him at a full gallop after the herd. We caught up to them, but the nearest I could get Sovereign was about ten yards away.

I fired, and out of the corner of my eye I saw a tuft of hair fly from the buffalo. At the sound of the shot Sovereign took another header into the air, wheeled and was off like the wind again. I spent the next hour firing at trees and anything else, and eventually got him to keep a more or less straight course. The next problem was to teach him to swerve when a buffalo fell, but I decided to wait for that until the next morning's shoot.

Among the eleven buffaloes we had brought down was a young cow, and Whittaker had several choice cuts from her. What a contrast was this steak to the first we tasted at Jim Jim! It was as good as anything that ever came from a bullock. With fresh onions and potatoes, and a tin of peaches to finish, we had a meal that could not have been surpassed.

The blacks were still gorging themselves, but they had such a supply that they were only concentrating upon the titbits.

Sitting around our fire, piled with buffalo-dung to keep at bay the mosquitoes, we chatted about the day's doings, particularly the tragic death of Wark-Wark. That, we were disposed to look at from another angle.

There were we, the born and relentless enemies of the buffalo, and there he was fighting for his life, and making a gallant job of it. Horse and man take great risks hunting; so, if either loses a life, it must be taken in the day's work.

I fell to wondering how many buffaloes would be shot in Arnhem Land each year. In the season of three months I knew Fred Smith shot up to three thousand, Hardy brothers about two thousand,[40] the Maraki shooters[41] the same (Paddy Cahill was not shooting then) and half a dozen smaller parties getting, say, a thousand each. That would mean that thirteen thousand carcasses were left lying on the plains to rot or be eaten by the dingoes and blacks.

Surely it would be possible to salt and export meat south, and to erect factories for the manufacture of beef extract. Then again, the buffalo calves could be domesticated as is done in India, and I saw visions of buffalo cattle-stations throughout the Territory. Why not? Once domesticated, the buffalo remains so, and is as docile as an old cow. I firmly intended to investigate these matters later.

Early the following morning we set off on the hunt again,

this time Whittaker mounted on my Dinah, and I on Sovereign.

I was none too happy about the first buffalo I came alongside. Sovereign was trying to pull away, but I got a crippling shot in, and the horse did just what I might have expected. He didn't swerve a foot, and tumbled head over heels; I with him. Neither of us was hurt, and I hoped that Sovereign, being an intelligent animal, had learned his lesson. The next couple of days' shooting showed he had. He became an excellent buffalo horse.

At the end of the first week we had sixty hides, stacked and protected from the weather, at Cannon Hill.

One day a boy came to me and said Bob Cadell "wantem tucker." I could not understand this, knowing that there was plenty of everything in the stores, so I asked Koperaki to tell him to ride back and find out actually what Bob wanted.

In due course he returned with a look of awe upon his face, and holding a piece of stick in a split on which was jammed a large sheet of paper. He handed it to me as though the missive might bite, and said it was from Bob Cadell. On the paper was written in large block letters - TEA, SUGAR, FLOUR.

This puzzled me considerably. I didn't know Bob could write, and I knew he could have helped himself to whatever he wanted. I tackled Bob about this later, and he explained:

"No more touchem tucker alonga store, boss. Might be you rouse."

I then asked him when he learnt to write. Puffing out his chest and grinning, he took me to our supplies and pointed to the bags of flour and sugar and the packets of tea. He knew what they contained, and had copied the lettering!

"But why write?" I asked.

"Nother fella myall black no more speakem English like you or me, boss. Thoughtem more better send letter."

Which I knew was so much bunk. Bob only wanted to show

off, and he certainly caused Koperaki's gang to hold him in greater respect.

The blacks never cease to marvel at the white man's method of communication. When one is given a letter to convey, he would not for the world let any part of it touch him. To "talk alonga paper" they regard as the highest form of the white man's magic.

CHAPTER XVI

BOB CADELL'S GIGANTIC BLUFF

AFTER three weeks' shooting, in which time we collected almost two hundred hides, we found the buffaloes had moved north. We followed their trail for several miles, then decided to let them go for the time being, and to return to our main camp.

It had been an exciting and profitable experience, but I don't know how we would have got along if it hadn't been for Koperaki and his boys. Had Whittaker and I depended upon only Bob and Jacky to do the skinning, salting, and packing, the going would have been slow and tedious.

It was good to get back to Cannon Hill, if for nothing else than to see the delighted smiles on the faces of Bob and Jacky. We found everything in order. I handed the boys a liberal supply of pipes, tobacco, twill, and food as extra reward for their good work.

We had only been back at camp a little while when a buzz of excited jabbering came from the blacks' camp. Looking over I was astonished to see most of them daubing themselves with paint and feathers, and dancing around waving their spears.

It puzzled me. But on glancing to my right I got a further shock to see that a neat gunyah had been built of paper-bark and twigs. And calmly squatting in front of it was Bob Cadell and a lubra! She was wearing a weird-looking costume made from a white flour-bag, Bob was smoking his pipe, and domestic contentment was written on their grinning faces.

I called Bob over and demanded to know where he had got the lubra.

"She likem me little bit, boss. Came alonga be my missus."

So that was it. The wily Bob had apparently taken unto himself one of the gins which had been left behind with Koperaki's wife and spare parts.

I was annoyed, and said:

"You gottem missus alonga Pine Creek, and Adelaide River. Too much missus belonga you."

"No more boss," he replied with a knowing grin. "This one pretty fella lubra. Bimeby I leave him here go back alonga nother one missus."

I pointed to the blacks making warlike preparations:

"Might be they killem you all about. You finish."

"No more killem me, boss. They been flite alonga me, I bin pointem bone, burnem rag, and writem paper all same alonga white man."

Well, it was news to me that Bob was a medicine-man or witch doctor.

I discovered some time later on indisputable authority, that the pointing of the bone is no fable. If a witch doctor, the same as Bob claimed to be, desires the death of any native, he points at him a human bone, chiefly portion of the lower leg, and on saying that his victim is to die by so many moons, no powers on earth can prevent his death. He simply walks away, and at the appointed time, gives up his spirit.

The "burnem rag" is also equally effective. The blacks believe that every star represents one of their lives, and when a star (or meteor, as we know it) falls, it signifies a death. Should a black discover any piece of wearing apparel belonging to him partly burnt, he knows it is his death sentence, and so he goes away and dies. If the witch doctor desires to get rid of an enemy he secures such a piece of apparel, singes it, and leaves it for his enemy to find. Of course he tells him a meteor has fallen - and there is shortly another black less.

The whole business was very disturbing. I sent Bob back to his gunyah and called Koperaki over.

Koperaki somewhat mournfully admitted that Bob possessed

the powers he claimed, and said there was nothing else to do but let him have the lubra.

By now the blacks had formed a line in front of Bob's gunyah and were singing songs of hate, and shaking their spears.

Bob was still sitting complacently with the gin, and in front of him was his dilly-bag of tricks. These consisted of teeth, bones, dried lizard-skins, claws, and other gruesome relics, and he slowly and deliberately emptied them on the ground.

This had a visible effect upon the threatening blacks, who moved away. They then split into two ranks about fifty paces apart and in open order, and began to indulge in light spear-throwing.

A spear would flash through the air, a black body would sway to right or left, a head would duck, or legs open and the spear would fly harmlessly past.

Such amazing skill was tremendously impressing. But if the exhibition was intended to put the breeze up Bob, which it undoubtedly was, then it must be marked down as a dismal failure. He took not the slightest notice.

I could see Koperaki believed in Bob's powers, but I also felt that if he ordered his tribe to kill Bob they would have done so despite the consequences. And it was with great relief when Koperaki said to me:

"Much better makem brother all same alonga us, and lendem lubra."

I gave him more tobacco, and a couple of tins of treacle, and on a word from him his warriors broke up, still muttering and making faces at Bob.

Calling my audacious lover over, I gave him a sound lecture and told him I was not concerned with his "pointem bone" or "burnem rag," but that if there was any more of that sort of thing, I would send him back.

My next fear was that Jacky Anyone would get similar notions and I said to him:

"You catchem lubra too, Jacky?"

"Me no catchem lubra, boss," he answered. "All about bin ugly fella."

Perhaps their lips were not thick enough or their noses broad enough for Jacky, but I was more inclined to believe that the exhibition of Koperaki's boys had scared him stiff.

"You no more touchem lubra belonga this country, Jacky. Might be they killem you dead," was my final and effective warning.

The last protest from the blacks took the form of a warlike corroboree which lasted well into the night. They chanted fearful threats to the accompaniment of sounding sticks beating on stones, and there the affair ended.

Whittaker had got a tremendous amount of enjoyment out of the business. Of course, Whittaker would.

I never heard of Bob Cadell's boasted powers being put into effect, but he was always treated with respect, if not affection. However, I have since thought that the old scoundrel put over a gigantic bluff that day, which luckily for him, and maybe for us, came off.

CHAPTER XVII

WITH PADDY CAHILL AT OENPELLI

AFTER pottering about camp on the following day, we agreed that I should pay Paddy Cahill the promised visit, and leave Whittaker in charge of the camp. So on the following morning I set off for Oenpelli with Jacky Anyone and Big Head, who knew the way. As the trip would take a couple of days, I had two packhorses.

We reached the East Alligator about twenty miles from our camp, and halted on the bank. The stream was some seventy yards across at this point, and flowing fairly strongly. Big Head got off his horse and walked up and down the bank for several hundred yards, at last finding a crossing. There we waited half an hour, intently gazing about us on the look out for crocodiles.

At length we decided it would be safe to cross, and I was mighty glad when we reached the other side. Crossing a river you know is infested with crocodiles is no pleasant feeling, especially when your horse has to swim some of the time.

I was now for the first time on the wonderful Oenpelli holding of which we had heard so much. And as I rode over the immense plain, heavy with luxuriant grass, and splendidly watered, I envied the man who owned such magnificent country.

I passed several herds of shorthorn cattle, the first I had seen since leaving Mary River. Their splendid condition gave further evidence, if such were needed, of the nature of this country of Paddy Cahill's.

Passing through a gate - there was a touch of civilization about this! - I saw ahead a group of black boys with something struggling in their midst. A colt had been thrown, and slapping it all over to get it used to being handled, was Paddy

Cahill in his shirt-sleeves.

He gave me his gruff and friendly greeting, and handing over my horses to his boys, we walked towards the homestead. It was a large, rambling place covered with bright, flowering creepers, and surrounded by wonderful mango and other tropical fruit-trees.

A porch led to the side entrance and out of it waddled past us twenty or so wild geese which Cahill told me had been hatched at the homestead.

I was taken into a cool mosquito and fly-proof sitting-room, and while my host went to find his wife, I had a look around. There was a fine library of several hundred volumes and the authors ranged from Huxley, Dickens, Thomas Hardy, Conan Doyle to Florence Barclay and Ethel Dell. The room was furnished with easy chairs, and a lounge, and it gave me a delightful sense of comfort and security.

I took an immediate liking to Mrs Cahill. Her calm, friendly gaze gave me the first breath of the south I had had since leaving Sydney. If her life there was lonely - and it surely was since she saw other white women about once in twelve months - she did not show it. Indeed, she looked completely happy and contented. As her husband placed his massive hand on her shoulder and introduced me, I thought: what a splendid pair of pioneers! And what a magnificent country this Arnhem Land could be made if there were more like her. (Should Mrs Cahill chance to read this story, I hope she will accept my gratitude, ill-expressed at the time, I fear, for her kindness and hospitality during my visit to her wonderful home in the wilderness.[42])

I was shown a room, and after a shave and clean up dinner was ready. It was a meal which remained long in my memory. There was the good old beef of the bullock with cabbage, turnip, potatoes, and pumpkin, a steamed pudding, and papaw, oranges, and mangoes as dessert. And to drink-gallons of rich cow's milk.

When the meal was finished, Cahill showed me over the place. The kitchen was spacious and well equipped, and in it were four or five neatly dressed lubras who did all the cooking and serving for the native hands, as well as helping Mrs Cahill to prepare foods. They had been trained by his wife, who, he said, was the only white woman living who could speak the native language of the blacks. I knew Paddy was one of the few white men in existence who also knew the Alligator River dialects.

Outside I was shown the butter factory. A splendid structure with cement floors, and even though in disuse, it had been kept spotlessly clean. Naturally, he told me the story of its failure, which was the same as that recounted by the skipper of the *John Alce*.

"Let's walk back to the garden," he said. "I want to get some fish for breakfast."

The connexion at the moment was not obvious, but before long I was enlightened.

We passed through an orchard of orange, mandarin, and papaw trees, with melon, passion-fruit, and granadilla vines growing in profusion, and by gardens of sweet potatoes, onions, squash, lettuce, and radishes. At the bottom was a lagoon covering many acres of land which provided a perpetual supply of fresh water to the homestead.

Paddy called out something, and a comely looking lubra appeared, to whom he spoke in her own language.

"I have a few fish-traps in the middle of the lagoon," he explained.

As the lubra reached the edge of the water she began gingerly to lift her dress, but was making slow progress.

No doubt for my benefit, Paddy called out to her in pidgin-English:

"You no longa young lubra. You old lubra. You no more be

shy alonga this fella."

I laughed outright at the thought of encountering modesty among the blacks.

The girl finally dropped off all her clothes and swam out to the traps, soon returning with a fair sized barramundi, a couple of freshwater bream, and what appeared to be a crayfish.

It was getting dusk, and we returned to the house. Paddy led me on to one of the wide verandas, and we sank into big easy chairs in the pleasant evening air - it is mostly cool at night in Arnhem Land - and lit our pipes.

Hearing a mob of dingoes howling in the distance, and remembering my fear of crocodiles when crossing the East Alligator, I was curious to know how the dingoes managed to make the other side.

"Well," said Paddy, "a mob, say, of thirty, will come to the bank and set up a yapping and a howling. This may go on for an hour, anyhow, long enough to tell all the 'gators around where they are. Then, at a move from their leader, they will race half a mile down the river and cross with safety."

I looked hard at Paddy Cahill. Was he gently stretching my leg? I let it pass.

We were chatting generally, when I happened to mention Jacky Anyone's fear of debil-debils, and this started Paddy off on an extremely interesting talk upon the mentality of the Australian black. Said he:

"We will never do anything with them. They have the minds of children, and are full of superstitions which we can never hope to eradicate. The missions are no doubt doing good and self-sacrificing work, but it is utterly impossible to bring the natives to reason along the lines of Christianity. The moment you try to bring them to the level of brothers, and I suppose the brotherhood of man is one of the bases of Christianity, then the black will regard himself as your equal, and consider it his right to associate with your women. Do you want that?"

I did not reply.

"The only thing to do with them in the Territory" he went on, "is to segregate them in areas and leave them alone. Not on any account should their tribal customs be interfered with. If one black hits another on the head, or runs a spear through him, don't interfere."

"Isn't it possible to teach them to farm for themselves?" I asked.

"Not a hope. If a bunch of them managed to grow a crop of potatoes, they would immediately eat, or try to eat, the lot in one sitting and go hungry afterwards."

"What about the half-castes?"

"Ah! There you have a problem that will never be settled. In the end the half-castes will outnumber the original black population, for the reason that there are so many whites and Chinese associating with the blacks, and a black woman always prefers to have a child by some other race than her own. Once the Chinese come into contact with the blacks, they can buy any gin with a pinch of opium. It is not pure opium, mind you, but the dregs left in the pipes after the Chinese have finished.

"A black will readily sell his gin to a white man or a Chinaman for a few grains of opium ash. Then the half-caste child comes along and is rejected by the whites and held in contempt by the blacks. If you create a half-caste colony you are going to strike trouble similar to the nigger problem in America. The only way out I can see is to encourage the British half-castes to mingle and marry with whites, and for the Chinese half-castes to be accepted by the Chinese."

(I found out later that many half-caste women had married white settlers and had turned out good types. I also met many half-caste men who were splendid in every way.)

"I'll tell you a true story," went on Paddy seriously, "which illustrates better than anything I know what an impossible job the missionaries have in trying to handle the blackfellow's mind. At the old Kopalgo Catholic mission station, there were a number of so-called converts.[43] They would listen as long as the fathers liked to talk, providing their tobacco was kept up. Among them was a black named Booradawa, an Alligator River boy. He was christened Paddy - perhaps after me," added Cahill with a grin, "and water was sprinkled upon his head in the approved Christian manner. Paddy, they thought, had the makings of their best convert. As time went on he asked permission to go on a walkabout, which was granted. Before leaving he was reminded of the many things he should not do, which included no meat on Fridays.

"A day or so after, one of the reverend fathers came across Paddy settled beside a hill, whacking into a shank of buffalo-beef. It was a Friday; and the priest knew that Paddy knew it was Friday.

" `What name this one, Paddy?' asked the priest, pointing to the bone.

" `That one fish, fader'

" `I told you, Paddy, you no more bin tellem me lie. That one beef, no more fish.'

" `That one fish, fader,' Paddy repeated. `I tellem you. Long time ago my name Booradawa. I bin go alonga you. You bin tellem me all about im Ole Man up above. You bin splinkle water alonga head sayem "Your name Paddy, no more Booradawa." I bin work alonga you long time. Bimeby me go walkabout, catchem buffalo beef, splinkle water alonga beef, callim fish, all same.' "

"The worthy father," said Paddy Cahill, "received one of the greatest shocks of his life. That is typical, Warburton, of the blackfellow's reasoning. How in God's name can you hope to alter that?"

"Too tough for me to answer."

The dingoes started howling afresh, and Paddy switched his

talk to them again.

"This is a wonderful country for those brutes," he said. "They get so much natural food. If ever the pastoral industry begins here properly, they will prove a pretty big problem. Sheep and goats would have no chance. The only thing one could do would be to poison all the buffalo carcasses about, and then some unfortunate wandering black would be sure to get it."

I could not help remarking on the glorious freedom from mosquitoes during the evening, and I asked Paddy how he had got rid of them.

"When I first came here," he said, "there were millions of them, but after clearing away all the jungle and undergrowth, I put a quart of kerosene on the lagoon, and ever since I have been doing so at regular intervals. It does not affect the water, and it certainly stops the mosquitoes from breeding. Two tablespoons of kerosene to fifteen square feet of water will keep the pest down anywhere."

Stretching his great frame and knocking the ashes from his pipe Paddy said with a yawn:

"I think we'll call it a night."

We did. And I went to my room to ponder on what this great pioneer bushman had said. It had been a talk of absorbing interest.

Early in the morning the household was astir. I walked outside and found Paddy getting ready an outfit for mustering. About half a dozen boys were engaged some little distance from Paddy, and I noticed that one of them seemed to be in command of proceedings. His manner was authoritative, and his methods business-like. I heard him say to them:

"Come on, boys; get a move on. Boss close up."

I asked Paddy who he was.

"Twenty-five years ago," he replied, "there was a shoot-up of blacks by the whites in revenge for the killing of a white man. This chap was then three or four, and I saved his life. He was the only one rescued from the massacre, and he's been with me ever since. That's the only way I know of doing anything with the blacks. Get 'em young."

Paddy took me over to the stockyards and showed me the outbuildings which had been built by the blacks under his direction. They had been constructed of rough bush timber with a tradesman's skill.

There were about sixty head of cattle, and the morning's work was to dip them and run them into a crush. In this they were jammed tight; torches of paper-bark were then lit, and the blaze run over the beasts to get rid of that most terrible of pests, the buffalo-fly.

This fly is smaller than the house-fly, and thousands of them will form a bunch on the animals and eat away skin and flesh.

There was too much fat on the Oenpelli cattle for the blood-sucking tick to cause any trouble, but Paddy assured me that the buffalo-fly was a definite menace. Paddy's methods of ridding the beasts of the pest were crude but effective. No better treatment was then known.

We strolled on to where some of the boys were building a fence. Paddy walked over and examined one of the holes, and his quick eye instantly saw that it was slanting upwards. He called over the boy who was handling the auger.

"This one hole no more good. No more straight fella. You want to makem hole all same you bin shoot im buffalo alonga gun;" and bringing an imaginary rifle to the level, he demonstrated. I immediately congratulated Paddy on the excellence of his methods of training.

"By the way, are there many blacks between you and the Gulf?"

"About fifteen thousand; and a pretty tough lot, too. A fighting crowd. I hate to think how many Malays and Japs have been killed by them."

"Have you ever come into contact with them?"

"Yes. Tribes often come down to the station. Men of magnificent physique, but silent and suspicious. I've always tried to get their confidence by trading and treating them liberally. Of course, I never know the day when they will come down with other intentions; but if they do they'll find me well prepared. I've a good intelligence service, and as you are going to be a neighbour, I'll let you know at the first signs of any trouble."

Realizing the potential danger, I thanked him warmly.

Still wandering around the marvellous holding we came to a couple of dozen pigs - some huge old sows, litters of young, and many fair-sized porkers, all, obviously, of Berkshire strain.

Paddy, who could not go long without telling a yarn, now proceeded to unload one.

"A little while ago an old sow was about to litter. When the blacks heard of this, they hung around the sty to watch the business. Before this event, twin calves and foals were the only records known to them. When the first and second came along, all was as it should have been; but on the arrival of the third and fourth the boys began to get excited; when the fifth and sixth were born, they were yelling; when the tenth and last appeared, they went mad. One of them rushed up to me at the house: 'Im pig alonga sty, boss, im plenty full up foal, im ten fella through.' They talked of that for weeks."

"That's a good one, Paddy," I said. But I quite believed it.

We next had a look at the cow-bails. About half a dozen Ayrshires and Shorthorns, all in magnificent condition, were waiting to be milked. The bails were spotlessly clean; and alongside the two black milkers were buckets of hot water, with which they carefully cleaned the cows' udders.

During that early morning stroll Jacky Anyone had been following me at a discreet distance. Knowing he wanted his tobacco issue, I beckoned him over. I was about to give him a stick, when Paddy said:

"Give him half. I can see you spoil your boys."

Perhaps he was right, but I gave Jacky the full stick all the same. Grinning hugely he said:

"More better you bin stoppem here long time, boss."

"Why, Jacky?"

"Good fella place. Full up tucker, milk, eggs, butter, eberytink."

Jacky had evidently been making the most of his stay. At breakfast we sat down to ham, bacon, and eggs, with toast and coffee.

"How do you like the flavour of the ham and bacon?" asked Paddy.

"Great," I answered, for it really was delicious. "Did you get it from Darwin?"

"Not on your life. That is home grown and home cured. This is the best pig-raising country I have come across in Australia. With adequate refrigeration we could produce sufficient pork to supply the whole of the continent. I have the advantage of the refrigerating room at the butter factory." And drawing a deep breath he added, with a touch of bitterness: "I wish to God people would wake up to what a great country this is."

Spreading another chunk of butter, excellent in colour and flavour, on my toast, I thought the same. A swift vision came to me of such a home as the Cahill's on our holding. It was much the same country.

I stayed at Oenpelli a couple of days, taking short excursions on the run with Paddy, and acquiring a great deal of invaluable knowledge.

Before taking my leave I discussed with him our future movements. He said that the buffalo herd in all probability had shifted farther up towards the coast, and that they should be found on the plains around Gaernin and Munganilida. We would find perfect camping-grounds at either place. He suggested we should make our first halt at Cobabby, some fifteen miles from Cannon Hill.

"Get one of Koperaki's boys to go to Fred Smith's at Kopalgo and ask him to send his lugger down to pick up your hides and the bulk of your stores. Your hides will go on to Darwin when Fred's sending his, and your stuff can be dumped at Gaernin. That's about thirty miles from your camp and the nearest point on the river to Munganilida. You'd be set then."

"That's a good thought, Paddy," I said gratefully.

"I'll give you one of my boys now who'll show you the way to Oenpelli landing. You can send your boys and horses around the way you came, so you'll shorten the trip home by a day."

With heartfelt thanks for their generous hospitality, I said good-bye to Paddy and Mrs Cahill.

CHAPTER XVIII

DANGER FOR BOTH OF US

WHEN we reached the river we waited until the tide was about on the turn. I was a little disturbed to see four big crocodiles asleep on a mud-bank some three hundred yards to my left. But the boy said it would be all right to cross, so we started.

He was in the lead, and we were about half-way across when my horse must have got his forefeet tangled in weeds. He pitched forward, rolling at the same time. The next thing I knew I was floundering in the water, yards-away from the horse, and being carried along by the tide.

I was heavily booted and spurred, and what with my revolver and other gear I had no chance of fighting against the current. Faster and faster I was being swept towards the crocodiles. I was terrified and helpless.

Looking around I saw the black boy had reached the bank and he immediately set his horse at a gallop in my direction. But what in God's name he could do I knew not.

He passed me, and swinging the horse sharply, plunged into the river. I then realized his game move and it looked a chance. He was now between me and the crocodiles, which were no more than a hundred yards away, and as I was swept near him he yelled:

"Catch im longa tail."

I made a desperate grab at the swimming horse and succeeded in clutching his tail.

The boy cleverly turned the animal, which struck out for the bank. We reached it, and I threw myself on the muddy ground, my heart nearly bursting.

When I got my breath I looked towards the crocodiles, now fifty yards away, and a shiver passed through me. I didn't want an experience like that again. I said to the boy:

"You plenty good fella." He smiled happily. You can pay a black no greater compliment than to tell him directly that he is a "good fella."

The boy brought my horse to me - he had been standing at the spot where he had reached the bank - and then moved up the river to cross back to Oenpelli.

Smothered in mud I rode into camp at Cannon Hill to be greeted by ill-timed guffaws from Whittaker. He, of course, passed his usual bright observation:

"What the hell's happened? Where's your gang?"

I told him all.

Next day Jacky Anyone and Big Head arrived with the horses and a splendid supply of fruit, vegetables, butter, bacon, and ham.

"Bacon and ham!" said Whittaker. "Let me at it."

I never saw a man enjoy a meal more.

We were full to the eyebrows, as the modern world has it. This, combined with the hot day, made us feel more ready than ever for the customary afternoon nap. We stretched out in the shade of some rocks and were soon asleep.

In an hour or so I awoke feeling fine. I glanced towards Whittaker, who was six yards away, to see if he was still out to it, and I could have fainted from sickness. He was lying on his bare back - he seldom wore a shirt - and across his chest was slowly passing a rock python some eighteen feet in length.

Whittaker's eyes were open, and glazed with terror. The reptile paused for a moment, swayed its head from side to side, and moved on. Foot by foot its great slimy length slid over Whittaker. The only thing that gave me any hope was the huge girth of the reptile, evidence that it had eaten recently.

Neither of us dared to move. Had we done so that terrible tail would have whipped around my mate, and in seconds the life might have been crushed out of him as we had seen the wallaby killed a short while ago.

At last, thank God! the tail passed over Whittaker and he was clear. My .32 and Whittaker's revolver barked simultaneously. The shots brought the blacks rushing over, and with their spears they finished off the writhing mass to which we had reduced the python.

We then opened it up and found inside a fair-sized wallaby, which probably saved Whittaker. Having satisfied their curiosity and lust to kill, the blacks would have nothing more to do with the python; probably because they were gorged with buffalo-meat. Incidentally, a black will never eat a poisonous snake he has not killed himself. He knows only too well the snake in its death-throes will sometimes bite itself and leave the poison there.

"Well, how do you feel, Whit?" I asked.

"Not so damned good," he replied shakily. "I've had the breeze up before, but never worse than then."

I poured him a spot of the sacred whisky, and he was soon himself again.

Whittaker agreed to Paddy Cahill's suggestions; and we decided to head for either Munganilida or Gaernin, via Cobabby.

The following day I sent a boy to Kopalgo with a note to Fred Smith, asking him to send his lugger down to collect our hides and the bulk of our stores. He had told Whittaker he would be only too pleased to do that.

Calling Koperaki over, I asked him if he would stay with us to the end of the shooting-season which, we expected, would be another three months.

"Which way you bin go?"

"We go alonga Cobabby, Munganilida, Gaernin; makem camp alonga Gaernin."

"We go alonga Gaernin too. All about blackfella go alonga Gaernin. Plenty yam there."

He explained that they were due for a change of diet. At Cannon Hill they had as much beef as they wanted, but very little vegetable food. They would get all the vegetables their systems needed at Gaernin; and, farther up the river, fish, turtle, and dugong. To be guided thus by apparent instinct seemed to me a pretty good way of keeping fit.

We spent that day getting our outfit ready, and after an early breakfast next morning were prepared to move off. I left a liberal supply of salt meat, tobacco, and flour for the boys who were to guard our hides and stores until the Kopalgo lugger arrived. We were taking with us only Bob Cadell, Jacky Anyone, Koperaki, and his two boys Big Head and Hobble Chain. The rest of the tribe was to follow on to Gaernin in its own way and time.

I knew they would stay with the guardians of the stores until all the food and tobacco were finished. But I knew also that those guardians would be faithful to their trust. Koperaki had said they would, and to betray him would be more than their unsainted lives were worth.

Since returning from Oenpelli, I had noticed Bob Cadell eyeing me rather furtively, knowing he was still in disgrace over that gin episode. He had done many odd jobs unasked, trying to restore himself to favour. But I was far from feeling friendly towards him.

That morning he came to me and said in a humble voice:

"Which one horse you wantem, boss?"

I replied severely:

"I tellem Jacky I wantem Dandy. You better catchem Club" (a big, strong animal) "for yourself. Might be you wantem take lubra alonga horse too."

I could see he didn't know whether I was pulling his leg or not.

He looked at the lubra, then scratching the dirt with his big toe and hanging his head, he muttered:

"That one lubra belonga me, no more all same white woman. She bin walk all time. No more ride."

I couldn't help smiling. When at last we moved off, Koperaki led the way on foot as usual. Once more on the plains, we early came across buffalo tracks which looked to be a couple of days old.

In the afternoon we reached the edge of what appeared to be exceptionally boggy country. Here Koperaki said, pointing to a thick fringe of trees about a mile away:

"That one Cobabby."

We could see where the buffaloes had forced their way through the bog, and thought it possible that we could do the same. We moved off, but, alas! had not gone many yards when we found ourselves in difficulties. My horse was soon down to his belly in reedy, muddy, sticky swamp. I jumped off, and turned to see what was happening to the others.

The horses we had bought from Fred Smith were trying to force their way through, but the others we had brought from Pine Creek were floundering in terror. Whittaker, still on solid ground, was looking on aghast. It certainly seemed as if our outfit would be smashed up in a general stampede.

I got back to where Whittaker was, turning as many horses towards the firm ground as I could. We got all but half a dozen packhorses clear, but these were so bogged that they were unable to move. They even seemed willing to give up the struggle.

Summoning Koperaki and the boys, we rushed into the swamp to free the horses of the heavy packs. To do this, we had to cut girths and harness. When the packs were removed, we fastened greenhide ropes to the horses and succeeded in dragging the badly frightened animals to dry ground.

Whew! It was a nasty half-hour.

When we got our breaths, I asked Koperaki if it were possible to cross.

"Might be," he answered.

Blast him and his "might be"! I was sick of hearing that.

"Might be no good, Koperaki. Which way we go? This way? Or that way?" (pointing up and down the river).

"More better down the river," he said.

I got a fresh horse and rode up and down looking for a passable way through the swamp, but had to give it up. We camped where we were that night, and early next morning skirted the swamp.

And at the end of the day we found ourselves at the scene of our first buffalo shoot on the Magela Plain, at almost the exact spot where Whittaker and I had crossed the swamp after the buffaloes! I cursed thoroughly at such a waste of time, and asked Koperaki what he had to say for leading us into such a mess. To be within a mile of Cobabby and to finish where we were was maddening.

"That fella swamp," he said, "all right alonga foot back. No more alonga horse. Bimeby all right, now too much wet."

I should have realized that old Koperaki, not being a horseman, would not know a horse's capabilities, so I forgave him. We crossed this swamp without trouble and made camp for the night. We then decided to cut Cobabby out and to make straight for Munganilida, Koperaki having assured us it was a safe track.

The following morning we made another start along what was practically the centre of our block, and passed at least twenty clear running streams bordered by dense palm thickets and undergrowth. This crystal-clear water ran on to the plains and kept it perpetually irrigated. What a country!

We made camp that evening near a billabong upon which were some fifty black ducks. After seeing that everything was settled, I took a shot-gun and told Koperaki to come with me.

As I preferred to have a crack at the ducks on the wing, I sent him on ahead to drive them towards me. After waiting some minutes there was no movement by the ducks nor any sign of Koperaki.

I lifted my gun to shoot, when a duck disappeared. Thinking it had dived I was about to shoot again, and another duck vanished. Wondering, I made a third attempt. To my astonishment the first two ducks appeared floating apparently lifeless on the water. Suddenly, there was a swish and flurry and the ducks left the water in a bunch - except three which were held aloft by Koperaki.

The old devil, as he told me afterwards, had slipped silently into the billabong, and, swimming underwater, had pulled the ducks down by the legs and wrung their necks.

Returning to camp I found Bob and Jacky were about to have a little sport of their own. At the end of the billabong they had discovered a crowd of pelicans; these Big Head and Hobble Chain had just frightened into flight. As they passed slowly overhead, Bob and Jacky hurled heavy sticks at them, bringing down a bird with each throw.

It was an amazing exhibition of a form of the black man's skill I had not hitherto seen. The sticks were any old bush sticks with a bit of weight, and were thrown perpendicularly. It was almost uncanny to see half a dozen of those great birds brought to earth in such a manner.

Many times afterwards I saw demonstrations of the stick-throwing art, but not once in all my years in the Territory did I see a boomerang thrown. I mention this because it seems to be a popular belief that the boomerang is one of the blacks' weapons in the north.[44]

From the pelicans' breasts I skinned the thick and white soft feathers, and rough-tanned the skin with alum.

Years later I had muffs made from them in Sydney.

Bob and Jacky had gone a little wild that day, going so far as to discard their shorts and boots, and to finish it they turned aside the damper and made a meal of the tail portions of the pelicans. This consisted chiefly of fat which, when cooking, sent forth a putrid smell.

We were early away again next morning, and over similar country, generously dotted with bubbling springs. About four o'clock Koperaki stopped in front of a running creek with a sparkling waterfall, and said proudly:

"This one Munganilida."

Cheers! After crossing the creek, we pitched our camp among the trees about a hundred yards from it.

CHAPTER XIX

PLAIN MURDER

LOOKING around we were entranced with the magnificence of what was to be our second shooting-camp. Giant Moreton Bay ash, and bloodwoods, heavy with foliage, and the green, luxuriant grasses told us how fertile was the loamy soil. And the spring water was sweet.

Many of these springs as far down as Mataranka are bitter with minerals. Fan and pandanus palms, rising to a great height, fringed the springs. Half a mile away were tall cabbage-tree palms; and dense scrub timber lined the banks of the Munganilida Creek.

There were thousands of birds, mostly magpies, jays, pigeons, parrots of all kinds, and kookaburras. The variety of kookaburra found in the north is called "swamp jackass." He is not so drab as his southern brother, but what he gains in brilliant plumage he loses in vocal efforts: he is gay, but can't laugh.[45]

As the day was hot and humid Whittaker and I stripped off and dived into the bubbling waters of the spring. It was balm to our dusty and aching bodies.

Next morning I took my .32 and .303 rifles, and with Jacky Anyone set out to explore. We followed the creek down and soon came upon even richer and more fertile country. It may seem that I have rashly exhausted superlatives in describing this country of Arnhem Land, but I can assure my readers that there is no finer country in the wide world.

I was more than delighted with what we were now passing through. How sugar-growing would prosper!

The soil, manured as it was by thousands of years of decayed vegetable matter, and with an everlasting supply of spring water, compared more than favourably with any of the world-famed Queensland canefields. I investigated these on my way south from the Territory.

Three-quarters of a mile from the camp we reached typical jungle country, into which disappeared a fairly wide buffalo-pad. Many fresh tracks and crushings in the reeds adjoining told me the big beasts were handy.

We skirted the jungle until we came upon a plain similar to the Magela, but not quite as large. A mob of geese was on the wet ground some distance off at the edge of the plain. Tethering our horses we went ahead to get a shot. We had not gone far when through the trees I saw a young buffalo bull, and said to Jacky:

"More better catchem beef alonga to-night."

Jacky looked alarmed. Buffaloes were the constant fear of his life.

"More better goose, boss."

Be hanged to Jacky and his worries! We were short of beef and I intended to try and get it, so I retraced my steps to approach the buffalo from another point, and keep hidden.

I crept to within fifty yards of the animal, and, taking careful aim, fired. The buffalo sank to his knees: apparently it was a fatal shot.

As I stepped out of the trees Jacky called out:

"Im dead, boss, im dead."

With my eyes on a herd out on the plain I was putting the bolt leisurely back and jamming in another cartridge, when Jacky screamed:

"Im no dead, boss! Im no dead!"

Looking round I saw the bull with head down coming at me full tilt. He was almost on me when I jumped behind the nearest tree, a small Moreton Bay, just before the buffalo crashed, shoulder on, into it.

There was a startled yell from above, and there was Jacky hanging precariously to a branch from which he had almost been dislodged. He had shinned up the tree on the first sight of the charging buffalo.

I assumed I had hit the buffalo in the centre of the skull but the bullet, deflected by the bone, had penetrated upwards and not touched the brain. However, he continued on his way.

Still after the geese, we came upon a glade and there was a buffalo cow with a twelve-month old calf. I had no difficulty in bringing down the young fellow, and at the sound of the shot the mother rushed away on to the plain.

Back at camp, I saddled a packhorse, took Koperaki and Big Head and proceeded back to collect the kill. I left Jacky behind to tell, no doubt, a harrowing tale to Bob Cadell or whoever else would listen.

Approaching the glade we dismounted and tied the horses. On reaching it I got a jolt to see the old cow standing over her fallen calf, looking in puzzled wonderment at it.

When the cow sighted us she gave a bellow of rage and came at us, hell for leather. We scattered, taking refuge behind the nearest trees, as the buffalo charged by. She came to a standstill, thrashed about madly for some moments, and then returned to her calf. After a good deal of manoeuvring I managed to get a shot in, and the beast fell, but almost instantly regained her feet. Then, to my disgust, I found the magazine of my .303 was empty. I had forgotten to examine it before leaving camp - an unforgivable oversight in the bush, one which can easily cost a man his life.

However, I had my .32 and thought there would be no trouble in finishing off the badly wounded animal with it. At a range of not more than twenty-five yards I aimed for the centre of the forehead; but the only effect the shot had was to cause the beast to shake its head as though a fly was worrying it.

Although I had eight more shots for the .32, I could see that further shooting would be futile. Koperaki came to me and said:

"I kill im all about, boss." Drawing a razor-edged knife which he always carried in his belt when on the buffalo-trail, he muttered something to Big Head. That individual, working from the side, got about five yards in front of the buffalo's head, and then began dancing about and waving his arms, something in the manner of a toreador. Like a flash Koperaki shot to the rear, his knife flashed, and the animal was hamstrung.

With a bellow of pain the buffalo sank on her hindquarters. I then rushed up to again try my .32 which I had fondly believed would kill anything. I fired into the eyes, into the curl of the forehead, behind the heart, and at every vital spot I could get a crack at.

It was a sickening business, but there was nothing to be done but go through with it. When I had finished, the animal was still alive. Koperaki then took a hand again. With one leap he drove his knife deep over the kidneys; repeated the blow; and at last the buffalo gave its final gasp. I was very upset, and swore that never again would I leave camp improperly equipped.

We wasted no time in loading a good supply of meat. I was anxious to get away from the scene, and we made back for camp as soon as we could. I told Whittaker of my stupid neglect. He called me a damned fool, which I was unquestionably.

One of our first and imperative moves was to be the construction of a stockyard, so the arrival from Cannon Hill early the following morning of Koperaki's tribe was a welcome sight.

We set to work straightway, selecting timber which would be the easiest to use. We only needed the stockyard until the end of the shooting-season, which would be in another three months. We erected posts, two close together and the next pair fifteen feet apart; between them we wedged rails cut from the palms. In a few hours a yard about thirty yards square was completed.

Our horses had kept remarkably fit, although they had much to contend with. The mosquitoes and the March-flies and the big green flies worried them. These were so bad in the daytime that we used to light dry logs throughout the bush to keep the horses from coming into camp to get protection from the smoke.

Taking Koperaki with him, Whittaker made a trip to Gaernin on the East Alligator, about eight miles away. He returned the same day and said there was a good landing with a salt-water creek running a couple of miles inland. He had tied a bottle to a pole with a note inside giving instructions to the men aboard Fred Smith's lugger regarding the dumping of our stores from Cannon Hill.

When Whittaker left camp he generally returned with something interesting. On this occasion it was one of the largest eggs I had ever seen; it was oval and rather dark brown in colour. Koperaki told me it had been laid by a plain turkey. We ate the egg for tea, and it was excellent.

Whittaker and I agreed that night to get down to the serious business of shooting buffaloes the next day; and providing the herd did not move on again, we would shoot there until the season ended. We had already seen several hundred, and indications were that there might be thousands.

So we set off the following day much as we had done before. There was little thrill about it. We were now fairly seasoned shooters; and although the dangers ahead were obvious, I don't think either of us gave them much thought. We were cautious enough not to take needless risks, and contented ourselves with bagging about a dozen beasts a day.

It was hard work; but in the six weeks' shooting we got just on five hundred hides. There was very little incident worth recording: each of us averaged about a spill a week from our horses, but apart from being bruised and shaken, no damage was done. People of the bush take such falls without comment, although, of course, there was always the danger of a buffalo turning and charging the fallen one.

At the end of the day's shooting we were usually about dead beat and ready to turn in soon after tea.

Koperaki's blacks had fallen into the more or less humdrum business of skinning the buffaloes and salting the hides, and finishing each day gorging themselves until their bellies were as swollen as toads'.

The only one of the outfit I felt sorry for was Jacky Anyone. Bob Cadell had his lubra, to whom he still seemed very much attached, but Jacky was a lonely little beggar. Although he feigned contempt for "them poor myall black," he was still scared of them; and he no longer had the companionship of Bob. One day he said to me:

"When you go alonga Pine Creek, boss?"

"Little bit close up now, Jacky."

"I bin wantem see im fader, mudder, and all about belonga me," he said plaintively. Poor Jacky, he was very homesick!

Sitting by the camp one night, smoking my pipe and chatting with Whittaker, I fell to wondering what my friends in Sydney were doing at the moment. For the benefit of Bob Cadell, Jacky, Big Head, and Hobble Chain, who were squatting a few yards away, I had been painting a rosy picture of the city, when it occurred to me to say to Big Head:

"You come Sydney alonga me?"

"Im big fella place, boss? Im full up house?"

"Yes, full up house."

"No more bush?"

"No more bush, Big Head. Full up house. You come alonga me?"

Big Head reflected for a moment.

"Full up house, boss. Where I bin sleep no more bush?" At this Bob Cadell roared with laughter.

"You poor myall blackfella," he said, in that superior way of his. "You no more savvy white fella house. Alonga Pine Creek blackfella live all same alonga white man. No more sleep alonga bush."

I couldn't let Bob get away with this:

"Well, what about you, Bob? You come?"

"Might be soon, boss, I take a stroll alonga Sydney."

A "stroll" to Sydney - that broke me up properly.

It was now about the end of August. We had a letter from Fred Smith saying he was sending the last of his hides into Darwin, and that it would be advisable for us to get on to our permanent headquarters for the wet season, which would begin in earnest in a couple of months.

This meant that a busy time lay ahead. One of us would have to go to Darwin to arrange for the next year's supplies; the horses would have to be returned to Bachelor Farm; and we would have to select a site on high ground and erect wet-weather quarters.

We had arranged for the shipment of our hides. In the weeks we were shooting, there had been a continual trek with hides to Gaernin; the last had been sent a couple of days previously. So that worry was off our minds.

Whittaker had told me that he did not think Gaernin would be a suitable spot for our home, as there was no permanent supply of fresh water. So instead of going there, as intended, we decided to follow the river to a likely looking headland which we could see about ten miles up.

CHAPTER XX

WE BUILD A HOME

ONE morning we got our original outfit together - Whittaker, myself, Bob and Jacky, and forty horses - and prepared to move off. Koperaki was not coming with us; he said he had certain tribal arrangements to make. I had noticed that during the past couple of days he had seemed very preoccupied, even worried. There had also been a good deal of mysterious activity among his followers. Their corroborees had been attended by many strange blacks, members of a tribe we had not seen before, and there was much spear-shaking and singing of warlike songs. I asked Koperaki what was the matter. Wagging his head he said:

"Might be im nother one cheeky fella black come up bimeby. Might be they bin fight."

So that was it! They were preparing for a scrap. Well, as long as it remained a matter between themselves, we were not concerned. With a promise to pick us up later, Koperaki and his boys gave us a yelling farewell.

We turned north and came out on another very fertile plain with the edges pierced here and there by the jungle. As it was getting towards dusk, Whittaker said he would go ahead and see if he could find water.

"Right-oh!" I said. "You go to the right towards the river, and I'll take the left. One of us is sure to strike it."

We left the two boys in charge of the outfit, and set off. Whittaker was out of sight, and I was about three hundred yards out on the plain looking for signs of water when some fifty buffaloes swept out on to the plain from a timber belt on the left. They came around me in a wide sweep and, to my horror, made straight for the outfit.

Bob and Jacky, realizing the danger, endeavoured to get our

grazing horses together and on the move. The horses, too, had become aware of the peril, and started off, but unfortunately in line with the charging buffaloes.

My only chance was to beat the buffaloes to it. I set spurs to Dandy, who responded magnificently, reached the buffaloes, and rode neck and neck with them for a few strides. But Dandy's great pace did the trick. I got up in time to head the leaders, and the buffaloes swept past with only a couple of yards to spare.

We had quietened the horses, and were starting them off towards Whittaker, who had showed up from somewhere, when the buffaloes reappeared not more than fifty yards away, having apparently circled us. This time there was no holding the horses, and they stampeded straight for the timbers. A wild yell from Whittaker, as he tried hopelessly to turn the leaders, and the next moment both us were racing through the trees on horses almost as terrified as our maddened outfit.

It was dusk, and the wonder was that we were not killed. As it was I got a heavy clout on the side of the head where a piece of shrapnel is still embedded, and reeled in the saddle, but managed to hang on.

We got through the woods safely, and found the horses had pulled up at the edge of a sheet of water which seemed to my dazed sight to be a couple of miles in extent. In the mad tear through the trees I had lost one panel of my saddle, my water-bag, and a stirrup-iron, and the blood was trickling from my head, which buzzed like a swarm of wasps. Old Whittaker was cut and scratched pretty badly, but otherwise unhurt.

We were successful in getting all but one of the horses together and hobbling them before dark. But as bad luck would have it, the one we could not catch had our blankets and immediate food requirements. That being so, the only thing to do was to get him. He made for the plain, and I after him with a rope. The brute led me a merry dance before I lassoed him.

I sent Jacky to the lake for a billy of water. He returned with a soupy liquid which, after being boiled, was pretty terrible.

Next morning an amazing sight greeted us. The sheet of water was literally alive with feathered game-waterfowl, pelicans, ducks, and geese were there in tens of thousands.

I took the can down for some more water, and found the cause of its soupy composition. The water was thick with the excreta of the birds. I strained it through a cloth, and after adding a pinch of Condy's crystals, boiled it. It was drinkable, and that's all one could say.

We shot a couple of ducks and grilled them, and immediately after breakfast set off to find two missing horses. Whittaker, dressed as he invariably was in a pair of shorts, went on foot in the direction of the river. Bob Cadell and I, riding, made towards another point, leaving Jacky to keep an eye on the camp. I soon left Bob and headed for Munganilida, near where I found the missing horses. It was dusk when I returned to camp. Bob and Jacky were there, but there was no sign of Whittaker. What the devil had happened to him?

Night fell and there was still no sign of him. I fired several shots from the double-barrelled gun at intervals, and with poles set alight to the dry branches of fan palms thirty and forty feet from the ground. They flared up in a great blaze which should have been seen for miles.

But no sign of Whittaker. I was getting very worried. Anything could have happened to him. He could have stumbled across a crocodile, been bitten by a snake, come upon a wounded buffalo, met hostile blacks, fallen and broken his leg, or a dozen other things.

I was too upset to sleep, so before day broke I got Bob to catch a couple of horses. They were ready at the first streak of dawn. Taking some food and a few drops of whisky, Bob and I set off.

We had not gone a quarter of a mile, when Bob picked up

Whittaker's tracks. Almost simultaneously there was a loud "halloo" from the right and there was my missing mate. I galloped over, delighted to see him. The old grin was present, but there was a twisted touch to it as though the man was in pain.

"I've had a hell of a time," he said, and began to rattle off what had happened. He had followed the tracks of the horses until mid-afternoon, when he lost them. After scouting around trying to pick them up, he decided to make back for camp. By then night was falling, and he got tangled up in the swamps. It would have been lunacy to try and cross them at night, so he camped. Unfortunately he had no matches to light a fire as a shield against the mosquitoes, and his shirtless back provided an unprotected target. They gave him hell.

He crept under a thick matting of grass to try and get some sleep, but the mosquitoes would soon find him out. All night long he had kept moving along the edges of the swamps getting only a few minutes peace at a time under cover of the grass.

Poor old Whittaker! His back and chest were a mass of red, angry looking lumps. He got tremendous relief when I applied the old-fashioned pain-killer remedy.

For the first time since I had been in the Territory I was feeling pretty dicky. The crack on the head the day before, and the all-night sitting, had induced a temperature. I began to wonder if malaria had got a hold of me.

After breakfast I felt a little better, and as we had no desire to stay there that day I said I was well enough to move off. We filled the one water-bag which was left and made a bee-line straight across the plain for the headland ten miles away. It was extremely hot, and my head was beginning to sing abominably. My eyelids needed propping open with matches. I don't know if it was due to dizziness, but when we reached the plain I saw a mirage for the first time. The headland we were making for seemed to be swimming in water, and pools appeared to be dotted here and there about the plain.

At some time or other the plain had apparently been flooded, and we knew by the number of small shells and the absence of grasses that it had been salt-water. There were innumerable craters several feet deep, which made the plain resemble a shell-torn field in France. We had to twist our way among them in a succession of hairpin movements which made the going slow and tiring.

I was bringing up the rear. In a violent collision with a packhorse, the one remaining water-bag burst, and we were left without water. In ordinary circumstances this would have mattered little, as we would reach our destination at the end of the day, but a fever of some sort had gripped me, and my tongue and lips began to swell until I had difficulty in speaking.

I put a small stone in my mouth and tried to suck it, but got no relief. I knew Whittaker had no water, and could see no use in worrying him, but I was having my first terrifying experience of what it must be like to die of thirst.

Good heavens, what a thought! I had only been half a day without water. I laughed at my fears, and my swollen lips burst and the blood trickled down my chin. It tasted like brine.

With unspeakable relief I saw the mirages disappear at last, and the trees take on their normal shapes. Another mile and we would be among them, where I was sure water would be handy.

I have never ridden a mile in more agony, and when we reached the welcome shade I almost collapsed. Out of the trees emerged a tribe of strange blacks which I rightly took to be some of Koperaki's crowd. Whittaker had now become aware of my plight, and grabbing a billy-can he pushed it into one of the blackfellow's hands and said:

"Ogo! Ogo!" (Koperaki's word for water.)

The black took the can and vanished, returning in a couple

of minutes with fresh clear water. I had sense enough not to gulp it, merely bathing my bleeding lips and allowing a trickle to pass down my throat.

I rested for a little while, and feeling revived we moved on again. For about half a mile we passed through the green, cool trees until we came across a bubbling spring, where we made camp.

Whittaker took a gun and brought back some game from which he made first-class soup. This and a cup of tea worked wonders in me. After a good night's rest, I felt a new man.

Breakfast of grilled duck and damper, and then we got a couple of horses and went up the river. Skirting dense jungle country for a mile and a half, we came upon mangrove-trees lining the river's banks for miles. Beyond these, on the other side, were rich plains, forest, and hills. We were looking towards Port Essington, one of the first settlements in Australia. Thereupon we made up our minds to visit it later.

The river was muddy and sluggish, and dozens of crocodiles were basking on the mud-banks. In the mangrove swamps around us were eerie croakings. Weird sounds emanate from mangrove swamps. If you have ever been in one, you will know what I mean.

On the way back we found a cleared gap which led us towards the centre of the jungle, which, we reckoned, was about a mile from our camp and half a mile from the river. At the end of this cleared space, and between us and the lagoon, we could see a huge banyan-tree, the space covered by the aerial roots appearing to have a diameter of about fifty feet.

The banyan-tree is native to India, and is a species of fig. It has heart-shaped leaves five or six inches long and produces a rich scarlet fruit, about the size of a cherry. The branches send roots downwards which in time become thick supporting pillars. In this manner the tree spreads over a great surface and lives for ages. There is a famous tree in Calcutta, which is known to be about a century old. Its main trunk is forty feet in circumference, and two hundred and thirty proper roots (supporting pillars) six to ten feet in circumference. Another in India has no fewer than three hundred and fifty proper roots and more than three thousand smaller ones. The whole tree covers a space sufficient to comfortably accommodate seven thousand persons.

There are many of these trees on the coastal areas in the Territory, and they are put to profitable use by the natives. The hanging roots are as tough as any hempen rope, and are used for all purposes that rope serves. The smaller ones are chewed by the gins into fibre, from which fishing-nets and lines, dilly-bags and other things are made with astonishing skill.

As this spot appeared to be the highest point on the headland, we decided to make it our permanent home, having satisfied ourselves on the two most important matters - we had easy access to the river, and would be out of reach of the flood-waters. The blacks' name for this locality was Kajadja.

Back at camp, and I immediately gave Bob Cadell a shot-gun with one cartridge and told him to go to the lagoon and get a few ducks. He brought back twenty, which he regretted almost at once, because I made him and Jacky pluck them.

After tea that evening I said to Whittaker:

"Well, what do you think of it, Whit? Do you for the wet season?"

"It'll do me for all time," he said. Just then I too would have been content with nothing more from life.

Even in that one day's brief exploration, I could see that the country about us would be ideal for tropical agriculture and grazing. The soil was wonderful; there was an inexhaustible supply of water; and it would be an easy matter to install a pump and irrigate the whole area.

Portion of it was ideally suited for coconuts; and it would

not take long to rip it up and plant cassava and peanuts as well as start an orchard. The plain in front of us would carry vast herds of cattle and horses; the jungle would be a home for thousands of pigs; and, the greatest asset, a navigable river was at the back door, a day and a half's steam from Darwin.

For the next few days we explored all about us, and could not fault this piece of our immense holding had we tried. At the end of one day's easy ride we returned to camp, hungry and contented in mind, when who should greet us but Koperaki. And his tribe was with him.

He had certainly promised he would pick us up later, but I had not expected to see him so soon. An important part of Koperaki's philosophy must have been: "When you're on a good thing, stick to it."

We gave him a warm greeting: we needed labourers.

But, our supplies of flour, sugar, and so on were getting dangerously low; there was scarcely enough to keep ourselves going until next year's stores arrived, without feeding over a hundred gluttonous blacks. Still, their help was essential, and I put the position frankly to Koperaki. I told him they would be paid liberally when the new stores arrived, and on this verbal I.O.U. he guaranteed that they would work where and when I wanted them to. That suited us, because all the reward they looked for would be tobacco, treacle, and, maybe, some Turkey twill. There were enough fish and game around to feed an army!

Well, the first thing to be done was to erect a signal on the river. Koperaki detailed a team of his boys who, armed with axes, soon had a three-foot track cut through the twenty yards of mangroves which blocked a way to the river. Then, as it was low tide, they waded out and sank a forty-foot pole into the bed of the river, and tethered to the top of it a pair of well-worn underpants.

Back to camp came the gang, and the next part of the

programme was to clear about half an acre of the dense jungle which surrounded the banyan-tree.

We had kept their stomachs well filled with buffalo-beef, goose, and duck, and Jimmy, that hairy old-timer of Koperaki's, played his accomplished role of fisherman to the party. Each morning before breakfast we could see him standing up to his knees in one of the waterholes, with his three-pronged spear poised. For minutes he would remain thus, motionless, then the spear would flash downwards, and up would come a barramundi weighing anything up to fifteen pounds.

Koperaki's lubras added to the fare for the tribe by gathering the delectable variety of yams which resembles closely the sweet potato, and by taking the hearts out of the heads of the young cabbage-tree palms - a dish quite as good as the cabbage of civilization.

It was hard going to clear that half acre, but the blacks worked like the devil. At last the job was over, and the banyan-tree stood there in all its tremendous majesty. There remained only the construction of our hut alongside it.

Here Whittaker came into his own and designed our hut. It was simplicity itself: one room, twenty-four feet by twelve feet with ten feet walls and a gable roof.

Our only tools were axes, tomahawks, and shovels; we did not possess a saw. I called Koperaki over and told him our plans. He said:

"I bin build im hut for you. You bin watch."

That sounded something like a proposition; nevertheless, we all intended to have a hand in the business.

Whittaker and I went into the jungle to cut some hardwood timber. After felling one tree, we barked it and carried it to where the hut was being built. Whittaker, as usual, was not wearing a shirt, and across his chest there suddenly appeared a big water blister surrounded by dozens of smaller ones. My arms were the same. Wherever the bark or sap (which was mustard colour) had come into contact with our skin it had raised burning blisters, and it was some days before we got rid of them.

During another excursion for wood, Whittaker discovered a "cheeky fella" yam, something like a small turnip. He cut a bit and we both tried it. In five minutes neither of us could speak. For the rest of the day our tongues and lips were swollen to twice their proper size.

Koperaki thought it a great joke. He told us these particular yams were poisonous, unless baked or boiled for twenty-four hours.[46]

After a couple of days' hard toil, the framework of the hut was erected. Then we set about making the walls and placing on the roof. We found a number of stringy-bark trees, and cutting around them we removed the bark from each trunk in one large piece. These bark cylinders we filled with grass, to which we set a light; thus drying up the sap on the inside.

Koperaki had taken a couple of packhorses to the paperbark swamps, and came back loaded. We split the bark crossways, and placed one piece upon the other in a manner which would prevent the water finding a way through the grub-holes.

In about ten days our hut stood complete, with the exception of the flooring. We placed sheets of paper-bark on the ground, which would do until we later decided to timber it. The hut Koperaki assured us would withstand the strongest blow in the Territory. And, remember, not a nail, or screw, or piece of wire was used; the timbers had been laced together with jungle ropes, and the blacks had made an expert job of it.

The next business was to sink a well, which we did about thirty yards from the hut, going down only about ten feet. I was engaged with two or three boys turning over the soil near the well, when Whittaker came along:

"What do you think you're doing?" he asked.

"Wait and see," I said.

When the digging was finished to my satisfaction, I produced a packet concerning which Whittaker had been very curious since we had left Darwin. And with Whittaker looking on, highly amused, I began to plant radish, lettuce, carrot, onion, papaw, and mango seeds, and a few peanuts. I expected them to spring up quickly near the well; then I intended to transplant them.

Under Koperaki's direction, the blacks had built their own huts about half a mile from us, but nearer the river. I was rather intrigued with Koperaki's own abode. He had built it on a platform on six-foot piles, and the front entrance was gained by climbing a ladder of sticks tied with jungle rope. This neat little home was to be shared by Koperaki, his wife, and child. His spare women, he said, would have to fend for themselves.

I naturally asked him why he had built his hut on piles, and he said that in the rainy season the crocodiles had a habit of wandering a couple of miles inland from the river, and he was not running any risks.

"What about us?" I asked. He explained we would be protected by the jungle, while he was nearer the river and more in the open. He had also another reason for his elevated home.

"Jungle country full up mosquito, sand-fly, eberytink. Blackfella got him no more net all same alonga white man. High up, wind blow this way, that way, all about blow im mosquito away."

Well, they certainly sounded to me commonsense reasons for having a lofty residence.

The huts of the other blacks were similar to the beehive looking structures we had seen at Jim Jim. I asked Koperaki why weren't his boys frightened of the crocodiles. He shrugged his shoulders as much as to say it was their own fault if they were too lazy or stupid to do as he had done.

The next and final work for the settlement of our home was to build a stockyard. We selected a site a quarter of a mile from the hut, and after cutting a four-foot track through the jungle, which would connect us directly with the yard, we began building; this time using timber from the Moreton Bay figs and bloodwoods. Lord knows how long we would be there, so we determined to make everything as permanent as possible.

In making the track and yard, we frequently dug deep, and I was astonished to see to what great depths the decayed vegetation went. It was truly magnificent soil. So much, for the time being, of our first real home in the Territory.

Whittaker and I discussed the immediate future. We agreed that he should go to Darwin to see about the consignment of our hides and arrange for next year's supply of stores. He was to take Bob and Jacky, leave them for that long-promised walkabout at Pine Creek, return to Bachelor Farm the ten horses lent us by Trower, and go from there direct to Darwin. He would pick up Bob and Jacky on the way back. I expected he would be away about two months - in fact he would not be able to get back to Kajadja if he were longer. The wet season would have begun, and the route we had followed originally, which was the only one, would be impassable.

It would mean a couple of months' loneliness for me. I decided to while away some of the time by making a trip to Kopalgo, for more horses to replace those Whittaker was returning to Bachelor.

In the couple of days before Whittaker left I became subconsciously aware of something missing from our midst. With a mild shock I realized that I had not seen Niogo, Koperaki's lively little four-year-old son about recently. The happy youngster was always running around the camp and playing with reed spears even at that early age. I suppose we had been too busy to notice his absence. I asked Koperaki where he had got to.

"Im very sick fella," he said. Probably too many yams, I thought, and promptly forgot about the little fellow.

Next day, however, Koperaki came to me again looking a picture of distress and misery.

"Niogo close up die," he said.

Both Whittaker and I had had ambulance training in France, and as we frequently doctored the blacks, we at once went with Koperaki to have a look at his sick son.

Niogo was lying on his bunk looking in a bad way. He was running a temperature of 104 degrees and his right upper-arm was swollen double its size, and there was a large lump in his armpit. We knew immediately that the boy had blood-poisoning. Examining the arm I could feel a big splinter of some sort embedded in the flesh.

Koperaki said he had put clay-packs on the wound, but Niogo was getting worse. Throughout that night we applied hot foments, in an endeavour to draw the poison, but in the morning the little fellow was sinking. We frankly did not know what to do. Obviously the wound should be opened at once, but if the child died after operating (and the odds were that he would die whatever was or was not done) we were none too sanguine as to how Koperaki would react.

Niogo was his one real passion in life. If Koperaki lost him, how would he regard us? So far he had proved a good and reliable friend; but should his beloved son die, would he hold us responsible, and go berserk? Although naturally concerned about our own skins, we were attached to the little fellow, and anxious to do everything possible for him. We told Koperaki the boy was very bad.

"Might be im die, eh?" he asked, with tears in his eyes.

"Might be, Koperaki," I said gravely. "But I bin cut im

alonga arm might be im live then."

He seemed distrustful of this, but I knew it was the only chance of saving Niogo, and decided to take the risk.

When he knew we were going to operate, Koperaki got his wife and old Jimmy to hold the youngster. He whispered something to him in his own language, and whether he told him to behave as a black should under torture I did not know. But when I made a deep three inch incision with a scalpel into the badly inflamed wound, the little fellow did not murmur.

I located the foreign matter, a piece of jagged wood which had been driven in deeply, and began to remove it with a pair of tweezers. As the splinter was being extracted Niogo must have suffered excruciating pain. He broke out in an ice-cold sweat, but not a whimper came from his bitten lips. What a grand little stoic the kid was!

At last I got all the splinter out; then thoroughly cleansed the wound and stitched it. I gave the boy a couple of drops of brandy, bound the arm, and left him to rest.

Early next morning we visited the hut and found Niogo's temperature had gone down, as also had the inflammation. And in a few days he was racing about the camp full of beans again!

When we told Koperaki his son was out of danger and would get well, we had a job to prevent him embracing us. Although Koperaki's wife seemed perturbed over the boy's accident, she took it with a sort of fatalistic philosophy, of which her husband, in this instance, had given no indications of possessing.

So great was Koperaki's joy that he would have promised us the moon. He was "brudder belonga us" for all time, and he said his tribe would do whatever we wanted. They would work for anything or nothing. We had saved his son's life, and Niogo, who would one day be the tribal chief, would be told when he grew older.

Whittaker was now ready to start on his long trek, and Bob and Jacky were hustling around, their faces wreathed in smiles at the prospect of a visit to Pine Creek. Bob was climbing on to his horse, when I went over to him:

"What about that one lubra belonga you here, Bob?"

"That one all right, boss. I bin gibbit alonga Jimmy," he said with a smug grin.

"She bin cry. More better I think you stop here."

He looked at me, and as I appeared to be in earnest, his lip dropped. He started to get off his horse when inspiration smote him.

"Might be that one lubra alonga Pine Creek die, me no longa go back, boss."

Then up spoke Jacky.

"I bin gibbit message alonga Bob, boss. Might be he bin lend im lubra alonga me."

Bob looked as if he could have murdered him on the spot. With a snort of contempt, he said:

"You only boy, no more man. Lubra no look alonga you."

Bob would have stopped had I told him to, but I had had my little joke, and let him go. He was so delighted that he put out his hand, which a black rarely does, and said:

"Good-bye, boss."

So the party moved off, and I faced the rather dismal prospect of being alone with the blacks for a couple of months.

CHAPTER XXI

I DOUBT KOPERAKI

FOR the first night or so I had a thoroughly miserable time. Koperaki's crowd, which had now increased to over two hundred, and in which were a good number of young and attractive-looking gins, had nightly corroborees of a pretty fierce character.

Although Koperaki had but recently pledged lifelong fidelity, I didn't know enough about the blacks to go so far as to place complete faith in him. The present good temper and humour of the tribe were evident; but they could be aroused easily to a pitch of ungovernable excitement, which more often than not had an outlet in a killing for the joy of seeing blood flow. Many times had I seen a dance or corroboree start in the best of joking spirits, and in a few minutes, without apparent cause, become transformed into an angry and sinister conclave.

I remembered my first encounter with Koperaki and his tribe, and I thought with a shiver of those suggested spears in the back, had I bolted.

Things seemed vastly different now Whittaker had gone, and although not afraid, I determined always to be on the alert.

As I say, the first couple of nights were extremely lonely. What with the din kicked up by the blacks, and the mopokes and screech owls in the banyan-tree, I had little sleep. The first time I heard the screech owl I was sure someone was being murdered. I broke out in a cold sweat, and grabbing my rifle, dashed outside to see a great owl screeching its way through the night.

The jungle was full of weird noises, and the fire-flies flitted about like an army of men behind lighted cigarettes. The bellow of the crocodiles in the lagoon added another mournful touch to the eeriness of everything.

My first job every morning was to tally the horses to see if the hobbles were all right, and that none were bogged or sick. Afterwards I would take a rifle or shotgun and explore the country for miles around.

On one occasion I went on foot with Koperaki looking for buffaloes. We were moving through the tea-trees when I spotted a young bull not fifty yards away.

To get a better shot I took cover behind a tree. As I raised my rifle I heard a hiss, and spinning round saw a big swamp tiger snake, one of the most fierce and venomous of all snakes, with its head drawn back ready to strike at my foot. I pulled the rifle down quickly and shot it; but when I looked towards the buffalo it was charging across the plain.

I then took my shot-gun from Koperaki and set off to stalk some geese which were in the swamp in thousands. Resting against a log to steady my aim, I was about to fire when there was another hiss and a huge water-snake glided from beneath the log. The country seemed alive with them. I eventually got eight geese with one barrel, and we set off back to camp.

Passing a small billabong Koperaki halted and pointed to the water; there was a green snake about seven feet in length. He promptly dropped my rifle, dived in and swam to the snake, caught it behind the head, and with his other hand broke its back and flung it on to the bank. He then swam out and finished the job by slitting open the snake's head with his hunting-knife. He wound it around his neck and we continued on our way.

We were winding along an old buffalo-pad with the grass growing high on both sides. It was getting towards dusk, and I was slightly in advance of Koperaki, more intent on looking up at the birds than anything else. Suddenly I felt myself seized by the arm and flung violently off the track, landing on my seat. The first thought that flashed through my mind was that Koperaki had gone mad and was going to kill me. I jumped up instantly and snatching my revolver pointed it at him.

Koperaki, however, was not looking at me, but was pointing to the ground, and I realized that if I had taken another step I would have put my foot on a swamp tiger snake. Its head was raised some eighteen inches, its forked tongue was darting in and out, and its body was tense and ready to spring.

I emptied the chamber of my revolver at it.

Koperaki had undoubtedly saved my life. A bite from these reptiles is so deep, and the action of the poison so rapid, that few survive. Being then a couple of miles away from camp I would have had no chance had I been bitten. I was sorry I had doubted Koperaki. I thanked him, shook hands, and the incident was forgotten. Koperaki would not touch the snake.

"Im all about cheeky fella that one, Garl," he said.

Curiously enough, Koperaki was the only black I ever met who would not call a white man boss, or recognize him as such. "Garl" was as near as he could get to my Christian name, and he always called Whittaker, "Whit."

When we got back to camp I gave the geese to the blacks to clean, and Koperaki told Jimmy to cook the snake he had carried round his neck. As there was a coal fire at my hut, he asked permission to do the cooking there. I watched the proceedings with interest. Jimmy threw the snake on to the coals, then grabbing it by the tail, drew it slowly towards him. Turning it, he repeated this several times. He then got hold of a foot's length at a time and twisted it, apparently to loosen the skin. This at length began to crackle, white flesh appeared, and the smell reminded one of roast sucking-pig.

When the snake was cooked Jimmy offered me a piece. It looked appetizing enough, but I could not come at it. Koperaki, Jimmy, and Koperaki's harem soon polished it off, but not before little Niogo grabbed a piece and cleared out.

Getting a bit fed up with my own company, I decided to make that trip to Kopalgo. So with Koperaki, Jimmy, and Hobble Chain, I made ready to set off, leaving Big Head in charge of the camp. I got a couple of exceptionally quiet saddle-horses - Hobble Chain always rode - and after much persuasion, succeeded in getting Koperaki aloft. Jimmy insisted on walking. Koperaki had taken an affectionate farewell of his kiddy and lubra, to whom I had given a couple of pounds of sugar. I was to remember this, forcibly, later.

Naked as the day he was born, hairy old Jimmy led the way, and Koperaki looked about as happy on that horse as a sailor would. He stuck it miserably for five or six miles, and then got off.

"More better walk," he said.

For the first couple of days we passed over open forest country, camping at fine waterholes. On the third day we ran short of meat supplies. I had anticipated getting a buffalo, but we had not come across a sign of one.

Old Jimmy had been busy pulling goannas from their holes in the plains. He must have collected half a hundred. Over these he ran his fingers carefully and kept only two, saying of the discards: "No more plenty fat."

This was the first evidence I had that a black will not always kill for the sake of killing, and moreover that Jimmy had an eye to the future. The goannas he had thrown away would no doubt live to fatten for another day.

Flocks of wild ducks were flying high overhead, suggesting a large waterhole near by. By nightfall we had not located it and were compelled to camp alongside a small billabong on which there was no sign of game. After a fruitless hunt for something to eat, I returned to the camp to be greeted by the extremely pleasant smell of sizzling goanna. The flesh closely resembled that of the snake. Although hungry, I could not stomach it, so tightened my belt and turned in.

At daybreak we set off again. Koperaki said the ducks would be "close up." Sure enough in half an hour we came across them in a large lagoon. So dense were the waterfowl that I could not see the water. There were geese and ducks of all varieties. Breakfast was assured, anyhow.

With one shot I got twenty-six. I was sorry for what might appear to be wanton slaughter, but it was unavoidable.

After salting the ducks left over from breakfast, we set off once more. Passing over some likely looking quartzite and ironstone country I gathered several specimens, and as there seemed every prospect of their holding gold, I tabbed the place for future reference. Leaving this mineral country we moved on to a plain. I asked Koperaki:

"How far Kopalgo?"

"Might be four feet. Little bit far."

The "four feet" touch amused me. I learned subsequently that the black man has no idea of distance. He invariably refers to it in terms of feet or yards or whatever first enters his mysterious mind.

On my reckoning, I figured Fred Smith's was about forty miles away, and knowing it was on the South Alligator, we turned in that direction. I was glad we did, for after a couple of days' travel, we came upon the saltpans about which the skipper of the *John Alce* had spoken so enthusiastically.

The salt water had overflowed on to these clay-pans, and the intense heat of the sun, setting up quick evaporation, had left acres of natural salt.

It was very coarse, and a small crushing plant, a corn crusher for instance, would be required before the salt could be used for hides. As the skipper had said, there was sufficient to supply the entire Territory.

Riding over to the banks of the river, I found it almost the same width as the East Alligator at Kajadja - about a mile. It was a muddy stream, flowing strongly, and full of crocodiles. On the other side were many dense patches of jungle. I wouldn't have swapped our place for it.

Knowing there would be no fresh water near the saltpans, we pulled out on to the plain and forest country again, and soon came across a number of springs and billabongs similar to those on our own side.

We camped alongside one of these. Next morning we approached a fertile plain, covered in beautiful green grass on which hundreds of buffaloes were grazing. They seemed to be in wonderful condition and quieter than those we had so far encountered.

Anxious to get to the other side and to avoid making a roundabout trip, I decided to cross the plain and risk the buffaloes.

My experience with cattle had been that they will not charge a man on horseback, whereas they will frequently come straight at a man on foot. After a good deal of persuasive argument, in which I pointed out the danger from the buffaloes, I succeeded in getting both Koperaki and Jimmy mounted, and off we trotted. Everything went all right until the buffaloes sighted us, and then a dozen of them lowered their heads and charged.

I put Dinah into a gallop and set off on a counter charge, at the same time firing six shots from my revolver over their heads. I didn't like to think what would have happened had they continued on their way, but the shots scared them, and fortunately for us, they turned tail and disappeared. Safely on the other side, Koperaki and Jimmy wasted no time in getting off their horses.

Next day we passed over country dotted with fan palms and I was not at all impressed with it. Still, one could scarcely expect to find rich and fertile plains everywhere, even in such an El Dorado as Arnhem Land. In the distance a line of mangrove-trees told us we were approaching the South Alligator again. I asked Koperaki which way lay Kopalgo. Pointing between two hills some six miles away, he said it was there.

Not wishing to reach Fred Smith's at night, we proceeded leisurely, and camped beside a billabong half a mile from the river.

Early in the morning I left the blacks, and taking my swag and revolver, made for the river on foot. At this point it was only about a hundred yards across; it was tidal, muddy and flowing swiftly.

On the opposite side I could see a landing-ground with a native canoe tied to a post. I fired two shots and sat down to wait. In about half an hour I heard a yell and saw two lubras near the canoe. I signalled them that I wanted to cross, and with swift, sure strokes they soon had the small craft over and I climbed aboard.

The lubras were jabbering excitedly to each other in a language foreign to me, no doubt speculating on what I was doing there. I supposed the presence of any stranger was an event of great importance to such a lonely outpost.

"Which way Fred Smith bin sit down?" I asked.

"Im bin sit down alonga Kopalgo."

"I bin go along."

Away they paddled. Both were fine-looking girls with that unmistakable touch of Malay in them, and they laughed and jabbered as the canoe rocked along. After securing the craft, one of them took my swag which she balanced on her head, and with hands on hips she led the way with rhythmical, swinging motion, along a made track through the bush. We had walked a quarter of a mile when we came in sight of Fred Smith's homestead, and I stood and looked. Some fifteen paper-bark, thatched huts, most of them small, were arranged in a circle round a much larger hut of the same construction. This I assumed was Fred's abode.

As we reached the clearing there was a scurry of fowls,

cattle-dogs dashed out barking, and about a hundred blacks appeared from the huts.

It was one sort of a welcome, but I wondered why Fred Smith was not there to greet me. If he was home, as the lubras had said, I knew he must have heard my shots from the river.

When I came to the fence surrounding Fred's hut, the path was blocked by a huge red bullock lying asleep in the sun. One of the lubras walked over him; the other grabbed him by the horns and pulled his head aside. The docility of the great beast surprised me. I heard the story concerning him later. I called out:

"Hullo! Anyone home?"

"Yes. Come right in."

In the hut, Fred Smith was propped up in two chairs.

"Sorry I couldn't meet you," he said. "I'm pretty sick."

Poor old Fred certainly looked it. He told me he was suffering from a bout of asthma, and had been ruptured in a fall from a horse the week before. He directed one of the blacks to take my swag into a room adjoining, and I sank into an easy chair and cast a curious eye at my surroundings.

My first impression was of the vast difference between Fred's quarters, and those of Paddy Cahill.

Here were two men of equal standing in the Territory, and of equal wealth - they were both making between two and three thousand a year. I have said enough about Paddy's wonderful home at Oenpelli. Fred apparently was content with a hut no more than twenty feet by eighteen divided into two rooms, with a kitchen at the back.

The room we were in was furnished with a couple of squatter chairs, a rough deal table, and hard-looking bunks; and propped against the walls and on the floor were rifles, guns, axes, saddles, and bridles. An unmarried bushman's idea of a home. Seeing my roving eye, he said:

"You can see I'm a bachelor. I only have myself to bunk

down at night, and this does me. I prefer to be under the stars, but occasionally I have to come back here. Have a drink?"

Happy thought! I swallowed a stiff gin and water and felt braced.

"I got your note about the hides, Fred," I said. "Damn grateful for what you've done for us. By the way, has your lugger been down yet?"

"I expect it back from Darwin any day. I'll load what hides I have here and send it down to Gaernin for yours."

"Fine," I said. "It must be a pretty big job looking after that lugger. Who've you got?"

"The boss of the show is a red-headed black, and he has four mates. He's been in charge of my lugger for years; and he knows the winds, tides, and seas along the coast so well that he's never had a mishap."

The idea of placing a black in charge of a seven-ton lugger, bringing stores worth several hundred pounds, and taking back hides worth fifteen hundred, gave me something of a shock.

He asked me if I was satisfied with our holding. When I told him I was more than pleased, he said it was quite the equal of Oenpelli.

"How is old Paddy?" he asked, with sudden interest. "We have just missed each other on the track lately, and I haven't seen as much of him as I would like."

I told Fred of my trip to Oenpelli, and added a few personal touches which made him laugh happily in spite of the pain I could see he was suffering.

"A great fellow is Paddy," was his comment. "And he's by a long way the best authority on the blacks I've ever come across."

When lunch was ready the fact was announced by the largest lubra I had ever seen. She was the cook. She stood well over six feet and was built in proportion, but without the vast balcony and gigantic beam of the cooks of tradition. Smiling there in white linen dress and with her mop of grey hair, she was an imposing and memorable figure.

Fred explained that when he had taken over Kopalgo from the old mission station many of the young gins and boys had been trained in housework, cooking, fishing, and carpentry. The cook was one of them.

"This one Polly," he said by way of introduction. "She boss all about this Place. She cook, keepem clean, look alonga garden, and boss lubra and blackfella all about."

Polly smiled delightedly.

"Good for you, Polly," I said. "I want im lubra all same alonga you."

"All right, boss. You send im lubra alonga me. I teach im."

I had no doubt she would make an excellent job of it.

It was a splendid meal. Delicious roast beef, four or five vegetables, home-made bread the equal of anything I have ever tasted, milk, butter, and any quantity and variety of fruit.

After lunch I left Fred to have a rest. He had eaten little, and was evidently a very sick man. I wandered around the place. The orchard and vegetable gardens, which were about thirty yards from the hut, occupied two or three acres, and were wire-netted to keep out such destructive agents as pademelons, bandicoots, and wallabies. The gardens were watered by pipes coming from overhead tanks.

Whether Fred had interested himself in tropical agriculture, or whether it was a legacy from the mission days, I knew not. Growing there, were coffee, cassava, kapok, cotton, peanuts, bananas, besides all the citrus fruits and vegetables that Paddy Cahill had cultivated.

I next had a look at the meat-house, which was a workmanlike structure with a thatched roof and openings at the sides to enable currents of air to pass through continually.

The method of killing, as Fred Smith told me later, was the

customary one. The beasts were shot with a .32 rifle, (yes, the rifle that could not kill that unfortunate buffalo cow!). They were skinned, the hides salted, and the carcasses quartered and taken to the meat-house on a horse-drawn sled.

There the meat was cut away from the bones. Roasts, steaks, tails, brains, and tongues were sent over to the house; the bones being given to the blacks who were always hungrily waiting. The meat left was salted, and a couple of days after, hung to drain and dry. It was the most wonderful corned meat imaginable; no matter how long it was left it retained all its flavour. Fred was sleeping soundly when I returned to the house so I had forty winks myself.

After tea we both turned in early, and I was quite prepared to sleep the clock round. I hadn't had much rest since Whittaker left, and I was looking forward to a couple of nights of complete unconsciousness. But this was not to be.

About one o'clock I was awakened with a start by the bang-bang of a shot-gun at the river, followed immediately by a hubbub from the blacks' huts.

"What the devil's the matter?" I called to Fred.

"The lugger's arrived."

"Anything I can do?"

"No, don't bother. The boys know what's wanted."

Within half an hour there was a yell from outside.

"You there, Fred?"

"Yes, come in."

Three blacks entered and dumped a couple of cases on the floor. I heard the musical jingle of bottles. Those boys certainly did know what was wanted!

Pointing to one of the boys, Fred Smith said:

"That's my skipper."

The fellow had none of the facial characteristics of the aboriginal; in fact his features were sharper than those of most white men. His mop of hair was the colour of burnished bronze - that colour which our modern henna queens strives so vainly for. He was dressed in khaki trousers and shirt and was twiddling in his fingers a felt hat. He appeared to be about thirty and had an air of authority and efficiency about him.

"How did you get on?" asked Fred.

"Little bit long time at Darwin, storekeeper man plenty slow. Big wind come up close up Mary River. We bin land stop there two days. Everything all right. I bin landem stores morning time."

After one of the boys had opened the cases, revealing four dozen bottles of lager and three of gin, they left us.

I knocked the top off a bottle and did the honours. Lord! how I enjoyed that beer. It was the first I had tasted in many months, and the Territory is thirsty country.

Sleep was now out of the question, so we settled ourselves for a yarn. I was anxious to get Fred's views on several matters, and here was the opportunity made to order. After remarking upon the cheerful, even happy types of blacks I had seen around, I asked Fred how he thought they should be treated. His eyes lit up immediately: I had broached a pet topic.

"I have been here almost all my life," he said thoughtfully, "and I have met blacks of all tribes from the so-called civilized blacks who hang around the goldfields and the towns, to the myalls. Give me the wild black to deal with and train every time.

"Take the 'civilized' blacks who have spent years in the townships or settlements. They have seen vegetables and fruit-trees planted and grow, but I've never heard of one attempting to plant them for himself.

"Take these blacks of mine. The lugger has just brought several tons of flour, sugar, tea, tobacco, and other stuff to keep them going throughout the wet season, providing they would carry on as if I was here. But I intend going to Darwin in a few days and then on to Sydney to see a specialist. I'll be away about five months. My gardens have been planted to their fullest capacity with green vegetables and fruit.

"As soon as my back is turned there will be a huge corroboree. Every black along the Alligator rivers and as far as the Mary River will be invited. The whole lot, my stuff and theirs, will be wolfed in about a week, and for the rest of the time I'm away they will be scratching for food. That has been happening every year as long as I can remember. It is a waste of time to tell them to do otherwise.

"And yet they are not ungrateful. Each year on my return I have found all the animals in splendid condition, new stockyards built, and a new hut built for me where the old one was. 'Boss all about good fella. Buildem nother sleep about,' is what I suppose they say.

"Further in their favour is that they are particularly kind to animals. You noticed Paddy, the big red bullock at the gate?"

I nodded.

"Well, his mother died when he was a calf, and the blacks brought him up. The gins used to give it so much of their spare cow's milk-supply that at times I thought he would burst. They made a real pet of the animal, and now you will often see him sleeping around their huts. The blacks and piccaninnies climb all over the great beast and ride around on him.

"Some time ago a man came here to buy bullocks. I ran them through the yard and cut off the sixty which he agreed to take. We signed the contract and he gave me a cheque - they averaged about £10 apiece. As he was droving them off there was a yell from the blacks, and I guessed in a minute what was wrong. I had mistakenly included Paddy.

"The blacks crowded around me howling for Paddy. I called the buyer back and offered him a tenner for him, but he said he had bought the lot, and that was an end of it. I warned him that he would never get the bullock off the run and that he was taking a personal risk in trying to. He laughed and went off.

"Next morning Paddy was back at the gate. Whether he had wandered back or been cut off by the blacks, I did not know. The buyer, very irate, returned to claim the bullock. I warned him again and he seemed on the point of losing his temper. 'Do you think any damn blackfellow is going to dictate to me?' 'Go ahead,' I said, 'but don't blame me if you strike trouble.'

"It took him the best part of that day to get Paddy away, while the blacks howled dark threats at him. I noticed that the blacks' camp was very quiet that night, and in the morning Paddy was back once more. Again the buyer returned, but this time to take a cheque for the bullock. He cursed my blacks roundly, and said they had stampeded his cattle and ridden Paddy home.

"Many a time when the country was in flood, and I would have eaten anything, I have suggested killing Paddy, but what a din the blacks raised! On one occasion the boys risked their lives, taking a canoe forty miles over the flooded waters for beef.

"That is one side of the blackfellow. Another is that he will never harm a child. And yet in some ways they are fierce and revengeful. Once, I had two or three boys shooting buffaloes for me. I gave them guns as I always did, but got something of a shock when one came back with a groove cut along his skull. They had had an argument over a lubra. I said nothing about it. If I hadn't given them guns, a spear would have been used, and there would probably have been one black less.

"They are faithful creatures too - perhaps you would call it foolish."

I then told Fred about Niogo and the splinter. He said I could depend on Koperaki for all time.

"I have known Koperaki for many years," continued Fred,

swallowing a glass of lager at a gulp. "He is the most intelligent and most independent black on the river, but what a staunch fellow he is. On one occasion Paddy Cahill ran short of flour. The river was flooded, and he sent Koperaki to me with a note asking if I could let him have some.

"Koperaki had swum the swollen torrent and waded through crocodile-infested swamps for a hundred miles to get here. He told me they had no flour whatever at Oenpelli, and I said I would send some over as soon as the flood-waters subsided. That was no good to Koperaki. He knew Paddy badly wanted flour, and he persuaded me to give him a fifty-pound bag. He returned with it on his head, taking wide detours to avoid swimming and arrived safely with the flour at Oenpelli. It was a supreme feat of strength, endurance, and bushcraft.

"Without the blacks this country would beat the white man. Unfortunately many of our own crowd do not appreciate them and treat them more like dogs than human beings. Many an Australian explorer has had his life saved by his own blacks only, unhappily, to die from the spears of hostile tribes."

I referred to the white man-black woman problem.

"I can tell you this, Carl," he went on seriously. "This country will never be settled without the presence of white women. No doubt you came across those settlements on the railway line. You found about three white women to every hundred white men, and you must have noticed how those white women are treated. Why, man, they're venerated as saints. Bring a white man before them and he will stand nervously fiddling with his hat, too tongue-tied to speak. A married man in these parts is an object of everlasting envy. Take the case of Mrs Cahill. There is no person more looked up to in the north than she.

"Any lonely white settler who has spent a little while in her company leaves with a feeling that some definite change has taken place within him. He loathes the thought of returning to his tent or rough bush hut with the blackened billy-cans and dirty frying-pans. He wonders when he will be in a position to ask a white woman to share his life. He realizes it may be years, it may be never. So he uncorks the rum-bottle and proceeds to deaden the hopelessness of everything. His passions are inflamed and a gin is the inevitable result.

"You take my tip, Carl, a lonely man in the bush is going to have a hell of a time to keep the passion out of his blood. There are only two things to do. Establish a home for yourself and bring a white woman to share your life, or work like blazes until you have made it worth while, sell out and go south.

"Most of us buffalo-shooters get our money fairly easily and make a trip south once a year to spend it. I would like to have a white woman here. But they won't leave the cities and the tinpot social life which seems to mean so much to them. In a way, I suppose, you can't blame them. If the Territory could only be made a little attractive!

"I have travelled extensively through the sugar areas and the rich settlements in Queensland where the women have everything they need. If those things could be brought here women might be induced to help settle this great country. That is the only key to the problem."

I interrupted enthusiastically:

"That's my intention, Fred. I want to make a definite settlement where I am and interest sufficient people to establish those things for white women here."

(There was then no such thing as wireless in the Territory, or the flying doctors, or the regular chartering of planes as we find it to-day. When it used to take days to get from Fred Smith's to Darwin, the trip is now done by plane in a few hours. Oh yes, the time is fast coming when the settlement of the Territory will be no visionary's dream.)

184

Fred was still talking and I was listening when the first streak of daylight crept through the window. I had been profoundly interested and impressed. We slept most of that day, and the day after Fred was feeling much better. He saddled up a couple of horses and took me over the run. I was as much delighted with the country as I had been with Oenpelli and East Alligator.

There were hundreds of pigs, and Fred told me he periodically sent fifty or so into Darwin, where the Chinese paid him as much as 1s. a pound for them. It was a profitable industry for him because they cost little or nothing to feed.

For my benefit he ran in about three hundred head of magnificent horses, each mob in charge of its own entire. It was an extraordinary spectacle to watch each stallion as he endeavoured to keep his own flock together.

I wanted ten horses to replace those Whittaker had taken back to Bachelor Farm. Fred told me to take my pick, barring a couple of his own buffalo mounts. He then told two of his boys to take those I selected some miles up the river to a point where they could cross, bring them down and leave them with Koperaki.

Next day was my last at Kopalgo, and I record with some reluctance that I assisted in the despatch of the last bottle of lager.

When I was ready to leave, Fred gathered several banana-plants and a bag of sweet potatoes, while Polly came along with huge loaves of bread sufficient to last many days. And as a parting gift, the old lubra handed me a box in which were a couple of kittens of opposite sexes. I bade Fred a warm farewell, thanking him for his many kindnesses and great help. He had his outfit ready to go in to Darwin. Still far from well, he was determined to make the trip. I urged him to go on to Sydney, and gave him a letter of introduction to a Macquarie Street specialist. Almost certainly he needed an operation.

I left, little guessing that I was never to see him again.

He went to Sydney, but, apparently, felt so much better on the trip that he didn't go to the doctor. Or, perhaps, he knew his end was at hand, for he soon returned, and died in Darwin hospital after a brief illness.

Fred Smith was a grand fellow. Both Whittaker and I felt his death more than we can say.

I was paddled across the river by the two grinning lubras who had first met me. Back at camp I got rather a surprise to see there some thirty bucks and lubras. I recognized one of them, Spider by name, having seen him at Fred Smith's. He said they were going to Koperaki's country for a walkabout.

The new horses were there, and the camp appeared to be in order, so with Koperaki, Spider, and Hobble Chain in the lead, I made a bee-line for Kajadja, leaving Fred Smith's blacks to follow their own way. Half-way across the plain we were hit by one of those fierce and sudden storms which in minutes turn brilliant day into night. Heavy rain lashed us, lightning split the heavens, and terrific thunder-claps made the earth tremble. In a moment the plain was a sheet of water and I was wet to the bone.

We made for the trees on the other side as fast as we could. Rather senseless haste since I couldn't get any wetter, and there was more danger in the forest than in the open. The horses were terrified. As we reached the timber there was a fiercer squall, a vivid flash of lightning, a shattering clap of thunder, and a huge tree was uprooted almost on top of us. The blacks scattered in all directions. The horses, unable to stand any more, stampeded, leaving me alone with Dandy. I had to dismount quickly to keep him in hand; he was rearing and plunging all over the place.

The storm gradually subsided and light misty rain began to fall. The blacks appeared from behind huge ant-beds and went after the horses. They soon found them, but I was dismayed to see the torn-off saddle-bags and smashed packages.

When we had them hobbled, and the damage repaired, dark descended. Rain was still falling and prospects for the night were exceedingly dismal. The first problem was to get a fire going; as every twig and leaf was saturated, it was a pretty considerable problem. But once more Koperaki taught me something. He slit open a branch of a dead pandanus palm and from the centre extracted some bone dry tinder-like fibre. I produced my waterproof match-box and a fire was soon crackling. I managed to get a little warmth into my chilled bones, but had no hope of drying my clothes. The rain did not let up for a minute - a most damnably unpleasant night.

At break of day we moved off. The drizzle was continuous and I was feeling weary and thoroughly fed-up. To make matters worse I couldn't see beyond fifty yards ahead of me.

We had been going for about three hours and should have hit the plain we crossed on the trip down. Another couple of hours, then Spider jumped from his horse and began to examine the ground intently. Seeing Spider and Koperaki scratching their heads and looking as silly and puzzled as it is possible for blackfellows to look, I demanded to know what was the matter.

With the expression of a sheep, Spider pointed to the ground and said:

"Horse track, boss."

Grinning shamefacedly, Koperaki added:

"This one horse track," pointing to our horses.

I realized what had happened. We had travelled in a circle and had cut our own tracks. It was the first and only time I have known a black to get bushed. When I got over my first feeling of annoyance, I was curious to know how the blacks actually did find their way in the bush. I said to Koperaki:

"I bin tinkit before blackfella no more get lost alonga bush.

You bin lost all about now."

He replied:

"When im sun up, and moon, im all right. Alonga rain im no more bin see long way."

Then, for the first time, I knew that the blacks were guided by the sun, moon, and stars, aided by landmarks. The knowledge upset completely my belief that they found their way as animals do by instinct.

Koperaki, who had quickly lost his embarrassment, said:

"You bin got em that one debil-debil alonga coat? Im bin talk which way we bin go."

He meant my compass, but the difficulty in using it was that I did not know where we were. We had been travelling north-west when the storm overtook us, and on starting off again the next morning we had apparently begun to move in a circle.

Retracing our tracks from the point where we had cut them, and taking numerous compass bearings, I found that we were on the northern sector of the circle.

I returned to where the tracks had been cut, placed a stick perpendicularly in the ground and drew a circle. Then I cut some sticks, each representing a mile. I reckoned we were about ten miles from the high ground we had passed over on the way to Kopalgo. And from the fact that we were on the north sector of the, circle, my compass calculations told me that our destination lay a few degrees north of west. The blacks had been watching me curiously, unable to understand what I was doing.

I now took the lead, and eventually reached the top end of a plain which apparently was the one we had travelled over previously. Koperaki had at once recognized it:

"Im all right now." And he looked at me with great respect, no doubt thinking I had been responsible for some sort of dark magic.

The sun at last broke through the scudding black clouds,

and I began to feel somewhat cheerful for the first time in a wretched twenty-four hours.

After such a tiring and frustrated day I decided to make an early camp. That evening Koperaki told me that the boys wanted to go for a walkabout, and that only he would remain. I had an idea they wanted to rejoin the lubras, and I knew it was no use trying to prevent them. In a body they disappeared into the bush.

Next day Koperaki and I travelled till evening without camping; then prepared to settle down for the night on a good camping-ground. I was hobbling out the horses when Koperaki approached me with a look of apprehension in his eyes.

"Nother one blackfella close up."

No sooner had he said so than about sixty blacks appeared, painted and looking very warlike.

I continued what I was doing as though nothing was amiss. The blacks halted about fifty yards away. Without looking up, I asked Koperaki who they were. He said they were not members of his tribe.

"Those blackfella no good. Very cheeky fella."

Two of them, evidently the leaders, each carrying several spears, came across and stood looking at me.

"Good day," I said. "What name?"

They answered in their own language. Koperaki understood.

They said they belonged to a tribe from the stone country and were on a hunting expedition. He didn't believe them, and told me he thought they were looking for trouble.

Koperaki talked to them severely. Whatever he said had the effect of making them appear uneasy. Finally, I threw them a few sticks of tobacco, which they accepted sullenly and withdrew to their followers.

"More better no more sleep to-night, Garl," said Koperaki. "That one cheeky blackfella all about."

I was beginning to feel far from pleased with the outlook. Unfortunately, I did not have much ammunition. There were only two cartridges for the shot-gun, and if it came to a show-down, I knew the duck-shot would produce better results than the .303.

After tea I took a seat at the foot of a tree, and with the gun across my knees, prepared to settle down for the night. Koperaki had taken up a position a few yards away. He was armed with a tomahawk and a .32 rifle. I had never seen him use a gun before, but apparently he was prepared now to have a go.

The blacks began to indulge in weird war-dances, working themselves into a frenzy. Evidently it was all for my benefit, and I certainly feared an attack first thing in the morning.

Koperaki mentioned one thing which consoled me a little. He said he had put the wind up the blacks by telling them that he expected all his tribe along any minute, and that he had explained with some force how it happened that his tribe was in that country.

Throughout the night I sat watching; it was a tremendous relief when day broke.

The blacks now moved close to my camp. With admiration I watched Koperaki stride through the mob of them as though extending an invitation to take the lot of them on.

Trying not to show signs of haste or fear, I got the outfit together, and we left with an air of assumed nonchalance, which I was far from feeling.

The blacks made no attempt to follow us. When we had travelled about a quarter of a mile, Koperaki suggested we should wait for a while. Knowing that he never did anything without a pretty good reason, I agreed. He made a fire, and quickly had a column of smoke going skywards with which he proceeded to send out signals.

We waited there perhaps half an hour. At last Koperaki gave

a grunt of satisfaction. About eight miles away, in the direction of Kajadja, smoke columns were going up.

"Im all right now," he said, grinning. "My tribe come up all around."

On we went, Koperaki forcing the pace. That day we covered a distance which normally would have taken us a day and a half. We were now only half a day away from home.

After tea that evening I heard loud cooees from the bush, which Koperaki answered. Presently several of his boys appeared, fully armed and carrying spare spears. Then Koperaki said:

"I bin leave you now. I tellem nother one boy go back camp alonga you." With which he left me and disappeared with his tribesmen.

CHAPTER XXII

THE FIGHT-BURIAL-AND INITIATION

I REACHED Kadjadja without seeing anything more of those "cheeky fella blackfella." Except for the watchdog, Big Head, the women, and youngsters, the camp was deserted. Big Head said, with a mysterious gesture, that the men had made for the bush. He had a hurried word with the boy who had accompanied me back to the camp, then:

"Might be we go walkabout. We bin back bimeby."

When they vanished, I knew that something pretty big was afoot.

The box containing the two kittens had been placed at the doorway of my hut. I took the lid off, the cats gave one concerted spit, and with tails bristling, flew up the banyan-tree. That was the last I saw of them.

I filled in time digging and planting the seeds and things Fred Smith had given me, feeling far from pleased with the outlook. If Koperaki's crowd came out of the scrap second best, it was good night me.

About dusk old Jimmy appeared.

"Which way Koperaki?" I asked him.

"Im alonga bush," he said noncommittally.

"Why did you come back?"

"Look out alonga lubra."

At the first sign of danger I guessed the lubras would disappear and Jimmy would go with them. The prospects for me seemed pretty dismal.

"More better, boss, lubra belonga Koperaki camp close up to-night," Jimmy suggested.

I agreed to this, knowing that if there was anything doing during the night, Koperaki's missus would give me early warning.

Jimmy brought the gin and Niogo over, and the three of

them settled down about twenty yards away. I was awake most of the night, and could see old Jimmy sitting beside the fire putting stick after stick on it.

Early next morning I saddled a horse and scouted around for several miles without seeing anything. That night was the same as the previous one, and the whole business was getting properly on my nerves. Just before lunch on the third day, Jimmy came running over to me, and pointing excitedly to a column of smoke a few miles away:

"Koperaki close up."

Two hours later Koperaki and his warriors straggled into camp. They were painted and carried fighting-spears. Koperaki had a hank of hair twisted around his head, and I never saw him look more fierce. The first thing he did was to pick up Niogo, throw him into the air, and kiss him hungrily. He took no notice whatever of his wife, who stood there silent and looking on.

"You bin fight?" I said.

"Plenty fight, Garl."

"You bin killem all about nother one blackfella?"

"Close up killem all about. Some fella bin run away"

"They bin killem you, too?"

"Little bit plenty."

"All right. Bring im over blackfella bin killem alonga spear"

(By "killem" the blacks mean wounded: if the injury is mortal, it is "killem dead.")

Koperaki went over to his own camp and I opened the medicine-chest and prepared myself for some gory work.

About half a dozen casualties were brought over, some of them being carried. The first chap I had a look at was in a pretty bad way. He had been speared through the side of the chest, and the broken and jagged ends of the spear were protruding from both sides.

Placing my knee in the small of the black's back, I grasped

the barbed end firmly and started to drag it through. The poor devil must have suffered agony, and I was on the point of vomiting as I felt the tissues tearing. At last I got it out and swabbed the horrible hole with iodine. Not once during the ghastly operation did the black utter a murmur!

I gave him a few drops of brandy and bound the wound, knowing full well that when I saw him next, providing he was alive, the bandages would have been pulled off and clay stuffed in the hole.

The next fellow had stopped a clout with some sort of axe and there was a deep gash on the back of his neck. This stitched up, the next customer was Big Head.

"They bin killem me alonga toe, boss," he said sadly.

Three toes had been broken and gashed.

"How happen, Big Head?"

"Im haxe."

Apparently a black had crashed the blunt end of an axe on his foot. I dressed the wounds and put the toes in splints, but I didn't expect them to stay long on.

Another of the warriors had two fingers cut off, while the rest of them had more or less minor spear-wounds and grazes. All were patched up.

That evening I went over to the blacks' camp to see how the patients were getting along, and if there were any more who needed attention. Many familiar faces were missing, and several of the lubras were wailing at the top of their voices and throwing dust and ashes over themselves. This meant that a corroboree and burial service would soon be in full swing.

As I had anticipated, the chap who had the spear through his chest, had pulled the bandages off and got someone to pack clay into the wound. He was in great pain. The only opiate I had was laudanum, so I gave him a dose and a half and hoped for the best.

The tribe was very excited, and the usually calm Koperaki

was like a mad thing. I thought it judicious not to ask questions and didn't stay any longer than was necessary.

A little later there was a hellish corroboree. There was much crying and wailing, and strange songs were sung, no doubt extolling the virtues of the fallen. I had not seen the bodies, but guessed they were hidden somewhere handy.

Here let me describe such a ceremony as had its beginnings with Koperaki's tribe.

A circular space is cleared in the scrub. About ten feet of the trunk of a tree which has been hollowed out by termites is cut off. The bark is removed, and the outside painted by the leading men with a design of lines and dots.

The body of the warrior is then rolled in a large sheet of paper-bark and placed full length in the hollow log. Wads of paper-bark are inserted at each end, and the cylindrical coffin is planted upright in the centre of the clearing with six or seven feet projecting. A black stone is placed as a capping and then the scene is deserted.

After a lapse of time, during which decomposition has taken place, the bones are removed, cleaned, often red-ochred, and the major bones and skull replaced in the coffin. At this period a bone is removed, generally an arm-bone, wrapped in paper-bark, and taken to the camp where a special ceremony is performed, the object being to find out who was responsible for the death of the person.

Some unfortunate black is always named, and a son or close relative of the deceased is deputed to seek vengeance. The bone is placed in an ornamental bag and the avenger sets off with it slung on his back and accompanied by several companions. Should the named one be discovered unprepared for the impeding retribution, he is promptly killed, but should he be ready, arrangements are made for a trial. The avenger throws spears at the accused, and if he is wounded he is finished off, but should he be unscathed, he is allowed to go free.

This, I believe, is the most usual ceremony; although here is another which is practised widely.

In this ceremony the body is placed on a bough platform of a tree.[47] When only the bones are left, the mother's brother and his son go up the tree and gather some of the long bones of the arm which they wrap in paper-bark. These are given to the mother and she keeps them as long as four moons.

Then she hands the parcel to her brother who makes arrangements for the final ceremony. A log coffin is prepared, all the bones are placed in it, and a ceremonial is held. Here the men, who are painted, assemble, but the lubras are not allowed to be present. They bring food at intervals, and return to their own camp some distance away.

A fire is lighted on the ceremonial ground by a black of the same totem as the dead person, and he takes two sticks from the fire and strokes the coffin with them. The other blacks sit around the coffin all night. In the early morning they take it, marching in single file, to the lubra's camp.

There a hole has been made in the ground in which the coffin is placed upright. The men then retire and squat about fifty yards away. The lubras weep and wail for some time and at last go away. This completes the ceremony, and the coffin is taken and placed in some hole in the rocks known only to the old men.

Although I have no first-hand knowledge of it, there is authoritative evidence that certain tribes in Arnhem Land eat the bodies of the dead. This evidence, which is to be found in Bulletin 2 of the *Northern Territory Bulletin,* Sydney Museum, 1912,[48] points conclusively to the fact that eating the dead is a frequent occurrence. When anyone, except the really old, dies, the body is first wrapped in paper-bark by the mother's brother's son, and left until morning when a big fire is made in a hole in the ground, and stones are heated on it.

All hair is then cut from the corpse and burnt. Paperbark is placed on the stones, then the body, another layer of bark, and the hole is filled in. This is carried out in the bush far from the main camp. The cooking is done by the mother's brother's son. While it is in progress the other blacks sit around and watch. The lubras are not allowed, actually, to see it, but are quite aware of what is going on.

When the mother's brother's son considers the body is cooked, he takes it out and places it on fresh sheets of paper-bark. Everything, including the intestines, is eaten. When the feast is over, the bones are carefully collected, wrapped in paper-bark and placed on a tree platform. After many moons the old men collect and plant them in crevices in the rocks, allotting different places to different bones.

I had heard rumours of this apparently revolting ceremony, and on several occasion[s] taxed Koperaki with it. Although he admitted that it was still a custom with certain tribes, he was loth to discuss it.[49]

In practically all tribes, when a child dies, the mother will carry the bones, wrapped in paper-bark, around with her for a long time, eventually placing them in the hollow of a tree out of reach of dingoes or wild dogs. After a further period, she will remove them and bury them in the ground.

After Koperaki's braves had been planted in their upright coffins, and the ceremonies and the moaning were over for the time being, there began further activity in the blacks' camp. Big Head and about half a dozen others were sent in many directions, and Koperaki told me that there was going to be "big fella corroboree close up."

The whole of the tribe, with the exception of Koperaki and his bodyguard, then abandoned their quarters, and moved a couple of miles south. I was told that they were preparing a new camp on the borders of a large billabong. Koperaki seemed to be watching for something: whenever I rode on to the plain, I could see smoke signals all over the country, and at practically every point of the compass.

One afternoon Koperaki came to me with a more satisfied expression on his face than I had seen for over a week. He said that in the next three or four days the big corroboree would take place. At certain times of the year, mostly after the early storms, he explained, a truce was declared and all the tribes as far as a hundred miles away would congregate at one spot.

"We bin makem young man alonga tribe," he added.

So, the famous initiation ceremony was about to take place, before about five or six hundred blacks. I was curious to know how they would be fed. Koperaki said that they would catch as many kangaroos, bandicoots, and whatever else they could find, but for most of the time they would be content to starve cheerfully in the sacred cause of initiation.

I decided to give him a hand to stock the larder. We saddled a few horses, and with Koperaki, Hobble Chain, and a couple of others, I went on a buffalo hunt. There was still a fair number of the big beasts around, and without taking unnecessary risks I got four.

Reinforcements were sent for, and the buffaloes were carved up and taken to the new camp, to the great delight of everyone.

That evening Koperaki, his wife, Niogo, and the henchmen left me to my own devices. Little Niogo looked wonderfully happy. He had a baby possum nestling in his woolly hair, and I could not help wondering how the animal existed, since there was no sign of its mother. Imagine my astonishment when some little while later I saw one of the gins with the possum on one breast and a piccaninny on the other!

I put in a couple of days alone, and with extreme impatience I was keen to know what was going on at the scene of the corroboree.

Unable to stand it any longer, I saddled Dandy, and arming myself with a .32 rifle, set off for the blacks' camp. Suddenly

Dandy pricked his ears and began to rear. Looking to my left I got a shock to see about a hundred blacks creeping through the trees in my direction. They wore hair-belts, carried fighting-spears, and were painted as though for war. I hastily withdrew behind dense scrub and watched. The procession was moving slowly on, and in the middle of it came a file of old men, elders of the tribes I concluded, carrying a spear in one hand and grasping a young blood of from fourteen to eighteen with the other.

This band was followed by another party of armed warriors. These wound in and out of the trees, almost doubled up as they moved on their mystifying way. They gave no sign of having seen me.

I tethered Dandy, and moving cautiously, climbed a tall tree. Making myself comfortable in a fork, I had an excellent view of the camp.

A clear patch of some three hundred square yards had been chosen, and in the middle of it dried grass had been heaped in circular fashion. This grassy cushion had a diameter of about ten yards.

Along two sides of the square patch lubras were squatting with paper-bark baskets and dilly-bags containing their belongings before them.

The strange procession of blacks then reached the clearing and I could see Koperaki was at the head. They padded softly and solemnly past the lubras, and when the boys came into view I saw the old men roughly push their heads to one side, and in the same movement cover the eyes with their hands.

After passing the two lines of lubras without being permitted even a glance at them, the boys were led into the centre and placed around the pile of grass and facing it. There were about thirty of them. The blacks next formed themselves in circles behind the boys until they were about ten deep, and had completely obscured the lubras' view.

An impressive silence was at length broken by the sound of a rich baritone voice, evidently that of the songster of the united tribes, which was followed by the massed choir rendering something like "H-a-a-a-r-r-r."

With one accord they then pushed forward closer to the boys.

The soloist would sing again, the blacks would chant, and there would be another forward movement until at last the boys were pushed face downward on the grass.

The blacks squatted, and apparently this was the signal for the lubras to rise. Stepping slowly and gingerly they came over to the blacks and behind them placed parcels wrapped in paper-bark. These I discovered contained cooked bandicoot, wallaby, yams, and other such delicacies. The lubras then turned on their heels without even looking at the boys and disappeared into the bush.[50]

I was extraordinarily interested, but unfortunately it was getting late, so with reluctance I crawled down the tree, mounted Dandy, and rode home.

I returned to my perch the next morning to see more of the weird proceedings. The circumcision of the youths - the most important part of the ceremonial - was carried out in swift, business-like manner, and the tribal markings applied. Horizontal cuts were made on the thigh, just above the knee, across the chest and abdomen, and occasionally on the forehead. These were kept open by packing clay into the wounds, so that when they healed definite ridges would be left for all time.

Different tribes have different markings. What they signified I was never able to find out.

Throughout the painful business the boys did not murmur. When it was over and other minor ceremonials attended to, they were full-fledged members of the tribes.

Later on they would be given a lubra, most likely the one

who had been promised to them at the age of about four, and they would place their own brands upon her in much the same way as a man would brand cattle.

Immediately after initiation is a dangerous time for these boys, and, for that matter, anyone else who happens to be near them. They want to blood their spears and are not at all concerned whose blood it is.

I had seen enough and again returned to my hut. Within the next day or two Koperaki's tribe began to drift back, and by the smoke signals in the distance I guessed that the other tribes were also on their way to their own hunting-grounds. They were given a certain time to make themselves scarce; at the end of that the truce was withdrawn.

When Koperaki appeared I endeavoured to pump him for more information about the ceremonial. From some knowledge which I inadvertently displayed, I fancy he guessed I had seen more than I should. However, he said nothing, and seemed disinclined to discuss the initiation at all.

"Bimeby Niogo be made man too?" I asked him.

"Might be I die before," said Koperaki sadly.

I laughed at this.

"Why, you young fella. No more die close up," I said cheerfully. The thought of Koperaki dying was too absurd.

"Might be I bin die. Might be they bin spear me."

"Where you bin go you bin die, Koperaki?"

"Might be they bin eat me, bin bury me all same nother one blackfella. Eberytink finish I bin die."

He then told me that a black man never dies from natural causes. His death is always declared to have been brought about by someone pointing the bone or burning the rag, or, and this was new to me, burning the excreta. Koperaki explained that the blacks always bury their excreta because if it is left on the ground and subsequently found burnt an early death is inevitable. This was an extremely sanitary custom, at all events.[51]

He did admit, however, that death from old age was not the result of some deadly portent, or one to be followed by retribution.

When a man gets too old to keep up with the tribe he is, in the gangsters' language, "put on the spot" and "taken for a ride." They can't afford to waste food on him or wait for his aged limbs to catch up with them. So a couple of the tribe take him many miles into the bush and sit him beneath a tree, where he passes away peacefully.

About this time Koperaki told me one of the gins was sick.

"Might be she have im piccaninny," he suggested.

I walked over to see if there was anything I could do and found that she was being attended to by her man. He had a fire going on which he had placed a number of stones, and beside him was a quantity of large green leaves.

Taking the hot stones from the fire he wrapped them in the leaves and placed them on the gin's stomach. I know he kept this going all night, and when I went across in the morning piccaninny twins had arrived. They both appeared to be lusty youngsters, but I paused to ponder on the fact that they were the first twins I had seen in the country. Koperaki declared twins were:

"No good."

He explained that it would be difficult for a gin to carry and feed two piccaninnies as well as cart along all her belongings, and the weaker of the children was always done away with.

The truth of this was borne out a couple of days later when I discovered that one of the piccaninnies was missing.

While we were on the subject I asked Koperaki how he accounted for the very low birth-rate in his tribe. Since I had first met them a great deal of promiscuous intercourse must have taken place, because some of the gins were openly passed on from one to another.

202

From what he told me, I gathered that they applied contraceptive methods, known only to themselves. Whatever they were the results seemed to be decidedly effective.

CHAPTER XXIII

THE CROCODILE HUNT

THERE had been many severe storms, and as it was getting on towards six weeks since old Whittaker had left, I was beginning to feel a little anxious.

Fred Smith's lugger had already picked up our hides, but there was yet no sign of the boat from Darwin with our stores for the wet season. I made many trips to the river, and one day rode to the coast about fifteen miles north in the hope of sighting the boat. It was a nice stretch of coastline. The tide there surprised me. It rose thirty feet. I camped the night, but as there was no sign of the boat next day, I returned to the hut.

The storms were becoming more frequent and my uneasiness was growing. If Whittaker did not arrive shortly he would have no chance of reaching Kajadja until after the wet season, two months hence, and I would be marooned. I cursed the outlook.

Then one evening the mental clouds lifted. Koperaki came over with the news that my party was not more than a day away: he had learned so from smoke signals. Again I marvelled at their bush telegraph.

I rode many miles in the direction I thought Whittaker would come, but on returning to camp found him waiting for me. He had taken another track. I almost fell around his neck. Nothing has ever pleased me more than his cheery grin did then.

And Bob and Jacky were with him, large as life. I must confess I hadn't expected to see them, having reckoned that the allurements of Pine Creek would be irresistible. They were dressed in new khaki trousers and shirts, and wore new hats and elastic-sided boots to which Jacky had attached a pair of spurs.

Both were holding new pipes, and their grins were like slits in a melon. I guessed that the entire new outfit had been donned that morning to impress me, and I told them they looked fine.

"How did you manage to bring these two back, Whit?"

"Ask them."

"I bin think you stop alonga Pine Creek, Jacky."

"More better I come look alonga you, boss," he said gravely. "Might be you bin get lost alonga this myall country."

He wasn't far out about the getting lost.

"What about you, Bob. How lubra alonga Pine Creek?"

"No good alonga me, boss. Meet im two fella lubra there together. They bin fight all about. No more sleep alonga night."

A hard citizen was Bob.

His eyes had been roving about the place, no doubt in search of his temporary maid. Sure enough there she was, grinning coyly behind a tree.

Whittaker was tired and hungry, so I hurried tea along.

We got our pipes going afterwards, and Whittaker handed me the mail, which I was mighty glad to get in spite of the presence of a few bills in it.

He gave me all the news from Darwin, the most upsetting of which was the prospect of an early and sensational flop in the prices of buffalo-hides. We would get from 35s. to 40s. clear for each of our five hundred hides, but Whittaker said we would be lucky if next season's shoot realized more than 6s. or 8s.

Europe was our biggest buyer, and apparently the postwar depression was setting in there, with the consequent stoppage of a great deal of machinery. As hides were used chiefly for belting, this news was a painful blow. Russia, it seemed, had dropped out of the market, and with Germany in revolution the prospects for two enterprising buffalo-shooters were pretty dismal.

One thing which relieved me was to hear that the *John Alce* was due with our stores in a day or so. She arrived next day, dumped our supplies, and left straightway for Oenpelli.

The wet season being due now at any moment, we took a couple of boys and went on a foraging expedition. We shot several buffalo cows, and a large quantity of all varieties of game. At the hut we had a fair supply of dried and salted tongues, but we were determined to have no shortage of any kind of food in the dreary months which lay ahead.

Back at the hut we set about preparing our kill. The geese and ducks we kept on boiling in the same water (liberally salted) until it became a rich concentrate. This we put into containers and sealed.

Most of the beef we salted. Some of it we boiled and boiled, of course with a good deal of salt, until we had an excellent substitute for beef-extract.

The seeds and plants we had put in were coming along nicely, and everything was in order for our entrenchment.

The horses were an anxiety; but both Fred Smith and Paddy Cahill had assured me that as the waters rose they would make their way to the high ground. All except a few had been unhobbled; the hobbled ones we kept handy in case of need.

The rains began with scattered storms, which soon developed into a steady downpour, light at first, but increasing until it came down in one huge sheet of water, and surprisingly quickly the plain was a lake.

This deluge lasted for an hour, then eased somewhat; but the rain continued to pelt down. For two days it rained unceasingly. The hut stood up to the downpour splendidly, and we were as dry as a bone.

Tired of being cooped up, we got a couple of horses, and taking Koperaki, we rode to the high bluff overlooking the river. We scarcely recognized it. The East Alligator had been converted into a raging, muddy waste of waters. Koperaki said that in a few days it would break its banks and flood the whole plains. It did.

Terrific downpours continued at intervals: ten inches would fall in an afternoon. There were a few fine breaks, and during these we seized the opportunity of getting out. I was amazed at how quickly the grass had grown: it seemed to shoot up overnight. We had to force our way through it to get from the hut door.

For six weeks it rained. We filled in the long days and longer nights reading and playing cribbage. A good supply of books had been delivered by the *John Alce*. But we got very much on each other's nerves at times. We had known each other many years, and we had put in many lonely times together, but this was the sorest trial our friendship had ever undergone. The incessant rain and the forced inactivity were getting us down. Even Bob and Jacky, camped near by, provided little diversion.

There was one occasion, however, when they brightened up the moment. The flood-waters had come up to our door. Jacky yelled out to me:

"Might be im halligator come alonga camp, boss."

Bob, of course, had to chip in.

"You bin tellem me halligator come up, Jacky, I bin fight im."

Jacky gave a snort.

"You bin fight im all right, Bob. I tink you bin throw im that one lubra alonga halligator, you run alonga tree."

And I believe Jacky hoped to the Lord Bob would. Bob had built a gunyah for his lubra and himself and Jacky was again out in the cold. Despite their squabblings, I fancy these two blacks were fond of each other, and things had never been the same since Bob appropriated the lubra from Koperaki's tribe.

Then there came a day which Whittaker announced was Christmas Day. We had kept a rough check on the calendar, and if it wasn't exactly the twenty-fifth of December, we agreed that it was near enough for us. We found later that we were a week late.

With the air of a conjuror [sic], Whittaker went to a place of concealment and produced half a dozen bottles of lager, three bottles of wine, a Christmas cake, and a pudding. That was a good start anyway. And during the morning, when scouting around in the wet, I was lucky enough to bag a sucking-pig, and some geese and ducks. What a party we had!

As the wine humanized and mellowed us, we got visions of a home better, much better, than Paddy Cahill's; of a motor launch travelling to and from Darwin; of groves of coconut palms, and banana plantations. We even mapped our dreams on paper. And after we had emptied the third bottle we went to sleep.

The sun was shining brilliantly next morning and, despite a couple of sore heads, the world didn't seem such a bad place.

After breakfast a native log canoe pulled up outside our hut, and there was Koperaki with a couple of his tribe. "Might be im rain finish little while," he said, which was the best news we had heard for a long while. The wet season was apparently drawing to a close.

I asked him if he had seen any crocodiles about. Pointing to a fringe of trees in about a foot of water which had bordered the lagoon before the rains, he said:

"Plenty alonga there."

I had always determined to have a crack at the crocodiles for the sport of it, and after our depressing seclusion the moment seemed opportune for a thrill or two.

"I think we bin shoot im to-day," I said. At that Koperaki and his boys began jabbering excitedly. Jacky was not fired with the same enthusiasm, but I decided to rope him into the party and leave Bob to look after the camp and his lubra.

We stepped gingerly into the canoe, and with great care sat

down. It doesn't take much to upset the wretched things. Jacky insisted upon taking a paddle, and he manipulated it as one might have expected. As soon as Koperaki had the nose heading in the right direction, Jacky would pull it round at a right angle. I told him to put down the paddle and sit still. That unfortunate boy never seemed to be able to do anything right, except, of course, to shin up a tree at the first sign of danger.

We reached the trees, and tethering the canoe and rolling up our trousers, got out. I told Jacky to stay put. We were wading knee-deep through the reeds, and I was not altogether taken with the scheme, half expecting any minute to put my foot into a crocodile's jaws. Koperaki, however, said everything would be all right, and on we went.

Suddenly he came to a dead stop, and quivering with excitement, pointed ahead. My pulses quickened as I saw a huge crocodile swimming slowly down the lagoon, not more than twenty yards away.

I suggested to Whittaker that on the count of three we both fire, which we did, aiming at the eyes. At the crack of the guns the great bulk of the crocodile literally heaved out of the water, crashed down again, and after thrashing madly with its tail, disappeared. We could not tell whether the shots had been fatal, although the water all around was stained with blood.

For the next few minutes we had the wind up badly; the beast might come at us underneath.

We waded on for another hundred yards, and I gave a startled jump as I saw a crocodile appear from the reeds not ten yards ahead. My first thought was to take to the nearest tree, but the second thought proved to be the soundest. Again Whittaker and I fired together, but this time aiming four shots behind the shoulder. With a bellow of pain the crocodile turned on his back, and I guessed we had got him. Koperaki, dancing with joy, cried:

"You bin kill im dead."

As the brute was still churning up the mud, we pumped a few more shots in for safety, and at last it became motionless. We waded over, the while keeping a sharp look out for others. I had not forgotten the one we had wounded.

The crocodile, which measured about eleven feet, was quite dead. Koperaki grabbed some jungle rope, made a noose and slipped it over the head, tying it to a tree. After a further hunt around we failed to see any more of the reptiles, and made back to the canoe, leaving Koperaki to bring the kill along.

Jacky gave a yelp of delight when we arrived. His face was an ugly grey colour; he was badly scared. Whittaker and I were standing talking as Koperaki made his way over, towing the crocodile right side up twenty feet behind.

A thought of devilment apparently entered his head. He gave a sudden and violent tug at the rope and the crocodile shot forward, giving every appearance of swimming. When Jacky saw it his eyes dilated in terror; he gave one leap, upset the canoe, and emptied himself into the water. As he rose from it there was the crocodile's head almost touching him. The poor little beggar gave an agonized scream, floundered out of the water, and flew up the nearest tree.

It was not until Koperaki straddled the crocodile that Jacky knew his leg had been pulled. Then, with downcast eyes, he slowly descended the tree. He looked sullenly at Koperaki, but as he was about as scared of him as he was of the crocodiles, he offered no comment. He whispered to me, however:

"You no more tell im Bob alonga this one."

I gave my promise and intended to keep it. I could not answer for Koperaki, who was still chuckling to himself. We tied the crocodile to the stern of the canoe, and paddled back to camp. Koperaki's blacks were waiting for us, and when they saw the crocodile they went wild with excitement. It was taken to their camp, and during a joyous corroboree that night they ate it.

Now that the storms and heavy rains were abating, ducks and geese began to make their appearance in thousands. They set about building their nests in the reeds on the edges of the swamps. The egg season was at hand.

Paddy Cahill told me he collected about twenty-five thousand goose eggs each year and put them in coarse salt for use in cooking. I thought at the time what a wonderful egg-pulp industry could be established.

In a few days the whole place was almost white with eggs. We ate really more than we wanted, and Whittaker experimented with a wide variety of cakes.

When the ducklings and goslings appeared, so did the snakes, goannas, dingoes, and hawks. These wrought havoc among them.

The crocodiles also were laying their eggs, as I discovered one morning when I saw one of them leave its nest and make for the river.

Crocodile eggs, which are firm though not thick shelled and about the size of goose eggs, are laid in layers in holes on the banks of rivers or waterholes. The disproportion between the newly hatched young and the adults is striking.

I had taken my .32 and was looking for plain turkey, having seen several of them fly over and land near the river. I got one bird weighing about twenty-five pounds, and was making to the hut when I saw a black jump backwards from the mangroves at the river-bank, and with spear poised leap in again.

I went over and was in time to see the finish of a fight between Koperaki and a sixteen-foot crocodile. He had one spear stuck well behind the reptile's shoulder, and was dancing around looking for an opening to drive home a second spear on the other side.

The crocodile, badly wounded, was trying to make its way

towards the river. Its great jaws were snapping, and it was lashing its tail with lightning strokes. With that terrible tail the crocodile knocks its prey into the water.

With amazing nimbleness Koperaki was jumping from side to side, but it took all his agility to keep clear. The crocodile's eyes were blazing green with ferocity and hatred, and I suggested firing a couple of shots, but he seemed keen to finish the job alone.

Koperaki then changed his tactics. He made a feint with his spear, and leaping across the crocodile's back, forced further home the embedded spear, and was out of the way again in an instant. The reptile gave a bloodcurdling bellow, and by its mad thrashing I guessed it was about finished. It was now within a few feet of the river, and thinking it might flop in at any moment, I fired.

Koperaki did not seem at all pleased at my interference, but I assured him I would not say anything about having had a hand in the kill. He made another dive, and this time succeeded in driving in the other spear, and that was the end of the crocodile.

He then raced back to camp, and in a few minutes returned with most of the tribe yelling and casting admiring glances at him. It is a rare achievement for a black to kill a crocodile of that size single-handed, and Koperaki was a great hero.

I told him if he liked to get a couple of horses he could do so, which offer he promptly accepted, and the crocodile was dragged to their camp. Koperaki gave the head to me. I placed it on an ant-bed with the mouth propped open for the ants to pick the bones, and eventually brought it to Sydney. It is now at my home, fallen to pieces because I had not bothered to wire it.

That night the blacks held another riotous corroboree, and the pungent smell of frying crocodile stayed in my nostrils for days.

We still had a couple of months to fill in before resuming buffalo-shooting, and as Koperaki had been telling me of the big turtles on Field Island, I thought we might as well go over.

Whittaker was on, so taking Koperaki, Bob, and Jacky, we started in the canoe. The island, Koperaki explained, was off the mouth of the East Alligator, about twenty miles from Kajadja. The tide was with us, and helped also by the flood-waters, we made good progress.

We saw dozens of crocodiles and had several long shots at them, but did not bother to investigate the results. We had plenty of ammunition, and it was good practice.

By mid-afternoon we reached a headland on the eastern bank and made camp for the night. Early next morning we set out for Field Island. In the open sea, the precariously balanced canoe bobbed about in the choppy waters until my heart was in my mouth. Bob and Jacky had turned green from fright.

I stepped on to the firm island with a tremendous feeling of relief. We dragged the canoe up on to the small, sandy beach, and going a little way inland, prepared camp.

The island appeared to be about three square miles in extent. It was lightly timbered, chiefly with fan and pandanus palms, and there were many rock-holes filled with fresh water. Pigeons were plentiful, but so far we had seen no turtles.

After tea we went to the beach in bright moonlight. Bob Cadell assumed leadership of the party. We had only gone a few yards when he stopped suddenly and pointed.

Several large turtles were coming out of the sea.

Koperaki dived into the bush and returned with a thin but strong sapling. When we reached the beach he pushed the sapling under the largest turtle and turned it on its back. He repeated this with a couple more, and we went back to the camp and turned in.

In the morning I told Bob and Jacky to hunt around and find some turtle eggs. The tracks on the beach to the nests could be plainly seen.

"What name egg belonga turtle, boss?" asked Jacky.

"All same duck egg, hen egg alonga Pine Creek," I answered.

The boys soon returned with their hats full. I broke several into a pan, put a fair amount of dripping in, and watched them cooking. After about half an hour the yoke was as hard as board, but the white still remained transparent. I then cooked some for a couple of minutes, and found them delicious. The white I discovered does not react to heat in the same way as that of other eggs.

As the tide was about to turn, we decided to move off to the mainland. We tied the captured turtles to the stern of the canoe and reached the other side without mishap. Koperaki hauled the turtles ashore and once more turned them on their backs. He cut off the head of one, and was about to remove the shell when I told him to wait until it died. We waited and waited. The creature was still alive, when I got tired of waiting, and I left Koperaki to finish the beastly job.

I learned later that, after the turtle's brain has been killed, life lingers long in the body. A headless turtle has been known to walk two hundred yards in twenty-four hours after decapitation. If the heart is removed and suspended in a moist chamber, it will sometimes continue to beat for two or three days.

Although I had eaten many good things in Arnhem Land, I can say in truth that never before nor since have I tasted anything so delicious as the turtle steak we then had. The blacks smacked their lips over it, but Koperaki said that dugong was even better. I had heard of this strange sea animal, and he promised to show me later where they could be found.

We finished the second turtle for breakfast next morning and pushed on to Kajadja, reaching there about midafternoon.

We had been away just four days, and no sooner had we hit camp than Bob made straight for his gunyah. I wondered idly why his lubra was not squatting in front waiting for him. He went inside, but came out immediately. There was no sign of the lubra. Sidling up to me, Jacky said, mysteriously:

"Might be they bin steal im lubra belonga Bob."

I looked around. There were plenty of gins about, but nothing of a vision in a gaudy print dress, which dress had been Bob's present brought from Pine Creek.

Jacky looked as though he knew something about the disappearance. I said sharply:

"No more bin tell im me lie, Jacky. You talk straight fella. What name this one?"

Jack shuffled his feet and said:

"Might be im Spider take im lubra, boss."

Spider, that boy of Fred Smith's, who had come with us! I had forgotten him.

"You bin tell im Spider take im lubra?"

Then he confessed:

"Might be, boss. Long time Bob bin have im no lubra. We bin good frens. Bimeby Bob catch im lubra. I no more bin catch im lubra. I got im no more brudder, fadder, nothing belonga me here. Might be Bob lose im lubra we bin all same brudder long time. Spider come up plenty time. I bin tell im Spider good fella lubra. Bob got im all about lubra eberywhere, Pine Creek, Adelaide River; too much lubra no good. Bob tink alonga imself all time. Might be he tink about nother one lubra he bin marry."

After a fruitless hunt around, Bob came over, and Jacky said to him:

"Which way lubra bin sit down?"

The wily Bob was equal to the occasion.

"I bin send im walkabout."

That evening Jacky shared the gunyah with Bob, and I heard him repeat half a dozen times:

"That one lubra got im plenty blackfella. More better you go alonga Pine Creek. You get im good fella lubra there."

215

And happiness for Jacky at any rate was restored once more. Spider and the lubra had disappeared into the bush and we didn't sight them again.

A few days after our return from Field Island, Koperaki came rushing over to the hut, in a state of great excitement, with the interesting news that he had sighted several dugongs on the river opposite our camp.

I hailed Whittaker, and we jumped into a canoe with Koperaki and set off on the hunt. When we reached the river we found the blacks had waded and canoed out and had, by shouting, forced the dugongs between themselves and the bank, and into the shallows.

The blacks secured a large female with its young one. Knives were got to work, the dugong was hacked into lumps, and the blacks marched back to camp singing lustily.

The usual rowdy corroboree was held in celebration, and the smell from the sizzling dugong fat was, if anything, worse than that of crocodile.

However, Whittaker and I tried a piece roasted. It was like pork, but not as good as turtle.

A brief description of this strange marine mammal may be interesting. The form of the body is fish-like, and the head is rounded and not out of proportion. The nostrils have valves, and the skin is hairless except about the mouth; the lips are thick. There is hardly any neck, and the tail is flattened horizontally. There are two fore-flappers, but no dorsal fin, and the bones are massive and heavy, which enables the animal to feed on the bottom. They are sluggish, inoffensive, and gregarious, and they never come ashore. Their food consists chiefly of seaweed. The habit of the dugong of lifting its head out of the water and of carrying its young under its arm has been stated to be a possible foundation of the mermaid myth.

The female only bears one at a time, and exhibits a curious affection. When the young one is speared, the mother is taken easily, giving the impression of not wanting to live. There are three varieties of dugong - one is found on the East African coast and in the Red Sea, the second is found in the Indian and Pacific oceans, and the third in the waters of eastern and northern Australia. The Australian species is valuable because of its oil, which is free from disagreeable smell, and is said to have the medicinal qualities of cod-liver oil. They are found up to about ten feet in length.

CHAPTER XXIV

WE ENTERTAIN A CONVICT - BIG HEAD'S TRAGIC DEATH

WE were pottering around the camp one morning, waiting for the next buffalo-shooting season, when Koperaki bolted up waving his arms in wild delight. He was more worked up than I had ever seen him. Pointing to a column of smoke in the distance, he said:

"Brudder belonga me close up."

That was the first I had heard of his brother. I said I would like to meet him.

Whittaker and I were having tea that evening under the banyan-tree, as we usually did, when out of the bush there appeared a black with a lubra, whom I took to be Koperaki's brother and his wife. They stood about ten yards away and looked at us.

He was a magnificent fellow, standing well over six feet, and powerfully built. He wore a hair girdle, had more tribal markings than I had seen, and carried two heavy, dangerous looking spears. The lubra was equally striking. She had a mop of beautiful reddish hair, and might have been the sister of the black skipper of Fred Smith's lugger. She was young, splendidly built, and altogether good to look upon.

Koperaki now arrived, and he introduced the black as his brother Romula.

"Romula!" grunted Whittaker. "Call him Sitting Bull. You'd think he owned the show."

We invited him and his lubra to eat, and I was staggered at his appetite. He polished off a couple of pounds of buffalo steak and looked hungrily for more, which we gave him.

It was not until I visited Darwin that I heard the story concerning Sitting Bull; it was a subject upon which Koperaki had never spoken. He had been working for Paddy Cahill, and one of his jobs was to assist in the butter-making. Then came a day when Paddy was entertaining a guest.

They sat down to a meal, and in a few moments the guest took violently ill, showing every evidence of strychnine poisoning. The butter had been tampered with. Paddy immediately gave his friend an emetic and had him removed to Darwin, where he subsequently recovered.

Sitting Bull was arrested, charged with attempted murder, and sentenced to penal servitude for life in Fanny Bay jail, Darwin. A few weeks later he broke jail almost under the noses of the warders and disappeared into the jungle.

He had picked up his lubra, and had travelled a hundred and fifty miles over crocodile-infested rivers, and through the country of hostile blacks, finally landing at our camp.

The police had no more chance of catching Sitting Bull than they have of catching any other black, unless by making some promise of pardon. In the case of Sitting Bull, however, it was said that the search was only half-hearted as it was believed that some other person had endeavoured to bring about the death of Paddy Cahill.[52]

The shooting-season was now approaching. We had spent several days getting our equipment in order, and at last everything was ready, with the horses in splendid fettle after the long rest.

Whittaker and I took a cruise around, and saw a large buffalo herd grazing on the plain near the South Alligator, a couple of days' ride from Kajadja. We decided to establish a shooting-camp there.

With an outfit of about forty horses and Koperaki, Sitting Bull, Big Head, Hobble Chain, Bob, Jacky, and some twenty other blacks, we bade a temporary farewell to our home.

When we reached the scene of the shoot we selected a site

alongside a good waterhole and made preparations for a stay of a couple of months at least. We built a bark hut with skillion roof and no sides, which we thought would provide sufficient protection against the weather.

The plain was still a little boggy, so we idled away a week or more in the sun. Whittaker made himself particularly useful by taking a party over to the salt-pans and bringing back about three-quarters of a ton. This the blacks smashed into small pieces, and salt for the hides was ready.

We started out at last, but gone was the exhilaration which attended our first onslaught upon the unknown the previous year. We rode out to the herd in the same matter-of-fact manner that we would after a few geese.

So we carried on each day, averaging about ten beasts without the slightest mishap. Then came a day when the buffaloes disappeared, and it turned out to be one of tragic memory. Leaving Whittaker at camp and taking Big Head, I set out to try and locate them. Big Head was an experienced buffalo-shot, and I had given him Dinah and a gun. If we came across the herd, it was my intention to get as many as possible there and then.

Some twelve miles away in the direction of Munganilida, we found them. We advanced at the gallop, and the buffaloes took to their heels. I had taken one flank and Big Head the other, and we soon overtook the herd. I brought down six bulls in quick succession, and by the shots on my left I guessed that Big Head was meeting with equal success. My wing then swung into the trees, and as it was hopeless to attempt to follow them, I turned, to gallop back to the other wing.

Then in a flash tragedy descended. Big Head was alongside a huge buffalo; as he fired, Dinah side-stepped suddenly to avoid an ant-hill, but crashed into it, throwing Big Head heavily, and coming down herself. The shot had not been fatal; it felled the buffalo, but he was soon on his feet again, snorting with rage. The great beast pawed the ground for a moment, then charged the fallen black.

He got his horns underneath Big Head and tossed him high in the air, and the boy's scream of agony and terror was terrible. Big Head fell to the ground, the blood spurting from him. The buffalo charged again, and with knees and horns, crushed and gored the life out of him.

For the moment I seemed rooted to the ground. But it all happened in a flash, and when I galloped up Big Head was dead. I pulled out my heavy .45 revolver from the holster and poured shot after shot into the buffalo until he rolled over lifeless.

A few yards away beautiful Dinah stood with her near foreleg hanging and broken. I shot her, with tears in my eyes.

I rode back and told Whittaker and Koperaki what had occurred, and we got a party and set out to gather the remains of unfortunate Big Head.

At the scene of the slaughter, I wondered grimly if I would be held responsible for the death of Big Head. Koperaki, however, seemed to size up the situation. With a tomahawk he hacked away at the buffalo until blood lapped our feet.

"Debil-debil belonga buffalo killem dead Big Head," he said. And I knew he did not blame me. He tenderly collected the torn and broken body of his comrade and wrapped it in paper-bark.

That night a burial ceremony was held, and the wailings and lamentations were louder and more full of grief than I had ever heard.

I thought how fortunate Whittaker was when the buffalo gored his horse instead of him. And I also realized that either of us might any day come to the same end as poor Big Head.

However, the next day saw us at it again, and we continued to shoot for nearly three months without any more serious

221

mishap than an occasional fall. Our fortune always lay in the fact that when we had spills the buffalo had either been killed or not maddened by injury.

We got about five hundred hides (making just on a thousand for the two seasons' shoot) and, abandoning the shooting-camp, we returned to our old home at Kajadja.

We had a note one day from Paddy Cahill which contained two pieces of bad news. The first was that Fred Smith had died in Darwin hospital. The second bit of distressing information was that the bottom had fallen out of the hide market, and we would be lucky if we got 2s. 6d. a head for the following season's work. The hides from the season just ended, he said, would bring from 6s. to 8s. Since we had been assured of getting from 35s. to 40s. a hide for the first season, it would mean that our total earnings would be about £1200. That was all right, but we agreed that it would not be worth while to shoot for 2s. 6d. or less a hide.

Paddy Cahill had also mentioned that a boat would be coming to his place from Borroloola, on the McArthur River, and he would give instructions for it to call and pick up our loading. That was a relief anyway.

The crash of the hide market upset our plans completely.

"If only we had some cash, Whit - a few thousands," I said, "we could make the show hum."

"What would you do with it?"

"In the first place I would make this place self-supporting, which would be an easy matter. I'd get a lugger, which would cost about £400, and erect a refrigerating plant similar to Paddy Cahill's, and a small canning factory, and tin game, turtle, and turtle soup. To begin with, I would send the stuff to Thursday Island. All this we could get going in a year, and it could be done with a capital of £3000."

"Well, why not let's try to raise the cash?" suggested

Whittaker.

"We will," I said. We decided to make that our move for the future.

CHAPTER XXIV

ZEBUS, TIMOR PONIES, AND OTHER THINGS

A SWIFT trip to Port Essington was to be our first step. We had heard that there was a good harbour there, and we were anxious to get some first-hand knowledge to determine whether it would be worth while taking up further land, having in mind the establishment of fisheries, and the exploitation of the trepang, tortoise-shell and mother-of-pearl industries.

Whittaker suggested that I should go. He was not feeling too well at the time and appeared to be sickening for a bout of fever. In any case, one of us would have to remain to meet the *John Alce* which was due any day with our wet season's stores. As we had made a drastic change in our plans we decided to send most of the stores back to Darwin, keeping only those necessary for immediate requirements.

I expected to be away about ten days, and got together supplies to last me for that period. I was a little worried at leaving Whittaker so short, particularly of such necessities as flour, tea, and sugar, as well as quinine, chlorodyne, and laudanum. But I was pretty confident that the boat would soon be there.

I told Koperaki that stocks were very low, and made it clear that there would be no surplus of anything for his warriors. He said that would be all right as they all intended to take "walkabout alonga Gaernin."

Intending to leave Bob Cadell with Whittaker I sent Jacky and Sitting Bull down the river where they would be able to cross with the horses, and the following day got word that they had arrived opposite the camp. I said "cheerio" to Whittaker; Koperaki paddled me across in his canoe; I picked up the outfit on the other side and with only the compass to guide me set off towards Port Essington. It was forty-five to fifty miles to the north-west. My last sight of Kajadja camp was the pair of tattered underpants fluttering from our pole, and Whittaker standing on the promontory waving his hat.

The first day we passed over what I took to be the western boundary of Oenpelli. It was easy going. But on the second day we struck trouble in the nature of saltwater creeks. Some of these we crossed, but soon found there was a network of them densely fringed with mangroves. We struck out north-east, but in no time were among the creeks again.

Turning almost due north we at last got clear of the creeks and came upon open forest country. Riding leisurely along the following day I saw in the distance what appeared to be buffaloes, but on looking through my binoculars I at once discovered that they were Brahmin cattle, or zebus.

These animals (easily distinguishable by a large hump on the withers) are native to India, but are also found in large numbers in Japan from where it is believed they were first imported to the Territory many years ago. They are tick resisting, and not subject to disease, and when crossed with our shorthorns the result is a heavier and hardier type. Cattle-owners in the north are now experimenting with this cross.

Taking a carbine, and leaving Jacky and Sitting Bull I worked Sovereign round and set off at a gallop after the herd. I took them by surprise and had little trouble in bringing down a fair-sized beast, shooting it in the same manner as I had done buffaloes.

Jacky came galloping up and jumped off his horse in great excitement. He pointed to the animal's horns, which are about three feet in length and have a vertical growth. "Buffalo-horn more better, boss. This one horn might be killem blackfella more quick." And forking his fingers he dug them into his stomach.

The terrors of poor Jacky's life were many, indeed.

We cut slabs of meat from the zebu, including a piece from

the hump, and found it excellent.

We continued over good country, well timbered and grassed. Suddenly my horse tossed his head and pulled up. Sitting Bull, who was riding with me, pointed to the left and there some fifty Timor ponies, bright chestnuts and bays with flowing manes and tails, dashed off.

These ponies, which are a little larger than the Shetland pony, but fine-haired, were also imported to the Territory many years ago. Instantly I thought of another line for our operations.

That evening we reached a large land-locked harbour on which a lugger lay at anchor, and I had a feeling we were at Port Essington. Making camp alongside a billabong, I left the two blacks and, taking my shot-gun, went down to the beach. I fired a couple of shots to attract the attention of whoever was on the lugger. In a few moments a man pulled up the lugger's dinghy, jumped in, and rowed over. He was a Japanese, and told me the land-locked harbour was Port Essington. He invited me over to the lugger - a pearler from Darwin.

I made myself known to the skipper, an Australian, who at once struck me as being as hard-bitten as any individual I had ever met. However, he gave me a hearty greeting, produced a bottle of rum, and we settled down to a chat.

Naturally, I was anxious to learn as much as I could about the pearl-shell, tortoise-shell, and trepang industries. I gathered that if there was not a fortune in them they should at least provide a substantial and profitable adjunct to our other schemes.

Trepang, also known as bêche-de-mer, is a sea-slug about eight inches long. It is found abundantly in the waters of northern Australia, India, Fiji, Tahiti, Macassar, Sumatra, and New Caledonia. It has a high and extensive commercial value in China as an aphrodisiac. When caught the trepang is gutted, boiled, slit open, and smoked dry. It is valued commercially according to colour, and in the following order: brown, black, red, white. "Talking of trepang," said the skipper, "I wonder if you've heard the story of a chap named R__ who was doing pretty well with the industry at Beacon Bay until he came to a sticky finish?"

I hadn't.

"Well, this man was being hunted by the police for some cattle-stealing near Victoria River. He was an expert bushman, and with a companion succeeded in reaching Field Island. The blacks gave them the tip that the police were approaching, and R__ left his friend at the island and made off in his own boat for Beacon Bay. His mate met the police and returned with them to Darwin. The Beacon Bay blacks were a wild lot, but R__ got on well with them and made all sorts of promises to induce them to help him to collect trepang. He must have been a bad-tempered brute, for one day a youngster annoyed him and he picked it up by the heels and dashed out its brains against a tree. Apparently the blacks were a bit scared of R__, but they waited their chance, and the inevitable happened. He was found fastened securely to the floor of his hut with spears. And the irony of the business was that the police were after him to tell him the cattle-stealing charge had been withdrawn.

"After the murder of the boy the blacks at Beacon Bay became fiercer than ever. For some reason they have shown particular hostility towards the Japanese.

"This same chap," added the skipper, "was responsible for a mild oil-rush. After making a fire somewhere near Port Keats (just north of the Fitzmaurice River) the rocks around the fire had burst into flame, probably indicating the presence of petroleum wax. Nobody has yet discovered the spot."

The skipper asked if I had come across any blacks on the trip up. When I told him I hadn't, he advised me to keep my eyes peeled. They were sure to be about, he said, and there was a chance I might run across trouble.

I declined an invitation to stay aboard the lugger for the night, and after being given directions as to where to find the ruins of the original Port Essington settlement and being presented with a welcome parcel of fish I left.

Next morning I moved up the harbour foreshores, came upon some headstones, and the ruins of a church - all that is left of what was once the settlement of Port Essington.

I spent another day pottering around and paid a second visit to the skipper of the lugger. From what I observed and was told, I came to the conclusion that Whittaker and I would be establishing a fishery there, as well as engaging in the trepang and pearl and tortoise-shell trades.

How little the fishing-industry has been developed in the Territory! In 1931-2 only forty hundredweight of fish worth £480 were produced in the Territory for export, and this in spite of the fact that it has been proved conclusively that the waters are teeming with them.

Naturalists working in conjunction with the survey-ship *Geranium* [53] in 1923-553 reported that the fish caught by them in the Pellew Islands, Darwin, and Cape Wessel included: sharks, sting-rays, wolf herring, herring, hair-backed herring, anchovy, catfish, eels, garfish, sunfish, mullet, sea pike, salmon, mackerel, trevally, pony-fish, soldierfish, grant perch, rock cod, coral-fish, red schnapper, grey schnapper, bream, silver belly, red mullet, whiting, batfish, butter-fish, flounder, sole, flathead, parrot-fish, and leather-jacket. [54]

And with this abundance available the people of Australia consume thirteen pounds per head of fish a year while in Great Britain the consumption is forty-two pounds!

Having all the information I required for the moment, I told Jacky and Sitting Bull to get ready for the return to Kajadja.

On the first day out Jacky was preparing a fire for lunch

when he did the sort of damn-fool thing one might have expected of him.

I had thrown him my box of wax-vestas, and a moment later I heard a mild explosion and a yell from Jacky. In shutting the lid he had apparently struck the head of a match and the lot went up in smoke.

"I bin burn im all about match, boss," he said needlessly, but I had my suspicions about that. A black can rarely resist the temptation to take a couple of matches for himself when he gets his fingers on a box.

I looked at him severely.

"Turn out your —— pockets."

He protested that he hadn't taken any, but I made him do as he was told. Unfortunately, he had only taken two. Two matches to last us four days!

We kept the fire going throughout the night, and in the morning I told them they would have to go without smokes until the next fire was lit.

This made a profound impression, particularly on Sitting Bull, who suddenly disappeared into the bush. He returned with half a dozen bone-dry cones, like the cones of the banksia, or bottle-brush. He handed half to Jacky, and they kept them smouldering until the end of the trip.

The next mishap was when one of the packhorses wallowed in a waterhole. Its pack-bag contained our flour, and when we dragged the horse out all the flour, with the exception of a couple of pounds, was ruined, as well as most of the food.

That evening I had noticed Jacky and Sitting Bull in earnest consultation. At length Jacky came over to me, and scratching the dirt with his big toe, and hanging his head in the manner so characteristic of him when simulating shyness, he waited for me to set the ball rolling.

"What name, Jacky?" I asked. "What you bin want?"

Still scratching and looking at the ground he said:

"Might be tucker close up finish, boss. Black man live alonga white man tucker all right. White man no more live alonga black man tucker. Might be white man die. More better we bin catchem goanna, anytink . . . you bin keepem tucker alonga self."

I was extremely touched by this thoughtfulness, and it registered another point on my long list in the black man's favour. I thanked Jacky and he grinned broadly.

For the remainder of the trip both he and Sitting Bull gave free rein to their primitive instincts, and lived on kangaroos, snakes, lizards, and similar luxuries.

When we reached the river I saw the old underpants flag still flying, and fired a couple of shots to let Whittaker know we had arrived. There was no sign of him, however, and we camped for the night. In the morning I fired several more shots, but again no appearance of Whittaker on the headland.

I began to feel a little worried. Telling Sitting Bull and Jacky to follow, I set Sovereign at a smart pace and crossed the river over twenty miles down, and then rode back along the opposite bank for a further twenty odd miles.

CHAPTER XXVI

THE END OF THE HUNT

I APPROACHED the hut by way of the blacks' camp, which was deserted. Along the track which linked us with the headquarters of Koperaki's crowd the young grass had grown, and all about there was evidence that the tribe had gone long since.

My uneasiness grew with every stride.

I hadn't expected to find the blacks there. I knew they would have gone on the promised walkabout. But where was Whittaker? And where was Bob Cadell?

The thoughts that tumbled through my mind as I galloped over the final fifty yards will never be set down in full. I had visions of Whittaker speared and mutilated . . . and of Bob Cadell with him. I had visions, too, of the hut deserted. Whittaker gone; Bob gone; no message; nothing.

And then again I thought what a damn fool I was. No doubt Whittaker was on some shooting-expedition with Bob. Yes, that's what obviously had happened.

And yet I felt - I knew - something was wrong.

I pulled Sovereign to a sudden halt within ten yards of the hut, and flung myself off.

I was dashing towards the hut door, when shuffling around a corner came aged and naked Jimmy.

I pulled up short and gasped:

"Which way boss bin sit down?"

Jimmy looked at me sadly and shook his head.

"Im dead," he said.

I swayed, feeling at once that it was true. Whittaker dead! So that was the end of our great adventure. Poor old Whit . . . great scout . . . great cobber. Those years at the war . . . the raiding-parties . . . the tight jams we got into.

And in a flash I saw before me, as though projected on

to a screen, Whittaker tossed from his horse on the way to Mary River when he flourished his stockwhip ... saw him shoot the head off a snake when it was about to strike at me ... saw his sly grin when he produced that first bottle of whisky . . . that marvellous shot of his which brought down the first buffalo ... saw him kicked fair and square when he tried to load the hide on the packhorse ... busy with his romantic letter-writing ... trying to shoot a pig with my revolver ... saw his rage and grief when Wark-Wark was disembowelled ... saw the python slimily crawling over his naked chest ... saw his brave grin when we found him after spending the night with mosquitoes in the swamps ... saw those days and nights of the wet season when we often felt like spitting at each other ... and that Christmas feast when he produced the wine and helped me build castles in the air.

In a flash I saw all these things, and many more - our life together with all its ups and downs mirrored before me in a manner horribly real.

What a swine I was to leave him sickening for fever or something. I should have postponed the Port Essington trip . . . I should have done this and I should have done that.

So Whittaker was dead. I had lost the best pal a man could ever have - staunch, game, ready for anything, never a grouch.

"lm dead . . . im dead . . . im dead."

The phrase kept repeating itself.

Well, I guessed he'd die with a grin on his cheerful —

"Im dead."

Blast me for an unthinking idiot!

"Im dead all about," or "Im bin killem dead" - that's what Jimmy would have said if Whittaker was dead. He must be sick or injured.

"Where? Where?" I yelled at Jimmy. "Where he bin sit down?"

And pointing a bony finger he indicated a huddled heap beneath the banyan-tree.

In a moment I was beside my mate. One look told me that if Whittaker was not dead, he was that near it not to matter much.

I dropped beside him and felt his pulse. It was barely registering. I slipped my hand beneath his shirt and his flesh was burning. His face was the colour of wood-ash, and glistening with ice-cold sweat. His eyeballs seemed to have been chiselled from their sockets, and the wrinkled lids let fall. He was unconscious, and breathing faintly.

I rushed over to the medicine-chest in the hut. It was empty. I then went to his pack-bag in which he kept his private belongings, and which was lying a dozen yards from him.

There was pinned to it a farewell note. He said he had dysentery and fever, and couldn't last much longer. The boat from Darwin had not arrived, and there was no food or medicine in the hut. He gave one or two instructions as to the disposal of his effects, and asked me to deliver certain messages when I went south.

As I read the tears scalded my eyes. What a hell of an end to everything!

I stood there helpless and impotent, not knowing what to do.

"Which way Bob Cadell?" I said to Jimmy at last.

He pointed down the river and said:

"Hoenpelli," and I gathered that he had gone to Paddy Cahill's a hundred miles away for assistance.

"Which way Koperaki?"

"Koperaki Oby Oby," he said. Oby Oby, I knew, was the name of a lagoon six or seven miles away, so I sent Jimmy off to find him at once. It was my intention to get Koperaki to bring his canoe, and if I could keep Whittaker alive until morning I would paddle him down to Oenpelli.

God, what a predicament! I wanted brandy and quinine. And all I had was a handful of tea, some rice, potato, and hard buffalo biltong.

I stripped Whittaker and gently sponged him, and succeeded in forcing a teaspoon of water between his cracked and bleeding lips. His eyelids flickered once, but I knew he was almost done. Hunting around again I was fortunate to find some wild honey, and I managed to get a little of this down Whittaker's throat. As dysentery tears the lining of the stomach I knew this would have a soothing effect.

Then taking my shot-gun I went to the lagoon, got a couple of ducks, boiled them, and made some rich broth. Whittaker opened his eyes and there was in them a look of mute appeal which sent a stab through me.

"Buck up, old boy," I said with forced cheerfulness. "We'll soon have you right. Try and swallow some of this."

He tried to smile, and managed to get down a little of the broth; then relapsed into unconsciousness.

I stayed with him throughout that long and terrible night, continually bathing his forehead and giving him occasional sips of water and honey. Listening intently to his breathing, I got the first glimmer of hope when I found it was more regular. He seemed to have settled into a natural sleep. At eight o'clock he woke, and actually smiled.

"I'll pull through now, Warby," he whispered. "Thought you'd never come."

Great! He was going to have a fight for it.

Then to my delight Koperaki and his followers burst into camp.

"Which way canoe," I asked him immediately.

"One fella alonga Gaernin; nother ones go Kopalgo," he said.

So the nearest boat was at Gaernin, sixteen miles away. It would be useless to send a boy for it since by the time he reached there the tide would have turned and he would be faced with the almost impossible task of paddling against it.

Time was too precious to delay, and I could see that the only thing to be done would be to get Whittaker to Gaernin.

By afternoon Whittaker had not had another relapse, and when I told him what we proposed to do he said that if we lifted him on a horse he thought he could hang there provided someone supported him on both sides.

As the only alternative was to carry him on an improvised stretcher, we hoisted him on to one of the old packhorses. Koperaki said he would ride on one side with me on the other.

Before we set out I must have said aloud: "God, if I only had some sugar." I was thinking that a sip of tea would act as a stimulant for the sick man, and almost before I was aware I had spoken Koperaki was at my side with half a cup of sugar. Where he got it from I did not know, but I imagined he had saved it for an emergency from the supply I had given him when Niogo was sick.

I felt like falling around his neck.

I quickly brewed some tea and gave it to Whittaker. He lapped it up in a way that pleased me immensely.

Just before we were ready to start Sitting Bull and Jacky appeared accompanied by Bob Cadell whom they had met on the way.

I told Bob to stay there and watch for the boat. Then, with Koperaki and I riding beside Whittaker and Jacky bringing up the rear we set off for Gaernin.

What a nightmare journey it was! We could only walk the horses, and with every spasm of dry retching Whittaker got we had to halt and hold him in the saddle. I kept giving him sips of water and honey to relieve his agony.

We reached Gaernin after two days' terrible travel, and with only a few drops of water in our one water-bag.

Whittaker was still alive but desperately ill. We lifted him from the saddle and placed him in the shade of a tree, and I went with Koperaki to locate the canoe.

We found it tied at the bank. When Koperaki saw it I thought he would have lost his reason: he tore his hair, lashed the air with his fists, and cursed in a dreadful voice.

The canoe had been half burned away, apparently the work of his enemies.

I'd never before seen a man in such a fearful rage.

"Killem all about bimeby," he yelled. And I had no doubt that he would carry out his threat.

The situation was tragic. Water was the pressing need for all of us. There being no permanent supply at Gaernin I told Jacky to take a spoon and go from hole to hole and collect what had remained of a recent shower. We boiled the muddy, brackish stuff, and it was better than nothing. I gave Whittaker a drop or two from the water-bag, and a little more of the duck broth.

Taking my .32 I went in search of food and shot the only game I saw - an emu. We made a meal of that. Whittaker appeared to be sinking, and he frequently lapsed into unconsciousness. It looked like the end. But next morning I was surprised and thankful to see that he had recovered a little and said he was willing to try and carry on the journey. The old boy's spirit was still there. I knew that would take a lot of quenching.

With over eighty miles to go to reach Oenpelli we started again, a desperate little band. Thirst had gripped us all, and I sucked a .32 bullet in an effort to relieve the pangs. We covered another eight miles that weary day when, with a shout of joy, Koperaki pointed to a broad sheet of water near a headland. We drank sparingly, but had all we could do to stop the horses from stampeding into it. We camped there the night, and in the morning Whittaker was still very low.

For the last three days we had been scanning the river

hoping and praying for a sight of a mast. The *John Alce* must arrive soon. Would it be soon enough?

Imagine my joy when Koperaki came running to tell me that he had seen the masts of the boat some miles up the river.

I feverishly saddled a horse, flung myself on, and galloped in the direction of the boat, aiming to reach a point where I could intercept it. The pounding of hoof-beats behind told me Jacky was following.

It was a furious race, but I got there in time. The *John Alce* was three hundred yards away. When she drew nearer I fired several shots; the anchor dropped, and a dinghy put off.

I was soon on board, being greeted by my old friend the skipper. It didn't take me many minutes to explain matters, come ashore again, and start back. I met Koperaki and Whittaker slowly coming along. The black had his arm around my friend's waist; even then he could scarcely hold him in the saddle.

At last we got Whittaker into the dinghy, and in a few minutes he was settled in the skipper's cabin sipping whisky and quinine while the skipper prepared arrowroot.

The skipper said he would go quickly on to Oenpelli, drop Paddy Cahill's stores, return to Darwin, and get Whittaker into hospital as fast as possible. I breathed freely for the first time for days.

Giving my friend a farewell pat on the head, and telling him to keep smiling, I left with some flour, sugar, tea, tobacco, and other stuff. The rest of our supplies I asked the skipper to take back to Darwin.

My next move was to return to Kajadja, take some of the horses to Brock's Creek, and catch the train to Darwin. On the way we encountered several violent storms. I must waste no time if I hoped to reach Brock's Creek before the wet season.

Still, I rode with a gay heart.

On reaching Kajadja I quickly got about twelve horses, collected the best saddles, the rifles, and some other gear, leaving the balance at the hut, to be picked up after the wet season. I said to Koperaki:

"I bin leave him all about everything here. Might be someone steal him."

"No more stealem. I bin killem they bin stealem," he said sternly.

With that I said good-bye to Koperaki and Sitting Bull, and left with Bob and Jacky for Brock's Creek. We reached there in six days after an uneventful trip, and camped at the Zap-a-pan mine. The first thing I did was to ride into Brock's Creek, and from the police station ring Darwin hospital. Whittaker was on the way to recovery!

I caught the train four days later. Bob and Jacky were to stay at Brock's Creek until I returned. Whittaker was up and about, and his own smiling self again when I saw him, although he had lost a couple of stone weight.

When he was well enough we put up at the hotel. After a few days of good food and beer, we began to make inquiries concerning the capital we needed to put those pastoral, agricultural, fishing, and other schemes into operation.

And here we approach the end of the story.

The business people we saw agreed with us entirely on the enormous value of the country. But they tossed the proverbial spanner into the works when they said we would have no hope of raising any capital in the Territory for development there.

"You can do it," they told us, "but you will have to go south for the money."

Well, that being the case, we would do so. After the wet season Whittaker would go south and try out the money market, while I returned to Kajadja and collected the remainder of the gear.

So we idled three months away in Darwin, having a well-earned rest, with an occasional splash of mild excitement.

When the weather cleared I left once more for Brock's Creek. There Bob and Jacky were waiting for me. I had pipes, tobacco, shirts, and boots for them; and, gaily attired, they set off cheerfully with me on the long trip to Kajadja again. When I entered our hut I was honestly surprised, in spite of Koperaki's assurance, to find that not a single thing had even been disturbed.

We got the remaining horses in (there were six foals with them) and, gathering the rest of the gear, moved off next morning on the return trip. I had seen no signs of the blacks at Kajadja, but on the first day out we met Koperaki and about seventy of his tribe.

They greeted me with excited yells; and when I distributed tobacco, treacle, twill, and ornaments they danced with joy. They camped near us that night. The following morning I said farewell to Koperaki, as fine a type of man, black or white, that I ever wish to meet.

Shaking my hand he said:

"Might be you bin stopem way little bit long time?"

"Might be," I said.

"I bin all same old Jimmy then," he said sorrowfully. "Die alonga bush. Niogo bin grow up. He look alonga you all time you bin come back."

So I left him, with the gins howling a mournful farewell.

At Brock's Creek I disposed of all the horses with the exception of Dandy, Sovereign, and a couple of buffalo mounts, which I put on agistment.

Bob Cadell was to return to his domestic troubles at Pine Creek, and Jacky, no doubt, to startle the natives with his imaginary exploits.

I told them both to look after themselves, and Bob said:

"I bin look after Jacky, boss. Two fella lubra Pine Creek. I bin gibbit im one."

"They bin old fella lubra," said Jacky with a snort. "Too much fight. More better I go alonga boss bimeby shoot buffalo. Buffalo more quiet."

And so I left my other two black friends.

In Darwin, at the hotel, there was a note for me:

DEAR WARBY, -

Gone with an expedition to Caledon Bay to look for those two white women from the *Douglas Mawson*.[55] See you later.

WHIT.

I had a beer.

Alex Warburton holding a shotgun used by his grandfather.

Senior Elder Jonathon Nadji, great nephew of Koperaki, welcomes Robert Warburton (son of Carl) to Cannon Hill.

Looking towards Cannon Hill from Hawk Dreaming - Arnhem Land.

Cahill's Crossing, East Alligator River, the border between what is now Kaka
National Park and Arnhem Land.

EPILOGUE

Carl Warburton and Lawrence Whittaker did not return to Kakadu. Their plan to obtain £3000 for a refrigerating plant, a canning operation and their own lugger, never materialised. Warburton left the Territory and returned to Sydney. It is not known whether Whittaker did join the search for survivors of the *Douglas Mawson*. It may have been an invented point, intended to resonate with the contemporary audience of the 1930s, harnessing the renewed public interest in the frontiers of Northern Australia fuelled by the Caledon Bay affair described in the Introduction to this edition. In March 1926 their pastoral lease was forfeited in light of their failure to comply with conditions requiring they improve and develop the holding.

What became of the Aboriginal protagonists of Buffaloes is unclear. Koperaki died some years later. His son Niogo later used the name Carl Warburton as his non-Aboriginal name, but died childless. Hobble Chain was survived by a son, "Hobble Ring", who was later a famed horseback shooter, well known to Yorky Billy Alderson (Cole 1988: 291). Another buffalo shooter who went by the name of Charles Whittaker, was an associate of Alan Stewart who ran the Nourlangie safari camp in the 1950s (pictured in Stewart 1969:39).

Shortly after Warburton left Kakadu, Paddy Cahill's Oenpelli station was given over to the Church Missionary Society. Most of Cahill's Gagudju workforce departed for the buffalo stations around the Mary and Adelaide Rivers. Very few remained at the time the missionary Alf Dyer arrived in 1925. The herds, gardens and homestead was restaffed by Kunwinjku people, who moved in increasing numbers into the region (Cole 1975: 23). Over the next fifty years, the peoples the East Alligator River floodplains dispersed and disappeared, so that by 1970 their population numbered but 4% of the pre-contact total. The Gagudju language retained limited usage until the early 1960s, but is no longer spoken (Harvey 1992: 6).

The buffalo shooting industry expanded after Warburton left, with a growing export market to leather manufacturers, especially in Turkey, for upholstery, industrial belting and handbags. Hide production peaked in the late 1930s when some 16,500 were exported, prompting the Northern Territory Administration to enact stricter licensing laws for commercial shooting. Shooting virtually ceased during World War II, then resumed for a decade with an annual yield of about 12,000 hides, until the market collapsed in 1956-7. Since then, buffalo have been shot for meat, supplying the Arnhem Land settlements, including the several missions, feeding thousands of Aboriginal people, and for export and domestic use in canned food and pet mince. Feral buffalo were all but eliminated in the 1980s-90s as part of the Brucellosis and Tuberculosis Eradication Campaign. Buffalo are now being bred in the Territory and southern states using disease free stock.

Warburton later sought his fortune in Queensland as a sugar-cane farmer, but failed. For a time he was said to have "led a good social life" among the artists and literati of Sydney, counting Norman Lindsay and others among his associates. In 1937 he produced a second book, a novel, *White Poppies*, also set in the Northern Territory. *Poppies* was a far-fetched and anachronistic tale of high adventure, romance and intrigue, decidedly less appealing than the laconic, auto-biographical *Buffaloes*. Warbuton's second book was, at the time of his death 25 years later, being worked into a screenplay for an Australian film company under the title "Mystery of the Bool Boons", which apparently never made it into production.

During World War II Warburton rejoined the military, training soldiers at Moore Park, briefly serving overseas in Palestine, before returning to Northern Australia where he worked on General Blaney's staff in Darwin. He was reportedly in Darwin during the Japanese air raids of 1942. In 1944 he married Thelma Ada Parkes at Annandale in Sydney. Their first son, Carl Jnr, died an infant of meningitis.

Warburton stayed in the service after the war. At Singleton in 1949, he was among the Army strike-breakers sent in to work the open cut mines, as part of Prime Minister Chifley's 'boots and all' approach to ending a crippling Miners' Federation strike. Carl's surviving son, Robert, was born at Denman in 1948. The family moved to Holsworthy where, amid increasing ill health and minor strokes, he was medically retired from the Army. The Warburtons then moved to Katoomba, where they ran some holiday flats. In his later years, Carl was called on to address Rotary and RSL functions, and sat on the council to organise the visit of Queen Elizabeth in the early 1950s. He was a popular figure with the Katoomba Aboriginal community, and his children remember sharing their house for short periods with numerous Aboriginal children.

Robert Warburton remembers his father as a usually quiet, reserved person who, like so many of his generation, kept his War memories to himself, but spent much of his life after 1919 trying to escape the ordinary and mundane. The Territory remained with him. He "daydreamed a lot", according to his son. But he was increasingly troubled by the inoperable head wounds he had sustained in World War I. Shortly after another major stroke in 1961, he died in Concord Hospital. He is buried in Rookwood cemetery, Sydney. He is survived by his wife Thelma, son Robert and daughter Carolyn.

ENDNOTES

1 Sergeant Herbert Rockcliff, 17th Battalion, was killed in action on 27 July 1916.

2 Private Robert Edward Hayward was born 1892 at Hillston, on the lower Lachlan River in western New South Wales. He enlisted on 19 February 1915, served with the 5th Field Ambulance and returned to Australia on 2 April 1919. He married shortly after the War and died in Sydney in 1945.

3 The Mocketts were Warburton's mother's family.

4 Warburton's claim to have been wounded in action at Passchendaele is not verified by his war records, although the 2nd Division did sustain heavy casualties in the attacks of 7-10 October 1917. Warburton's 17th Battalion lost almost 200 men. On 25 October he was selected to attend Officer's College in England, reporting in November to No.4 Officers Cadet Battalion, Oxford, four weeks after his was supposedly wounded.

5 Warburton received wounds to his head and left side on 17 July 1918. At that time the 2nd Division of the AIF held the southern portion of the Australian front line near Villers-Bretonneux. Warburton's 17th Battalion was involved in assaults on German positions on the Roman road.

6 Whittaker actually arrived back in Sydney three months after Warburton, in August 1919.

7 The British-made .450 calibre Martini-Henry rifles were adopted by the British Infantry in June 1871, replacing the Snider-Enfield, with carbine versions entering into service from 1877.

8 Condy's crystals, or potassium permanganate, is a powerful oxidising agent and mild disinfectant. It had multiple uses, including the control of black spot and powdery mildew.

9 Chlorodyne, a liquid medicine for diarrhoea and dysentery, was also taken to assuage pain from headaches and rheumatism.

10 Edmund Besley Court Kennedy (1818 - 1848), Assistant Surveyor of New South Wales, was killed while on an expedition from Rockhampton to Cape York.

11 The Darwin meatworks was conceived by the Federal Labor government in 1912, and was built by the British-based conglomerate, Vestey Brothers, which also acquired some 7000 kilometres of Northern Territory pastoral land. The meatworks operated briefly between 1917-1920. It was closed for a combination of reasons, including difficulties with the Australian Workers Union.

12 The aviators Ross and Keith Smith completed the first England-Australia flight in a Vickers Vimy bomber when they landed at Fanny Bay, Darwin, on 10 December 1919.

13 Miles Staniforth Carter Smith (1869-1934) was Acting Administrator of the Northern Territory from 1919-1921. He was later an Administrator of New Guinea.

14 Rum Jungle, according to author Douglas Barry (Barry 1982), received its name when 80 gallons of rum intended for the goldfields at Pine Creek was consumed there by a group of teamsters. Uranium was discovered at Rum Jungle in 1949, and five years it became the site of Australia's first large scale uranium mine, operated by the Commonwealth Government's Australian Atomic Energy Authority. Major environmental damage to the area was evident from the early 1960s, and mining ceased in 1971.

15 The Territory historian, Ernestine Hill, related the "fable of the Magic Pumpkin" grown at Batchelor. The gigantic pumpkin, lauded by Gilruth as evidence of the success of the government farm, was reputedly stolen en route to Darwin (Hill 1951: 275-6).

16 In the late 1890s, Brocks Creek had the largest Chinese population outside Darwin.

17 Fannie Haynes (1869-1945) and Tomas George Crush

(1865-1913) built the Federation Hotel at Brock's Creek in the 1890s. Fannie Haynes, a British immigrant, came to the Northern Territory goldfields at Wandi with her first husband, then later married Tom Crush, a miner, who became the Northern Territory's first Labor Member in the South Australian Parliament from 1909-1911. After Crush's death she married the "one-legged bushman", Henry (Harry) Haynes (d.1945). Fannie remained at Brock's Creek until World War II, when she was evacuated to Adelaide. She died in Sydney on 5 February 1945 (Hill 1951: 407-8).

18 Alluvial gold was discovered at Pine Creek, 250 kilometres south-east of Darwin, in 1871. The area became the Territory's largest goldfield two years later after the discovery of the Union Gold Reef. The railway from Darwin to Pine Creek was built between 1885 and 1889.

19 The story of Elsey Downs station was told by Mrs Aeneas Gunn in *We of the Never Never* (1908).

20 The "shag" was probably either a cormorant or darter, waterbirds that proliferate the paperbark swamps of this region.

21 The setting aside of land for lease to returned soldiers was part of the Northern Territory's small contribution to the ambitious soldier settlement schemes orchestrated by Australian governments after World War I. Some 37,000 returned serviceman were placed on farms in an attempt to create employment and rural development. Most were financially ruined by the end of the decade. Numbers of returned soldiers came to the Territory to take up farms around Katherine and the Adelaide River.

22 Warburton, Whittaker and a Mr Cyril John Jones applied to the Land's Board in Darwin for a pastoral lease on 28 May 1920, paying a deposit of £10 to reserve the land while they set off to conduct a personal inspection. On 2 August 1920 they filed a formal application for 600 square miles on the "Western bank of East Alligator River", paying the remaining £50 and undertaking to invest £1000 in developing and improving the land. Pastoral Lease No.2424 was approved a week later, commencing 1 October 1920. They made an apparently successful application for Repatriation Assistance funds, but after failing to undertake the necessary expenditure on improvements, the lease was forfeited in March 1926 (Department of Lands Correspondence Files 1915-1925, Northern Territory Archives Service, Darwin).

23 A Birkmyre fly was a waterproof fabric suspended over a rope with the corners pegged into the ground to create a basic, portable shelter.

24 Either the large Black Fruit Bat (*Pteropus alecto gouldii*) or the Little Red Fuit Bat (*Pteropus scapulatus*).Native fruit bats are often referred to as flying foxes due to similarities in the shape of the head and snout.

25 Apparently the grave of the buffalo shooter, Barney Flynn, who worked with Joe Cooper on Melville Island in the late 1890s. According to Alfred Searcy, Flynn died of a snake bite while shooting buffalo in the Alligator Rivers area (Searcy 1908: 235). Flynn was referred to by Banjo Paterson in the *Bulletin*, 31 December 1898, and recalled by Paddy Cahill in Ernestine Hill's *The Territory* (Hill 1951: 371-2). According to Tom Cole, Flynn was speared by Aborigines on Bamboo Creek (Cole 1992: 223).

26 The freshwater or Johnson crocodile (*Crocodylus johnstoni*) nests in sandy country adjacent to the Arnhem Land escarpment.

27 Among those who mistakenly referred to the endemic species of salt water crocodile (*Crocodylus porosus*) as alligators was Phillip Parker-King, who named the East, South and West Alligator Rivers during his voyage of exploration on the *Mermaid* in 1818.

28 A "jackass" or "laughing jackass" are terms for kookaburras.

29 The Victoria River Downs cattle station near the junction of the Wickham and Victoria rivers was established in the late 1870s as a 16,000 square mile lease granted by the South Australian Government to C.B. Fisher and J.M. Lyons. Later it was part owned by the Kidman brothers. In Warburton's time it belonged the Perth-based Bovril Australian Estates.

30 The early British outposts were on Melville Island (Fort Dundas, 1824-29) and on the mainland at Raffles Bay (Fort Wellington, 1827-29).

31 In Asia buffaloes had been domesticated for thousands of years. Attempts to domesticate buffalo in Northern Australia in the 1920s, as on the Woolner Aboriginal Reserve west of the Adelaide River, were deemed a failure, probably on economic grounds (McKnight 1971: 753). Buffaloes bred in captivity at the Berrimah Research Station in the 1960s were indeed docile, and others captured from the wild were found to be easily tamed, though they had a tendency to damage fences by rubbing against them to relieve irritations from lice (McCristal 1966: 115).

32 Buffaloes are subject to some diseases, especially bovine tuberculosis, and are susceptible to malignant catarrhal fever, for which reason they were kept away from sheep.

33 The jew lizard (*Amphibolurus barbatus*), also known as the bearded dragon from the pouch beneath its jaw which distends when the animal is threatened.

34 This could be the Oenpelli Rock Python (*Morelia oenpelliensis*).

35 Contrast this with Baldwin Spencer's more disparaging remarks on rock paintings at Oenpelli: "The blackfellow certainly has the capacity of seizing intuitively on the salient features of all animals that he draws, however crude his drawings may be" (Spencer 1928: 808-9). This particular cave may be that known as "The Small Labyrinth" on the northern side of Hawk Dreaming, distinguished by a painting of a speared kangaroo at the cave entrance (Edwards 1974: 47-8).

36 This could be the nocturnal Narbalek wallaby (*Petrogale concinna*).

37 Possibly a reference to the operations of D.G. Colivas, who established a saltworks at Ludmilla Creek, Darwin, in 1920. The industry survived the closure of Vestey's meatworks and supplied salt locally for twenty years (Powell 1982: 152).

38 The British explorer Ernest Giles undertook overland expeditions in the Australian interior across the Nullabor Plain, the Victoria Desert and the Gibson Desert in the late 1870s.

39 Paddy Cahill came to the Territory with the drover, Nat Buchanan, in 1883. He died in late 1923 in Melbourne (Mulvaney 2004).

40 Harry and Frank/Fred Hardy of Burrundie, Adelaide River and Mount Bundey.

41 Vestey's Marrakai station, between the Adelaide and Mary Rivers, east of the Stuart Highway.

42 Mrs Cahill was Mariah Pickford.

43 The Kapalga mission on the South Alligator River was actually an Anglican mission. Established in 1901 by A.H. Lennox and A.M. Gathercole, it was administered by the Adelaide-based Northern Territory Native Industrial Mission and abandoned around 1903 when the mission was transferred to Greenhill Island in Van Diemen Gulf. In Warburton's time, Kapalga was the head station of the buffalo-shooter, Fred Smith (see Chapter 21).

44 Boomerangs have not been used in this region for thousands of years, since the emerging woodland environment made them ineffective. Once used for hunting and fighting, boomerangs are depicted in some of the older styles of Arnhem Land rock paintings.

45 Blue-winged kookaburra (*Dacelo leachii*) of northern Australia. Its distinctive blue wings and rump distinguish it from the laughing kookaburra (*Dacelo novaeguineae*).

46 This was probably the poisonous Round Yam. They need to be carefully prepared by roasting or curing in the sun. When John Lewis' party was in this area, a police trooper bit into a yam. "I thought he would have died. His tongue swelled to about four times the natural size, until he could scarcely get it into his mouth" (Lewis 1922: 131).

47 The regional custom of preparing burial platforms was first noted by Lt. Stokes at Port Essington, who related it to the customs of the Arafauras or "Mountain Men" of New Guinea (Stokes 1841: 14-15). Visiting gentleman to Port Essington like John Sweatman and Lambrick raided the platforms for skulls (Sweatman, in Allen and Corris eds. 1977: 146). The custom was described at length by Baldwin Spencer (Spencer 1914: 251) and by Lazarus Lamilami (Lamilami 1974: 42).

48 This is probably an article by Baldwin Spencer titled `An introduction to the study of certain native tribes of the Northern Territory' in the *Bulletin of the Northern Territory*, No. 2, Melbourne: Home and Territories Department, 1912, referred to in Spencer 1914: 232.

49 The evidence of cannibalism among Australia Aborigines is ambiguous. There are hundreds of historical accounts in which non-Indigenous Australians reported evidence of Aboriginal rites and practices involving the flesh of deceased persons. Yet in most cases the authenticity of the claim is highly doubtful, involving insufficient, subjective or dubious evidence. In western culture, cannibalism was imagined to be an inherent characteristic of `uncivilised' or `savage' peoples - part of the luggage of preconception and prejudice that Europeans brought with them to Australia - and it was widely and easily accepted that such practices existed among Aborigines. Spencer wrote: "I have never come across any tribe in which cannibalism pure and simple, that is, killing human beings for the purpose of eating them, is practised, but amongst [some] northern tribes, almost every individual, whether death be the result of natural causes or due to violence, is eaten" (Spencer 1914: 254).

50 Warburton may have witnessed the first stage of a complex series of initiation procedures described by Baldwin Spencer as the "*Jamba* ceremony". The initiates are led to the specially prepared ground, called "*Tjaina*", where they are taught of the forbidden foods (Spencer 1914: 123-33).

51 Baldwin Spencer described this "very curious form of magic" called "*Tjilaiyu*", in which a person's faeces was burnt in an elaborate ceremony designed to remove the victim's spirit protector and expose him to danger. "Because of this, everyone is most careful to cover over and hide from view all excrement, one result of which is that Kakadu camps are more cleanly than those of many other tribes" (Spencer 1914: 257-60).

52 The Aboriginal man, Romula, was met and described by Elsie Mason as Paddy Cahill's "faithful black henchman" who rode to and from Burrundie to collect supplies and mail for Oenpelli (Mason 1915: 104). The 'Romula affair', which took place in 1917, was aired in Justice N. K. Ewing's Royal Commission into the NT administration in 1920, in relation to concerns about Cahill's violent management of his Aboriginal workers, and an apparent miscarriage of justice in Romula's trial. Cahill visited Romula in Fanny Bay Gaol in may 1918 (Mulvaney 2004: 62-4, 119-21, 125-6).

53 The HMAS *Geranium* was commissioned in 1920 as the first Royal Australian Navy survey ship, until 1927.

54 The list of fish species here altered slightly for the reprint of the 1934 edition, and was shortened for the 1944 2nd edition.

55 The coastal steamer, *Douglas Mawson*, was wrecked in the Gulf of Carpentaria on a voyage from Burketown in March 1923. Its twenty passengers disappeared without trace. The discovery of wreckage on the western shores of the Gulf a year later stirred rumours that female survivors had been captured by Aborigines. A police party sent by the authorities in Darwin established a base at Caledon Bay. Sir Hubert Wilkins, collecting specimens for the British Museum in that area, described the police expedition as a "punitive party". In the 1930s, the persistence of rumours concerning white women and children prompted the Northern Territory Administrator to reinvestigate the issue. Donald Thomson discredited the rumours.

SELECTED SOURCES AND FURTHER READING

Barrie, D., 1982 *The heart of Rum Jungle:* the history of Rum Jungle and Batchelor in the Northern Territory of Australia. Self published, Batchelor (NT).

Cole, Tom, 1988 *Hell West and Crooked.* Angus and Robertson, Sydney.

Cole, Tom, 1992 *Riding the Wildman Plains: The Letters and Diaries of Tom Cole 1923-1943.* Pan Macmillan, Sydney.

Edwards, R., 1974 *The art of the Alligator Rivers Region.* Canberra: Alligator Rivers Region Environmental Fact-Finding Study, Canberra.

Elkin, A. P., 1934 `Review of Buffaloes, by Carl Warburton', *Oceania* Vol 4, No. 4: 479-480.

Gunn, A, Mrs., 1908 *We of the Never Never,* Hutchinson, London.

Harris, S.G., 1962 `Historical Development of the Buffalo Industry at Oenpelli', *Australian External Territories* Vol. 7, No. 2: 33-9.

Harvey, Mark, 2002 *A grammar of Gaagudju.* Mouton de Gruyter, Berlin and New York.

Hill, E., 1951 *The Territory.* Angus and Robertson, Sydney.

LamiLami, Lazarus, 1974 *Lamilami speaks, the cry went up : a story of the people of Goulburn Islands, North Australia.* Ure Smith, Sydney.

Leichhardt, L., 1847 *Journal of an overland expedition in Australia, from Moreton Bay to Port Essington, a distance of upwards of 3000 miles, during the years 1844-1845.* T. & W. Boone, London.

Letts, G.A., 1962 `Buffaloes of the Northern Territory', *Australian Territories* Vol. 2, No. 5: 10-16.

Lewis, John., 1962 *Fought and won.* W.K. Thomas & Co., Adelaide.

McGregor, R., 2004 'Develop the North: Aborigines, Environment and Australian Nationhood in the 1930s', in *Colonial Post: Journal of Australian Studies* No. 81, Richard Nile (ed). API Network and University of Queensland, St Lucia.

Mason, Elsie R., 1915 *An Untamed Territory: The Northern Territory of Australia*. MacMillan and Co. Ltd., London.

McCarthy, F. D., 1954 'Buffalo Hunting in Arnhem Land', *The Australian Museum Magazine* Vol. 11, No. 8: 252-6.

McCristal, Vic, 1966 *Top End Safari*. K.G. Murray Publishing, Sydney.

McKnight, Tom L. 1971 'Australia's Buffalo Dilemma', *Annals of the Association of American Geographers* Vol. 61, No. 4: 759-73.

Morris, John, 2000 'Memories of the buffalo shooters: Joe Cooper and the Tiwi (1895-1936), *Aboriginal History* Vol. 24: 141-151.

Mulvaney, John, 2004 *Paddy Cahill of Oenpelli*. Aboriginal Studies Press, Canberra.

Powell, A., 1982 *Far country: A Short History of the Northern Territory*. Melbourne University Press, Carlton.

Searcy, Alfred, 1909 In Australian Tropics. George Robertson, London.

Searcy, Alfred, 1912 *By Flood and Field: Adventures Ashore and Afloat in North Australia*. G. Bell & Sons Ltd., London.

Spencer, B., 1914 *Native Tribes of the Northern Territory of Australia*. Macmillan, London.

Spencer, B., 1928 *Wanderings in Wild Australia*. Macmillan, London.

Stewart, Allan, 1969 *The green eyes are buffaloes*. Lansdowne, Melbourne.

Stokes, J.L., 1841 *Discoveries in Australia during the voyage *of the HMS Beagle 1837-1843*, T. & W. Boone, London.

Sweatman, John, 1977 *The Journal of John Sweatman: A Nineteenth century Surveying Voyage in North Australia and Torres Strait*, in P. Corris and J. Allen eds. University of Queensland Press, St Lucia.

Woerle, Frank and Colin Thiele, 1897 *Ranger's Territory: Adventure in Australia's Far North*. Angus and Robertson, North Ryde (NSW).

INDEX